The Blockchain: A Guide for Legal and Business Professionals

2016

Shawn S. Amuial,

Josias N. Dewey,

and

Jeffrey R. Seul

THOMSON REUTERS®

For Customer Assistance Call 1-800-328-4880

Mat #41985410

About the Authors

Shawn Simon Amuial is an attorney at Holland & Knight in its Miami office where he primarily focuses his practice in the areas of real estate and technology. In addition to his legal practice, Shawn is a co-director of LegalTech Labs, a legal technologies incubator also located in Miami. A self-described tech and real estate junkie, blockchain technology initially caught Shawn's attention due to its ability to transform the legal industry through the implementation of smart contracts. Shawn received his B.S.B.A. from the University of North Carolina at Chapel Hill and J.D. from Emory University.

Josias "Joe" N. Dewey is a partner at Holland & Knight in its Miami office where he represents a diverse portfolio of clients in the banking and finance, real estate, technology, and gaming industries. In addition to his legal practice, Joe spends his time developing a smart contract platform called "contractCode." A self-taught coder from a young age, Joe's intrigue with the brilliance of blockchain technology and its logical intersection with law and business propelled him to be one of the legal industry's leading experts on the topic. Joe regularly publishes articles on blockchain technology and has been a guest speaker and panelist on the matter at conferences around the world. Joe received both his B.A. and J.D. from the University of Florida.

Jeffrey R. Seul is a corporate and mergers and acquisitions partner in Holland & Knight's Boston office and serves as chair of the firm's Technology Industry Sector Group, a cross-disciplinary team of lawyers with deep tech sector domain expertise. He advises clients on a wide range of corporate transactions and activities, including helping launch, finance, and scale companies; helping financial and strategic investors deploy capital; representing sellers as well as financial and strategic buyers in mergers and acquisitions; and negotiating and structuring major commercial and intellectual property transactions, including joint ventures and other types of strategic alliances. Jeff's experience prior to joining Holland & Knight, includes time on the front lines of the start-up world, serving as vice president and general counsel of Groove Networks, a software company acquired by Microsoft in 2005. He also has served on the boards of several companies, including C3 Technologies (acquired by Apple), Energy Materials Corp., and Movimento Group. Jeff received his B.A.S. from Regis

College and his J.D. from the University of Colorado. In addition, Jeff received an LL.M from Harvard Law School and a M.T.S. from Harvard Divinity School.

Preface

This book is written for professionals, such as lawyers, accountants, and consultants, as well as business executives who want to know more about how blockchain technology might be able to help their business. No prior experience with blockchain technology is necessary, nor assumed, and the first chapter of this book is intended to provide our reader with everything he or she needs to know in order to understand more complex implementations and concepts associated with the technology. In addition to blockchain novices, we believe that this book will provide knowledge and insight to those with a more in-depth understanding of blockchain technology by developing and emphasizing a legal and business perspective. This intersection of law and business with blockchain technology will ultimately shape the future of blockchain technology—although it's easy to see how many might feel it's the other way around.

Introduction

What started as an experiment in money less than 10 years ago has become a technology on the precipice of radically transforming industries across the globe. In fact, until very recently, the term blockchain was synonymous with Bitcoin, as Bitcoin was the only implementation of blockchain technology for the first several years since its inception. While blockchain technology started as a solution to digital money, it is now becoming important to many people outside of financial institutions. Industries from agriculture to diamond mining are beginning to understand the impact of blockchain technology and its development is growing exponentially.

While there is no way to discuss blockchain technology without discussing Bitcoin, the focus of this book is, in fact, blockchain—the technology that underlies Bitcoin—rather than Bitcoin itself. That said, a disproportionate number of examples and explanations in this book will be based on Bitcoin's implementation of blockchain technology. The reason for this is simply because Bitcoin remains the most mature and "pure" blockchain implementation that exists today (and likely for some time to come)—more on this later.

Throughout this book, we will be introducing a number of rather complex concepts. We did our best to simplify these concepts (and pertinent definitions), but we suggest that our readers frequent the chapter summary points, definitions glossary, as well as Chapter 1 in order to most effectively keep up with the text. Furthermore, you will notice that certain key concepts may be described more than once (and in different contexts) throughout the chapters—again, our aim is to reaffirm key concepts in an effort to make more complex concepts digestible.

We hope you enjoy our book and encourage you to reach out to us with any comments, questions, or feedback—our contact information is located at the end of the book.

Josias Dewey

Summary of Contents

Table of Contents

CHAPTER 3. BLOCKCHAIN PROTOCOLS

CHAPTER 4. DECENTRALIZED AUTONOMOUS ORGANIZATIONS (DAOS)

Chapter 1

The Fundamentals of Blockchain Technology

§ 1:1 Summary of important points

- Blockchains are best thought of as a ledger, just like an Excel spreadsheet, except that they are maintained in a decentralized manner rather than on a centralized server.
- Blockchain ledgers generally keep track of "transactions." Transactions are grouped together in a data structure called a block (i.e., blocks are just groups of transactions that have been processed together).
- Each block on a blockchain includes some hash (reference point) to the last block so that any attempt to change a prior block has a cascading effect on each subsequent block. This relationship between blocks is what gave rise to the term blockchain.
- Every user on a blockchain sees and maintains the same copy of the ledger through a concept called "reaching consensus." There are different ways that a blockchain can achieve consensus, but it must have a reliable consensus engine to ensure the accuracy of the ledger.
- Blockchains can be public, in which case, anyone can participate, or they can be permissioned, in which case,

1

only authorized participants can access and add transactions to the ledger.

- While it can be difficult to trace digital tokens because of the use of alphanumeric addresses rather than names, most blockchains are not truly anonymous, but rather incredibly transparent.
- The term wallet describes software or hardware that securely stores cryptographic tokens, such as Bitcoin.

§ 1:2 The basics: What is a blockchain, and how does it work?

Blockchain may be one of the least understood of the technologies currently thought to be driving a Fourth Industrial Revolution.[1] The involvement of complex cryptographic mathematics and a general association with Bitcoin and its checkered past are factors contributing to this lack of understanding. That's not to say that blockchain technology is not complex; it can be incredibly complicated at a very granular level. To gain a fundamental understanding of blockchain technology, and more importantly, how it will affect your business or profession, you do not need to understand all of those complexities. In fact, one of our primary goals in writing this book is to abstract away these complexities so that our reader can focus on appreciating use cases that might be important to them, while having sufficient understanding on how things work to appreciate the limitations of the technology as well as those areas where it will likely excel.

The term "blockchain" refers to a system that has numerous components which, when operating in conjunction with each other, can solve incredible problems across a broad array of industries and even society more generally. We will discuss each of these components in more detail throughout this book, but first, let's start with some basic definitions: A blockchain is commonly described as a decentralized peer-to-peer network that maintains a public, or private, ledger of transactions.[2] Now, let's break that down:

[Section 1:2]

[1]"Extreme automation and connectivity: The global, regional, and investment implications of the Fourth Industrial Revolution," UBS White Paper for the World Economic Forum, Annual Meeting 2016.

[2]https://bol.bna.com/what-is-a-blockchain/.

A Blockchain is a Decentralized Ledger

The individual components that make up the blockchain will be easier to understand if we reinforce the basic premise that a blockchain is a ledger.[3]

When you read "Ledger," think of a simple database (like an excel spreadsheet) that can store all sorts of information (i.e., someone's name, age, address, etc.). For example, currently the Federal Reserve Bank maintains a ledger with respect to credits and debits between it and its member banks. That ledger is considered centralized because all of the transactions are manually inputted by one party (a bank employee or software controlled by the bank). As a result, the member banks must trust the Federal Reserve Bank to properly maintain the ledger so that the member banks can accurately determine their current position vis-a-vis the Federal Reserve Bank. Under this framework, if a member bank has a deposit made into its account with the Federal Reserve Bank, the deposit is processed electronically and the centrally kept database at the Federal Reserve Bank is updated to credit the member bank's account (and most likely debit another member bank's account in the same amount). Ultimately, this centralized approach is responsible for keeping track of where most of our money resides.

Blockchains tracking the transfer of virtual currency, like Bitcoin, essentially maintain a similar ledger that keeps track of the transfer of Bitcoin from a transferor to a transferee. However, in contrast to the Federal Reserve's centralized ledger, a blockchain ledger is considered *decentralized* because transactions are stored on (several thousand) computers connected to a common network via the Internet. These computers are known as "nodes." Each node contains a complete history[4] of every transaction completed on a particular blockchain beginning with the first transactions that were processed into the first block on that blockchain. The first block of transactions for any blockchain is typically called the "genesis block" since it represents the beginning of time for that blockchain. This all begs a simple and obvious question—how does any blockchain protocol

---

[3]As you work through this book, repeat this to yourself as it will reinforce a very basic and pragmatic understanding of this technology. Ledger . . . ledger . . . ledger.

[4]While it is possible for some nodes to operate with an abbreviated ledger, we will ignore this concept for now because it introduces an unnecessary layer of complexity.

ensure that each ledger maintained by an individual node is identical to the ledger that other nodes connected to the network maintain? The answer to this question is a function of the network to which each copy of the ledger is connected.

Maintained and Verified by a Peer-to-Peer Network

As indicated above, all of the nodes are connected to a common network via the internet. This network consists of a peer-to-peer platform whereby each node or computer that stores a copy of the blockchain ledger is connected via the Internet, but in a completely decentralized manner. In other words, there is no single server to which all the nodes attach. So, when we refer to the network, this describes all of the peer-to-peer nodes operating under the same set of rules (commonly referred to as a "protocol") which are embodied in computer code that one has downloaded onto their computer (now considered a node on that network). Thus, at the heart of every blockchain is an agreed upon protocol that ensures that only information upon which the network reaches consensus[5] will be included in the blockchain. In other words, a *network* of computers all running a common software application (rather than the Fed) must come to agreement upon whether a change to the blockchain should be made, and if so, what that change should be. This consensus is driven by all of the nodes (i.e., all ledgers) operating under the same rules (i.e., a protocol) for determining how consensus is reached within the network. Let's apply this concept to the Bitcoin[6] protocol in an effort to better understand the mechanics of how the Bitcoin network reaches consensus.

Bitcoin's ledger is set up for the primary purpose of keeping track of ownership of the entire supply of a cryptocurrency also called Bitcoin. It is a recording of all of the transfers (or transactions) of Bitcoin from one person to another. This is analogous to an Excel spreadsheet which contains an entry for every dollar transferred from one

---

[5]Consensus occurs when the nodes operating on the network (usually at least a majority of the nodes) agree that the proposed transaction is indeed "valid." The different approaches to reaching consensus are discussed in greater detail in Chapter 3.

[6]The term "Bitcoin" can actually refer to one of three things. The first is the protocol itself (i.e., the software code that creates and maintains the distributed ledger). The second is the network of nodes (being computers that run the Bitcoin protocol) that receive, verify, and re-broadcast transactions involving Bitcoin around the globe. The third is the digital currency itself (e.g., that item costs 1 Bitcoin).

person to another, dating back to the first dollar printed.[7] If I want to transfer one Bitcoin to my friend, Alex, I would type in a command on my computer (or node) alerting the network of my desire to transfer one Bitcoin to Alex. Once I broadcast my intent to execute the transaction, other nodes connected to the Bitcoin network will immediately and automatically verify whether the proposed transaction is indeed valid (e.g., I am not trying to spend Bitcoin I already spent before). This validation process is done by the nodes tracing through the history of all of the transactions that have been completed and verified on a particular blockchain ledger (the Bitcoin ledger in our example), all the way back to the first transaction included in the first block.[8]

While my transaction involving Alex has propagated throughout this robust peer-to-peer network, there is still one last step left—my transaction needs to be memorialized into a block on the Bitcoin blockchain ledger. We've used the term "block" several times already and it will get much more attention throughout the remainder of the book. As such, now is a good time to pause and explain to the reader that "blocks" are simply a convenient way to aggregate transactions into larger groups (or batches) for processing purposes. The transactions bundled up and included in a block do not necessarily have any relationship with each other (just as a batch of checks being processed by a bank may have no relationship to each other), other than a temporal relationship (i.e., they are all recent transactions not included in the prior block). Since all of the valid transactions have already been validated and propagated by the nodes that form the blockchain network, why do we need to aggregate these transactions into blocks? The answer is surprisingly simple. Without an orderly and sequential system of organizing transactions, the nodes that make up our blockchain network would lack the ability to verify transactions in the first place. But why blocks? Why not just add each transaction to the ledger as and when those transactions have been verified

---

[7]For purposes of this analogy, please disregard the fact that a legitimate debate probably exists for what constitutes the first "dollar" in U.S. monetary history.

[8]Blocks are groups of transactions that have been processed together. Each block on a blockchain includes some hash (reference point) to the last block, so that any attempt to change a prior block has a cascading effect on each subsequent block. This relationship between blocks is what gave rise to the term blockchain.

against the then current ledger. What purpose or benefit does the protocol gain by grouping transactions together?

In theory, our decentralized ledger could exist as a never ending Excel spreadsheet. Page after page, cell after cell, nothing but continuous sheets of transactions. This could serve as the basis of our ledger, but it would lack the tremendous security feature that the use of blocks provides. More specifically, the immutable nature of the ledger is rooted in the aggregation of transactions into blocks. It is the aggregation into blocks that permits us to create links between transactions—essentially the "chain" in blockchain. Each block contains a reference to the block before it. This reference is unique and one of the most ingenious ideas that Satoshi included in Bitcoin's protocol. Rather than simply referring to the prior block by some random numbering system (e.g., Block 1, Block 2, Block 3 and so on),[9] each block (including all of the transactions that were bundled up into that block) are subject to a specific mathematical algorithm that results in a unique "hash." If you change any aspect of that block or any transaction within it, then subjecting the block to the same algorithm will produce a different "hash." So each block includes the hash of the prior block.

This resulting relationship between all of the blocks makes it exponentially more difficult to alter a prior entry in the ledger. If we used a ledger that did not rely on blocks, each linked to their predecessor, then someone with computational power of x could alter a prior entry for malicious purposes. With a block-based system, a malicious actor would need computational power of x to the y power, where y is a very large number.[10] The need for greater computational power will become even more obvious later in the book, but common sense tells us that more power is needed because we have to alter more data. Not only do we need to alter the data for the specific transaction we wish to change, but every block thereafter has to be altered because the hash in each

---

[9]This might confuse some readers who have looked at Bitcoin and noticed that blocks are in fact referenced for many purposes by a linear numbering system (i.e., Block 1, 2, 3, 4 and so on). This numbering system is for a different purpose which exists for the purpose of having an easy to use reference system. It is separate from the unique block hashes that are used to form a relationship from block to block.

[10]This is where having a Ph.D. in mathematics would be helpful—but for our purposes, just recognize that the y value here is so large that you would need an amount of computational power that only certain state actors possess.

of those blocks will no longer be valid. So for my transfer to Alex to become final, that transaction will eventually be bundled up with numerous other transactions broadcast throughout the network and become part of the next block. The responsibility for bundling transactions and processing blocks is handled by a unique subset of nodes commonly referred to as "miners." We will discuss the process and mechanics of mining in greater detail, but for purposes of our crash course, simply understand their role as the historical record keepers. To put things into further context and come full circle, if Alex decides to transfer the Bitcoin I sent him to his friend John, then the process starts over—except now the blockchain ledger reflects Alex as owning the Bitcoin I once owned.

The remainder of this book will flush out many of these concepts in much greater detail, but now you have a basic idea of what blockchains can do and some of the primary mechanics. More importantly, you can begin to understand some of the unique characteristics of blockchain technology. The most important of which is the absence of any trusted participant in the process. Unlike our example involving the Federal Reserve Bank, our Bitcoin example had no similar participant. In Bitcoin, we have constructed a secure, completely digital form of money without the need for a central bank. As the remainder of this book will show, blockchain technology has the potential to eliminate the need for not only central banks, but countless other trusted intermediaries, which will ultimately drive down transactional costs and make possible types of commerce previously not feasible.

§ 1:3 The basics expanded

Section 1:2 walked you through some fundamental concepts embedded in blockchain technology. In the subsequent chapters, we will walk you through a more detailed explanation of all of the steps needed to effectuate the transfer of the virtual currency Bitcoin and expand on this knowledge by working through transactions implemented on other blockchain protocols, such as Ethereum. Before doing so, let's build on our understanding of the Bitcoin ledger. As noted before, Bitcoin's ledger is set up for the primary purpose of keeping track of ownership of the entire supply of a cryptocurrency Bitcoin. It does this by adding an entry into every ledger connected to the Bitcoin network each time any amount of Bitcoin currency is transferred from one person to another (or even to yourself).

Units of Bitcoin are stored by reference to public addresses[1] so that any participant in the Bitcoin network can verify that same information. Each public address is an alphanumeric string that is derived from the public key associated with the unspent Bitcoin. Now is an appropriate time to introduce another central component to blockchain technology—public key infrastructure (or PKI for short). PKI is generally considered the most secure form of encryption in widespread use today. In simple terms it works by using a mathematical equation to produce a pair of alphanumeric keys, known as a public and private key. The public key can be given out to others and shared freely. In fact, for communication purposes, people often include their public key along with their e-mail or other contact information. The private key, however, must be kept secret. Anything encrypted using the public key can only be decrypted with the private key. Existing computational abilities are not sufficient for brute force attacks to crack PKI encryption, which is why they are considered so secure. In addition, it is not possible to derive the private key from its corresponding public key—as the mathematical relationship between the pair of keys is a one-way street. Said another way, we can confirm the relationship of a private key to a public key, but not the other way around.

Each public address that represents an amount of Bitcoin starts as a public key. Because public keys are lengthier, an algorithm is used to shorten them for purposes of generating public addresses. What's important to understand is that the public key and the corresponding public address derived from it are randomly generated every time someone transfers Bitcoin (or were previously generated in the case of a transfer to an existing public address). The Bitcoin protocol has PKI built into its codebase. So when you transfer Bitcoin, the protocol can handle the creation of random public/private key pairs. For example, I own approximately one-tenth of a Bitcoin which is located at the following public address: 1CmYceGTrRCjdWgnkgZ5uKrMDVj2nBoNf4. You can verify this on the Bitcoin ledger by visiting https://blockexplorer. com/ and inputting that alphanumeric string in the search bar. You will see that this public address represents ap-

---

[Section 1:3]

[1]Units of Bitcoin are stored by reference to public addresses instead of individuals' names, and for this reason, Bitcoin is considered pseudo-anonymous.

proximately one-tenth of a Bitcoin. In fact, any Bitcoin ledger maintained by any participant in the Bitcoin network will verify that same information—and thus, there is "consensus." When I transferred that Bitcoin to that public address, I used a Bitcoin wallet (more on wallets later) to automatically generate that address as part of the public/private key generation which the wallet did for me. Now if I want to receive Bitcoin, I can give people the above public address and they can send Bitcoin to it (feel free to test it out by sending some Bitcoin to that address . . . just kidding).

As is apparent by now, my ownership of Bitcoin has nothing to do with physical possession of any tangible coin or other artifact. My ownership is based solely on my knowledge of the private key that corresponds to that public address. So, just like an e-mail or text encrypted with my public key that can only be decrypted by my private key, the Bitcoin at that public address can only be spent by having the corresponding private key. Later in this book we will talk more about PKI and key management in general. As we will see, one of the impediments to greater blockchain adoption is developing workable solutions for managing private keys, especially at the enterprise level. It's also worth noting that the recent policy debate surrounding Apple and other large tech companies who are caught in a fight with law enforcement and national security agencies over encryption and the need for "back doors" for government access is all rooted in the effectiveness of PKI. Even the NSA and FBI lack the ability to circumvent PKI. Ironically, the concept of a "back door" to circumvent PKI encryption is only relevant for those individuals using a third party application for PKI encrypted text messaging where the third party provider may have access to the private key. Any sophisticated user who wants to avoid any possible back door can use an open source solution and generate her own public/private key pairs. Ultimately, PKI boils down to a mathematical equation and there are no back doors for mathematics. No matter how clever you are, 2+2 will always equal 4.

So let's revisit my Bitcoin transfer to Alex, but this time with a little more depth into the key concepts we discussed so far and outline each concept step by step and in its most logical sequence of events, which is generally as follows:

1. The first step is to **build a transaction,** which is done by generating the computer code necessary to provide all of the information for the transaction (in many ways similar to writing out a check). The transaction (as evi-

denced by computer code) has an input and an output (like a payor and a payee). The input describes the public address from where the transferred Bitcoin will be taken. The output tells the network where to send the Bitcoin (or more exactly, how to update the blockchain ledger to reflect the change of state with respect to the Bitcoin that are the subject matter of the transaction).

2. Once the transaction is built, **it must be "signed."** The process of signing a transaction lays at the heart of ownership of any digital asset on any blockchain as this is the method used to prove we have the private key associated with the public address from which we are spending our Bitcoin. To reiterate, the concept of ownership within the context of a blockchain means having the ability to transfer or otherwise control the interaction of the blockchain asset with the blockchain ledger. In the context of a blockchain, this ability is almost universally tied to being able to input a private key that corresponds to the public address on the blockchain. These public/private key pairs discussed above form the basis of ownership within a blockchain. Another ingenious aspect of PKI and its implementation within blockchain technology is the ability to prove control of, or the ability to "sign" with, a private key without any need to disclose the private key to anyone. Instead, by using mathematical tools, an individual can prove possession of a private key without the need to disclose it. This is another example of why PKI is a superior security tool over traditional username/ password databases.

3. After signing the transaction, it must be **broadcast over the Internet** so that it can be received by nodes running the blockchain protocol and these **nodes can continue to propagate the transaction** throughout the entire network of nodes. These nodes all verify that the transaction is not defective in any respect and ensure in particular that the asset being transferred has not previously been spent by the transferor.

4. Finally, **miners bundle up transactions into blocks** of aggregated transactions and append each block to the prior block; thereby extending the blockchain and ensuring that all of the nodes have a **current, immutable history of all transactions** ever logged on the blockchain.

Building the Transaction

Assuming I have a sufficient amount of Bitcoin, the first step in the process is to build a "transaction" that complies with the Bitcoin protocol. The actual construction of the transaction can be done on or offline. As long as a person has access to the public address or addresses for his or her unspent Bitcoin (in Bitcoin terminology, this is often referred to as "unspent transaction outputs" (or "UTXOs" for short)) and a public address for the receiving party, the sending party can prepare the data structure (i.e., input the computer code necessary to prompt the transaction—see Figure 2) of the transaction offline.[2]

Signing the Transaction

Once the transaction has been constructed by writing the appropriate computer code, it must be "signed" so as to prove the sender is in possession of the corresponding private key, which we discussed above. So now I've built my transaction, which includes one or more UTXOs from which I will use to fund my transfer to Alex, the amount of BTC[3] that I'm transferring to him and the public address that Alex gave to me (and for which Alex holds the private key). In addition, I've "signed" the transaction with my private key—securely permitting, once broadcast to the network, the dispatch of BTC from my public address to Alex's.

Broadcasting the Transaction

At this point, the state of the Bitcoin blockchain remains unchanged with respect to my Bitcoin. I still control my Bitcoin and the public address provided by Alex still shows a zero balance on the blockchain. This is because my transaction is not yet known to the Bitcoin network. Accordingly, the next step in the process is for me to broadcast the signed transaction to the Bitcoin network. Note that this is the first step that requires access to the Internet. Once I broadcast my transaction to the Bitcoin network, the nodes running the Bitcoin protocol will be alerted that a new transaction

---

[2]One quick note about UTXOs. Unlike some blockchain protocols, like Ethereum, Bitcoin does not use an account concept. Instead, every transaction that sends Bitcoin must originate from one or more UTXOs. This will become clearer as we discuss the differences between various blockchain protocols later in the book.

[3]This is short for Bitcoin similar to USD (for Dollars) and EUR (for Euros).

has been broadcasted on the network. When a node receives my transaction it will immediately (and automatically) verify to make sure that the transaction is valid (e.g., I'm not trying to spend Bitcoin I already spent before!) and properly signed. Once validated, each node initially receiving the transaction will in turn propagate the transaction to other nodes, and this process will continue to be repeated until a large number of nodes have received and validated the transaction.

As previously noted, the Bitcoin network (like other blockchains) is a decentralized system where nodes form peer-to-peer relationships with other nodes, who in turn have other relationships with other nodes and so on. This makes a blockchain network very resilient against any sort of single point of failure. This is especially true of the Bitcoin network because of the large number of nodes that make up the network. There are several thousand Bitcoin nodes located all across the globe. For current information on the number of locatable nodes and their geographic disbursement, check out https://bitnodes.21.co. While my transaction involving Alex has propagated throughout this robust peer-to-peer network, there is still one last step left—my transaction needs to be memorialized into a block on the Bitcoin blockchain.

Mining the Transaction

This last step will be accomplished when a Bitcoin "miner" bundles my transaction up with dozens of other transactions, solves a cryptographic puzzle and successfully mines the next block in the blockchain. Within that block will forever exist my transaction, and from that point on, the BTC transferred to Alex will now be a UTXO requiring Alex's private key to be spent. We will discuss the process of mining in more detail elsewhere in this book.

§ 1:4   Application of cryptographic solutions to control ownership of digital assets

As we have noted, public key infrastructure (PKI) is one of the most fundamental components of blockchain technology. The ability to securely control any digital asset or state represented on a digital ledger is fundamental to the value of blockchain technology. Some commentators, however, have raised concerns about the possibility that future computers, such as those that may utilize quantum computing, will be powerful enough to use brute force attacks to destroy the effectiveness of public key cryptography. In other words, computers may become so computationally powerful that they could run through all the possible alphanumeric combinations in a short enough period of time so as to "guess" the correct private key. While this is certainly a possibility, it does not likely pose any risk to the ultimate efficacy of blockchain technology. To conclude otherwise assumes that the cryptographic components of blockchains will stay static in the face of advances in cryptography. There is no reason to assume this will be the case. To the contrary, the cryptographic component of blockchain technology is modular in the sense that new techniques can be used to replace or supplement existing techniques. So if quantum computers become the mainstay of cryptographic computation, then there is no reason to believe blockchains will not also use quantum techniques to ensure the security of the network. Finally, if public key cryptography fails, then so will all the encryption currently used by the World's financial institutions and governments. So, society will likely have much bigger issues.

§ 1:5 Transactions and blocks

Before going any further, it is useful to reinforce the importance of the organization of transactions into blocks because this structure provides a significant barrier to manipulation—and hence, is the primary reason blockchains are considered immutable. Once a transaction is a part of the blockchain, its place in history can't be changed.[1] This results from how transactions are grouped (or blocked together) and the relationship between one grouping of transactions and the prior groupings before it. Again, for purposes of explaining this concept, we will focus on the Bitcoin protocol, but the same concepts apply to virtually every (if not all) blockchain protocols.

As transactions are broadcast throughout the Bitcoin network, miners (discussed in detail in the next section) group these transactions into "blocks" (which simply refers to a collection of transactions)—see Figure 1 for a graphical

---

[Section 1:5]

[1]This statement assumes a blockchain with a significant enough "network effect" and adequate distribution of power within the network. While the Bitcoin network has avoided any material issues, the collapse of a DAO on the Ethereum blockchain ultimately led to a rollback of the ledger, all of which will be discussed in more detail in Chapter 4.

depiction. Once a miner successfully mines a block, that block is subjected to a cryptographic hash. This hash is then carried forward and becomes a part of the next block to be mined, which block is then subjected to a cryptographic hash. This process continues over and over again so that every block is back-linked to the blocks before it. As a result of every block being connected to its predecessor block, it becomes impossible to easily go back and change a record in a prior block (which becomes increasingly more difficult the more blocks back you go). For example, let's say that the current block in a blockchain is block 155103. If you attempted to modify a transaction in block 154103, the cryptographic hash of that block would change, and thus, have a cascading effect inasmuch as the cryptographic hash for the following 999 blocks would also now need to change since each one ultimately tied back to the hash of block 154103. The computing power necessary to override the consensus established after so many blocks is simply impossible on a mature network like Bitcoin. In fact, after six blocks have been mined, it is generally considered mathematically impossible to alter any prior transactions. This does not mean that you must wait for six blocks to have a reasonable degree of certainty with respect to a transaction as it is highly unlikely that a transaction will change after just one confirmation or block.

Figure 1. Graphic depiction of blockchain

Block 1	Block 2	Block 3
Header	Header (includes hash of Block 1)	Header (includes hash of Block 2)
Transaction 1	Transaction 1	Transaction 1
Transaction 2	Transaction 2	Transaction 2
Transaction 3	Transaction 3	Transaction 3
Transaction 4	Transaction 4	Transaction 4

Bitcoin's Wiki[2] provides a good example of what an example Bitcoin transaction looks like in Bitcoin's scripting language.

Figure 2. Bitcoin's scripting language

```
Input:
Previous tx:
f5d8ee39a430901c91a5917b9f2dc19d6d1a0e9cea205b009ca73dd04470b9a6
Index: 0
scriptSig:
304502206e21798a42fae0e854281abd38bacd1aeed3ee3738d9e1446618c4571d10
90db022100e2ac980643b0b82c0e88ffdfec6b64e3e6ba35e7ba5fdd7d5d6cc8d25c
6b241501
Output:
Value: 5000000000
scriptPubKey: OP_DUP OP_HASH160
404371705fa9bd789a2fcd52d2c580b65d35549d
OP_EQUALVERIFY OP_CHECKSIG
```

---

[2]URL: https://en.bitcoin.it/wiki/Main_Page.

As previously described, the first part of the transaction describes the input from where the transferred Bitcoin will be taken, and the second part (output) tells the network where to send the Bitcoin (or more exactly, how to update the blockchain ledger to reflect the change of state with respect to the Bitcoin that are the subject matter of the transaction). The scriptSig operations code allows nodes to verify that this transaction was signed by the holder of the private key (without the need to actually disclose the private key as part of the transaction), thus verifying that the transaction is authorized. The operation codes at the end of the output component of the transaction operate to "encumber" the newly transferred Bitcoin with a condition that the recipient must sign (with its private key) any future transaction in order to spend her new Bitcoin (i.e. the transferee must now authorize, using its private key, any change of ownership of such Bitcoin).

§ 1:6 Incentive structures: Proof-of-Work (Mining) vs. Proof-of-Stake

Nodes operating on a protocol are responsible for validating transactions and helping to maintain consensus. These nodes, however, must be capable of working in a trust-less manner. Accordingly, a solution is necessary for what is called the Byzantine Generals Problem. The dilemma faced by the generals is how to coordinate amongst each other in battle when the lines of communication may be compromised, such that information you are receiving is meant to deceive you. The solution requires that trust be removed from the equation entirely. This is where miners fit into the Bitcoin protocol.

In addition to nodes that propagate transactions, other members of the network are responsible for creating new blocks that are added to the blockchain. These people are generally referred to as "miners." Mining transactions requires that the operator of the mining node expend resources in terms of computing power and electricity. Accordingly, in order to ensure a robust network of mining nodes, blockchain protocols provide incentives to miners by issuing them newly issued cryptocurrency (e.g., BTC) if they successfully mine a block (i.e., a collection of transactions together with certain additional information, such as the hash of the previous block). Currently, the most commonly used incentive/mining structure is known as "proof-of-work." This structure actually addresses two distinct, albeit related, concerns. The first of which we just mentioned, being a way to provide incentives to people to participate in the network (which also helps introduce new "money supply" into the system). The second concern addressed by "proof-of-work" is to minimize the risk of an attack on the network by a malicious actor.

If operating a mining node and engaging in mining is too easy (or too cheap), then the network risks one or more people colluding to operate a sufficient number of mining nodes whereby they could crowd out the other miners (known as a 51% attack) and manipulate the ledger for their own interest. In order to minimize the risk of this attack, "proof-of-work" requires that miners expend scarce resources—significant computing power, which in turn requires a significant amount of electrical consumption. The introduction of scarce resources makes it incredibly expensive for any one person or group of colluding people to take over enough of the network mining to engage in malicious behavior. Though, it should be noted, with the growth of mining in China increasing significantly over the last few years, there has been a growing concern about a 51% attack. Since "proof-of-work" is implemented differently on different blockchains, we will focus on how "proof-of-work" operates on Bitcoin.

After the completion of each block, a new mathematical problem (also known as a "nonce") is generated, and a new competition begins among the miners for the next block. Each miner starts the process by aggregating a certain number of transactions that are yet to be added to a block (transactions yet to be included in a block are said to be waiting in the "transaction pool") and proposes to add that block to the ledger.[1] Only one miner, however, can successfully add a block, which is done by solving the mathematical problem generated once the previous block was mined. Winning the competition is based on repeatedly hashing a mathematical problem until by chance the solution is generated. The more computational power applied, the faster a solution can be found—this is nothing but a brute force effort. The Bitcoin protocol is programmed so that a new block is mined approximately every 10 minutes. This pace of mining is

---

[Section 1:6]

[1]A miner may discriminate between which transactions it wishes to aggregate into a block based on the potential payout that transaction has set for the miner once the miner successfully mines the block in which the transaction is aggregated into.

ensured because the protocol dynamically adjusts the level of difficulty in solving the mathematical problem based on the combined computing power mining at any given time. As the aggregate amount of computational power increases, so does the difficulty. The dynamic adjustment keeps the block interval at 10 minutes. This reward system is responsible for aligning the incentives of miners with the security of the network.

When Bitcoin was first introduced, people mined for Bitcoin with general purpose computers. The successful miner was rewarded with 50^2 brand new Bitcoins (together with all of the transaction fees associated with the transactions to be bundled up into the solved block). Over time, miners began to utilize graphics processing units (GPUs), often utilizing several GPU cards in an open air case called a "mining rig." This form of mining, however, was short lived with the advent of application specific integrated circuits (known as ASICs). These ASICs were designed and manufactured to do one thing very well—Bitcoin mining. It wasn't long before GPU mining was no longer economically viable. Over the last few years, advancements in ASIC technology continually led to miner heartbreak as manufacturers often failed to keep up with orders and timely deliver equipment. In many cases, by the time ASIC mining equipment was delivered, faster and more efficient ASIC designs had hit the market. In addition to increasingly more powerful and expensive ASICs, massive mining operations began to operate all over the globe with concentrations found in areas where low cost electricity was readily available.

Today, all but the very largest mining operations have little chance of being the successful miner of a block. As a result, almost all miners now participate in a mining pool. A mining pool is an operator who aggregates the computational power of hundreds or thousands of individual miners. Miners are then compensated based on their contribution to the pool in terms of computational power. While pools require miners to share in rewards, it ensures them a steady flow of Bitcoin that roughly approximates the computational power of their mining equipment. Otherwise, even large mining operations could potentially go years without successfully

---

[2]The Bitcoin protocol has a pre-programmed system of diminishing rewards. Every 210,000 blocks, the reward is halved. In November of 2012, the reward was reduced to 25 Bitcoins and was further reduced to 12 and one-half Bitcoins in July 2016.

mining a block. The days of Bitcoin mining being dominated by basement hobbyist are long over, having been displaced by mining operations that utilize more computational power than the World's most powerful supercomputers—combined.

Proof-of-Stake

Not all blockchains rely on a proof-of-work consensus algorithm. Instead, a "proof-of-stake" consensus model is used.[3] In a proof-of-stake model, the influence of each node participating in the network is dynamic and constantly adjusted based on their economic stake in the network. There are different methods and mathematical models used to determine the specific methodology used to determine this weighting, but the general idea is to allocate it generally based on the relative loss each node would suffer as a result of a network failure or breach. Economically, this model makes sense from an incentives stand point—at least on its surface. The idea is that someone with a significant amount of the network's assets would not want the network to fail or suffer a breach because that person's network assets would decline in value as the utility of that network diminished. This assumes, however, that a malicious actor could not easily "short" his position on another exchange in order to profit from a decline in the price of that network's assets. To address this, some models require nodes to post a certain amount of cryptocurrency as a bond in order to ensure their efficacy as a participant in the network. Another form of consensus that does not rely on proof-of-work, and which is often used in conjunction with proof-of-stake methodologies, is to hold multiple "rounds" of consensus voting by participating nodes, until a certain percentage of uniformity is reached. The threshold set is typically tied to a mathematical calculation whereby the probability of a failure is considered acceptable.

§ 1:7 Distinctions between permissioned and non-permissioned blockchains

Some of the most significant research and debate within the blockchain community centers around the efficacy of "permissioned," or closed, blockchains versus unrestricted, or open, blockchains. Financial institutions have a natural aversion to using publicly accessible databases to conduct

---

[3]Chapter 2 includes a more in depth discussion of different blockchain protocols and their consensus algorithm.

transactions involving customer information. There are several other problems for using public ledgers, including the fact that anyone can operate a node or run a mining operation. Arguably, these individuals should be subject to a financial institution's know your customer (KYC) and bank secrecy act (BSA) requirements—something that is not possible on the Bitcoin or Ethereum protocol (Ethereum is discussed in more detail in the next chapter). As a result, many commentators and industry players believe that blockchain solutions adopted by financial institutions and certain other businesses (e.g., law firms) will need to be permissioned systems that rely on nodes and mining performed by only those participants who are selected by the business community establishing the permissioned blockchain network. For example, a blockchain solution developed for banks would look like the Bitcoin protocol, except that the nodes and miners (assuming a proof of work system of consensus is used) would all be operated by the banks who make up the participants in the system.

Others have argued that such systems cannot provide the reliability that an open network like Bitcoin provides because the permissioned systems lack the robust network that ensures efficacy in the system. These individuals believe that adequate encryption techniques exist to protect customer information through encryption rather than closing off the system. There is merit to this position, especially given recent advancements in blockchain algorithms which permit participants in the network to validate transactions without knowing the identity of the parties to the transaction or the amount of the transaction. Accordingly, such a system, if implemented properly, could protect customer data while allowing bank participants to take advantage of a more robust network, such as the Bitcoin protocol.

The arguments for a permissioned system driven by concerns over privacy may be misplaced if one steps back and accepts the fact that bank databases are essentially operating on open systems today. All bank information, including sensitive customer information, are stored on networked databases that are connected to a very public Internet. These databases are protected by encryption, passwords, and firewall technology. If all the same (or in some cases, better) technological protections can be implemented on a public blockchain, then what is the real difference between the current, centralized databases accessible through the Internet and the proposed public blockchain networks? It seems then that the most legitimate concerns about public blockchains is not keeping sensitive information private, but rather the stability and certainty of continuity with respect to the community of miners and operators of nodes.

If only member banks are permitted to operate nodes and mining operations within a closed network, then there is a very high degree of certainty that the network will always reach consensus on the protocol (i.e., the rules governing the ledger). If, on the other hand, a group of banks is piggy backing on the Bitcoin network and the Bitcoin miners decide to adopt a hard fork[1] that alters the rules governing the ledger (e.g., they decide to roll back certain transactions), this could be problematic for the banks using this system. The recent DAO implosion[2] within the Ethereum community (which is covered in more detail in Chapter 4) shows how quickly a blockchain community can lose consensus on how a network should operate and that it is possible for the network to alter "immutable" records if a majority of the miners elect to adopt a "hard fork" and change the network protocol. This should be very disconcerting for any institution considering the public version of the Ethereum protocol.

§ 1:8   The issue of anonymity or lack thereof

Because of Bitcoin's popularity as a currency for conducting business on the dark-net (see Chapter 7 for more on the dark-net and the tools used to access it), it has had to defend itself against guilt by association. One of the largest illicit businesses on the dark-net is the illegal sale of narcotics on marketplaces that resemble eBay, except the products being sold are heroin, cocaine, crystal meth, and virtually every other controlled substance made. Virtually all such transactions are conducted in Bitcoin because it is pseudo-anonymous. We qualify anonymous with "pseudo" because while Bitcoin does not use names to identify parties to

---

[Section 1:7]

[1]A hard fork is a change to the Bitcoin protocol that makes previously invalid blocks/transactions valid, and therefore requires all users to upgrade (https://en.bitcoin.it/wiki/Hardfork).

[2]The largest Decentralized Autonomous Organization (DAO) to date, known as "The DAO," had a market capitalization of approximately $130,000,000 at one point, but ultimately failed when a flaw in the code was exploited and tens of millions of dollars in cryptocurrency was taken contrary to the intention of The DAO's creators.

transactions, each transaction is recorded and available for the World to view on any Bitcoin Blockchain explorer. For this reason, absent certain additional measures, individuals can be linked to Bitcoin transactions. For example, if I have an account with Coinbase (one of the most popular online wallets and trading platforms), and I purchase $1,000 worth of Bitcoin from Coinbase, that Bitcoin will be associated with a public Bitcoin address. Coinbase's internal records will include a database that shows the individual's name who owns the Bitcoin associated with that public address. Accordingly, if I then use that Bitcoin to purchase narcotics on the dark-net, it is conceivable for law enforcement to trace that Bitcoin back to my Coinbase account and link it to my true identity.

The lack of full anonymity is not only a concern for those engaging in illicit transactions, but also has implication for keeping customer information private if banks or other businesses use an open, public distributed ledger to implement transactions on the blockchain. As mentioned in section 1:6, efforts are underway by several start-ups to develop open ledger platforms which allow for fully anonymous transactions. For the most part, these technologies are aimed at facilitating the conduct of sensitive transactions on open, public ledgers (rather than facilitating illicit business). More specifically, if parties can engage in transactions on open, public ledgers without the identity of the participants being known or the specific terms of the transaction being available to the public (such as the amount of a money transfer), this would go a long way in solving at least one of the primary concerns about banks and other businesses have about using open, public ledgers instead of closed systems. Nonetheless, there still exists concerns about the lack of control (or vetting) of those who operate nodes and mining operations on open, public ledgers, such as Bitcoin and Ethereum.

§ 1:9 Wallets

No introductory discussion about blockchains would be complete without explaining the concept of "wallets"—a software and/or hardware that holds the private key(s) associated with one or more public addresses. The vast majority of transactions on Bitcoin and other blockchains that utilize a cryptocurrency are completed with the assistance of a "wallet." A wallet can take the form of software or hardware. For an example of a software wallet, you can visit bitcoin.org and download a free software wallet. Alternatively, if you are very security conscious and concerned about storing your cryptocurrency on a computer that may be accessible from the Internet (i.e., having your computer and wallet hacked), you can purchase a physical device (see Figure 3 below) sold by Ledger, Trezor, or a host of other manufacturers. These physical wallets benefit from the added protection of not being connected to any network. As discussed above, transactions can be created and signed without any network connection. As such, a physical wallet only needs to connect to a network for a brief moment in order to broadcast the transaction. Most physical wallets process transactions within a trusted environment within the device's circuits, which further reduces any risk of a security breach when the device does need to connect to a network to broadcast a transaction.

Figure 3. An example of a hardware wallet

Whether software or hardware, wallets make interacting with blockchain networks much easier. Private keys that are needed to sign and spend cryptocurrency are stored in the wallet. For security purposes, these private keys are encrypted and locked in the wallet. In order to access a private key, the user of the wallet must create a unique password or passphrase and enter that password or passphrase every time the user attempts to sign a transaction. In addition to providing a secure environment to store private keys, some wallets are also programmed to build transactions for one or more blockchain protocols. This is helpful for the average consumer who would have difficulty creating transactions programmatically. With a wallet, the user enters the information necessary for a transaction—namely addressee and amount—using a friendly graphical user interface. All of the heavy lifting occurs behind the scenes, including the coding necessary to broadcast the transaction on the blockchain network. This is particularly important when using an untrusted device to connect to the Internet, such as a retailer's computer.

As the first blockchain protocol, it should not be surprising that there are a large number of wallets designed for operation with Bitcoin. Other blockchains, such as Ethereum, also have a variety of wallets available for consumer use. Some wallets, such as Jaxx or GDAX, allow users to hold Bitcoin and Ethereum in the same application. To the user, the experience is identical to having one wallet that contains U.S. Dollars and Euros. Technically, however, there are two separate wallets since the programming necessary to structure transactions in Bitcoin and Ethereum are different.

As we move on to more detailed examinations of blockchains other than Bitcoin, it will become apparent that wallets are necessary for those protocols, like Bitcoin, that allow consumers to exchange cryptocurrencies in everyday commerce. On the other hand, those blockchains developed for specific industries may not require the use of wallets. Web portals or other digital clients will be a sufficient user interface. For example, a blockchain protocol and application built thereon, designed for managing supply chain information (see chapter 2), a user does not need a wallet, but rather a user interface that allows it to track items through the supply chain, so a web portal and/or mobile application will do fine for these purposes.

Chapter 2

Smart Contracts

§ 2:1   Summary of important points

- In addition to being used as a digital currency, block-chains can implement more robust functionality.
- The term smart contracts is generally understood to mean programming code that is executed on the block-chain in a manner that changes the state of every parti-cipant's ledger.
- There is some confusion created by the misconception that all smart contracts are legally binding agreements.
- There exists Federal and fairly uniform state legisla-tion that, with certain limited exceptions, recognizes the validity of electronic signatures to the same extent as traditional "wet ink" signatures.
- Smart contracts are being most actively developed in the financial services and supply chain industries.

§ 2:2   Smart contracts—Basics

Unlike the term "blockchain," there is no agreed upon def-inition for a smart contract.[1] However, we venture to estab-lish three basic elements of a smart contract: (i) the proposed transaction (which, of course, will reside on a blockchain) would involve more than the simple transfer of virtual cur-rency from one party to another, (ii) the transaction involves two or more parties, and (iii) the implementation of the transaction is autonomous (i.e., human intervention will not be required once the contract is initiated). Just like with a simple transfer of virtual currency, smart contracts are coded and digitally recorded on the blockchain by and through the efforts (albeit autonomous) of nodes and miners.

There are many benefits to smart contracts versus tradi-tional contracts. The key benefit of smart contracts lies in the heart of its most critical and coveted feature: automation. Since smart contracts require little or no human interven-tion, they are generally much cheaper, faster, and less ambiguous (they are code-based, after all) in execution and leave almost no room for human error—once set into motion. On the same token, since smart contracts are code-based, any error in the contract's code may result in an irreversibly faulty transaction.

§ 2:3   Terminology

There are few blockchain related concepts that create the

[Section 2:2]

[1]https://bol.bna.com/what-is-a-smart-contract/.

confusion and the level of disagreement than the concept of "smart contracts." Firstly, there are several different meanings assigned to the phrase "smart contracts." In the context of blockchain application development, the term "smart contracts" has nothing to do with the traditional notion of a legal contract. Instead, a smart contract refers to a snippet of programming code that gets executed on the blockchain, for the most part, in an automated fashion. Unfortunately, this term is often used interchangeably when referred to the idea of implementing legal contracts on the blockchain—something that many also refer to as a smart contract. To avoid unnecessary confusion, it is preferable for the speaker to distinguish between a smart contract, on the one hand, that just refers to code being executed on the blockchain versus a smart contract, on the other hand, that refers to implementing a legal contract on the blockchain.[1] For example, in the code context, transmitting the following to the blockchain is considered a smart contract:

contract
Hel-
loWorld {

        event Print(string out);
        function() { Print("Hello, World!"); }
}.

Obviously, the above bears no relationship to a legal contract, with its required elements of offer, acceptance and consideration. Before turning our attention to the concept of implementing legal contracts on the blockchain, let's continue to discuss the code-based smart contract. In this context, smart contracts represent a significant advance over the basic scripting language that only maintains unspent transaction outputs on a distributed ledger (e.g., Bitcoin). While the Bitcoin protocol contains a basic scripting language that allows for some programming functionality, it is not nearly as robust as the Ethereum Virtual Machine (EVM) that is incorporated into the Ethereum Protocol or

---

[Section 2:3]

[1]Hyperledger uses the term "chaincode" to describe code intended to be executed on a blockchain. The authors feel that is a much better description as it avoids any confusion with respect to contracts intended to constitute legally enforceable agreements.

similar protocols with turing-complete[2] programming capabilities. The effect of this is to add a fully-functional computer to a blockchain. So not only can we store cryptocurrency in a blockchain, but now we can store and implement computer programs on a blockchain, such that when called, the computer code will run on every node connected to the network. These sorts of smart contracts are what allow for the creation of decentralized autonomous organizations (DAO) among other high-level systems.

Some blockchain protocols, like Hyperledger, are a hybrid between Bitcoin and Ethereum. This hybrid approach permits the development of a blockchain environment using a turing-complete programming language (e.g., Go in Hyperledger), but once established, users only have available those functions that the architects of the blockchain have created and made available. This approach has a certain appeal for industry-specific blockchains. This approach allows for the development of data structures and functions necessary to fully implement a blockchain serving a particular purpose or industry—and nothing more.

One might question any blockchain protocol that doesn't expose a turing-complete programming language to its users, like Ethereum does. Why limit functionality? *The DAO* implosion[3] discussed in more detail in Chapter 4 is a good example of why increased functionality can be problematic— increased functionality requires more code, which results in a higher probability of code errors (or "bugs"), which can (as with *the DAO*) have a substantially negative impact on a platform and its users. So, while many consider Bitcoin's limited scripting language a limitation, others see it as an advantage because it provides the functions and capabilities that are necessary to accomplish its purpose—and nothing more. This approach minimizes the possibility of others trying to implement smart contracts not properly vetted, which can lead to catastrophic outcomes.

---

[2]Turing-complete languages (named after Alan Turing, an English mathematician and early computer scientist) is the name given to programming languages that allow its users to write applications that have no limitations in terms of the logic that can be implemented. In other words, they are general purpose programming languages rather than limited scripting languages like Bitcoin utilizes.

[3]The largest DAO to date, known as *"The DAO,"* had a market capitalization of approximately $130,000,000 at one point, but ultimately failed when a flaw in the code was exploited and tens of millions of dollars in cryptocurrency was taken contrary to the intention of *The DAO's* creators.

It's also important to note that even Bitcoin's scripting language still allows for a considerable amount of native functionality. For example, when transferring Bitcoin, a user can require that more than one party "sign" any subsequent transaction involving the transferred Bitcoin. This is called encumbering that Bitcoin with a "multi-sig" requirement. This allows for parties to create escrow like arrangements whereby Bitcoin funds cannot be unlocked without both the recipient's private key and a neutral third party's key. Or, for example, a company can create a joint signor arrangement, similar to that which might be established with a checking account—so that two or more individuals must "sign" any Bitcoin payments.

In addition to multi-sig capabilities, Bitcoin's scripting language also allows messages to be embedded into transactions using the OP_RETURN function. Under Bitcoin Core standards most nodes will not accept an OP_RETURN message if it exceeds 40 bytes. With the implementation of Bitcoin Core 0.12.0, this data cap will be doubled to 80 bytes. While the ability to embed messages may seem like a trivial function, in reality it permits the addition of useful functionality. Because of Bitcoin's immutable records (which are all time stamped), this feature permits the simple implementation of notary public services. These capabilities can be implemented with a minimal amount of coding.[4]

While blockchain technology (with the possible exception of Bitcoin) is still young and subject to much development, there are already concerns about the lack of standards and interoperability between different blockchains. The W3C, the organization responsible for maintaining uniform standards for the Internet, has taken an interest in working towards developing similar standards for blockchain technology. The ultimate question is how do you allow different blockchain technologies and the smart contracts built on top of them to communicate with each other? While only time will tell, the need for interoperability between blockchains is still debatable.

§ 2:4 Basic mechanics

Armed with a basic understanding of what code-based

---

[4]For a quick and easy implementation, see Bitcoin 21's Tutorial: A Bitcoin-Payable Notary Public. URL: https://21.co/learn/bitcoin-notary-public/#a-bitcoin-payable-notary-public.

smart contracts are and what they can do, we can turn our attention to the basic mechanics of how they work. As you think about smart contracts, the most important concept to remember is that they simply consist of computer code that executes on a distributed manner (blockchain)—in other words, the computer code runs on every node that is a part of the blockchain protocol implementing the smart contract.

§ 2:5 Basic mechanics—Programming smart contracts

Code-based smart contracts are embodied in computer code. The type of code depends on the blockchain protocol on which the code is intended to be implemented. For example, a smart contract implemented on Bitcoin will be written in Bitcoin's scripting language, while a smart contract intended for deployment on Ethereum will most likely be written in Solidity or Serpent. In the case of Ethereum, both Solidity (currently the most popular Ethereum language) and Serpent, are ultimately compiled into byte code (a lower level set of instructions that are machine readable but difficult for humans to understand), which byte code is then executed by the Ethereum Virtual Machine (or EVM). The bug that led to *The DAO* implosion was a bad function written in Solidity.

The fabric implementation of the Hyperledger protocol utilizes the Go programming language to establish the "chain code," which establishes the functionality that will be available on any particular blockchain based on the fabric protocol. Clients that interact with that blockchain will do so by using a very popular JavaScript based framework known as Node.js. As noted above, this framework for industry specific blockchains has the strength of allowing industry participants to determine what functionality is desirable on the blockchain and then being able to implement it through the use of a very common web-building framework like Node.js. There is no shortage of competent JavaScript and Node.js coders, which will make the implementation of client software much more accessible to companies who may not have the resources to hire people to code languages like Solidity which are unique to Ethereum.

For code-based smart contracts to achieve their full capabilities, they need to be able to respond to extrinsic information. For example, a self-implementing futures contract for oil will need a way to verify the price of a barrel of oil at the close of trade on a particular day. This is easier said than done. Because smart contracts of this nature are self-implementing, the introduction of any corrupted or manipulated extrinsic information can lead to disastrous results.

One approach to solving this problem is through the use of oracles, which are entities that provide smart contracts with extrinsic information. Unlike the nodes and transaction validators who form the basis of a functioning blockchain, oracles must be trusted entities who submit information to a blockchain or smart contract through cryptographically signed messages. Extrinsic evidence introduced to a blockchain must be cryptographically signed in order to confirm that the person submitting such information is in fact the trusted person and not an imposter.

§ 2:6 Basic mechanics—Sidechains

Because Bitcoin's purpose was to solve a problem with digital currencies, its scripting language is not turing-complete. Yet, the Bitcoin protocol itself is the most mature and considered to be the most secure blockchain in existence. Sidechains are an effort to utilize the best parts of the Bitcoin protocol and couple it with a more powerful system for generating smart contracts. One company pursuing this technology is Blockstream. Blockstream's solution is to transfer assets (further described below) from one blockchain to another by embedding the departing asset transfer in the initial blockchain (most likely Bitcoin) and embedding a cryptographic confirmation of such departure on the corresponding asset created on the second blockchain. The first blockchain is referred to as the parent chain, and the second blockchain as the sidechain. In essence, this permits parties to "check out" digital assets from Bitcoin to another blockchain where more complex smart contracts can be applied to their relationship, while the parent chain continues to provide long-term immutable record keeping. The Elements Project[1] is an open source community project that is using similar technology to extend functionality to the Bitcoin protocol through the use of sidechains. As part of the project, Elements has developed a component known as "Confidential Transactions" that allows individuals to transfer cryptocur-

---

[Section 2:6]

[1]URL: https://elementsproject.org/.

rency on a blockchain with only the participants to the transaction being able to see the amount of the assets transferred. Technologies like this could one day be useful in bridging the gap between permissioned and public distributed ledgers.

Figure 1. Concept of Sidechains

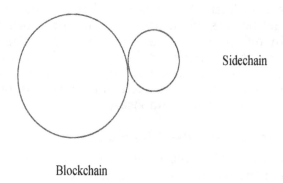

Sidechain

Blockchain

As Figure 1 helps visualize, the point at which the blockchain and sidechain come into contact is the where the "peg" between chains occurs. It is also where the security of one chain must hand off responsibility to the other, at least until data is returned back to the primary blockchain.

The difficulty in implementing sidechains is to maintain the trustless nature of the system as assets pass from one protocol to another. Blockstream uses a technique it describes as a two-way peg. The general idea is that the asset being transferred between sidechains is pegged to both blockchains through the use of "a simplified payment verification proof," with the ultimate goal being a mini-proof of work system to maintain a trustless state during the transition of assets between blockchains. Ultimately, only time will tell whether the concept of a sidechain becomes a viable product, but sufficient resources are being devoted to proof-of-concepts in this area to justify close attention being paid to any progress in its implementation.

§ 2:7 Smart contract use cases

There are potential use cases for blockchain technology in almost every industry. Before proceeding further, however, we have one word of caution. There is a tremendous amount of hype surrounding blockchain technology—just as there was with the Internet when it first became popular. That doesn't mean that blockchain technology will not ultimately be as revolutionary as many suggest, but expectations should be tempered in some cases. First, blockchains are not always better than traditional centralized systems. There are simply instances where centralized systems provide a better and less expensive solution for particular problems. Second, smart contracts (with the exception of some basic multi-sig like contracts) are still in the developmental stage and are not ready for prime time as of the publication of this book. As *The DAO* implosion discussed in Chapter 4 shows us, much further work and research are needed before complex smart contracts will become prevalent and safe in the real world. Part of the complexity of smart contracts is not the code itself or the ability to make out the logic of particular relationships, but rather the complex game theory and microeconomic theory that can come into play when trying to rely solely on deterministic code to govern an entire relationship between two or more parties. Lawyers have difficulty accomplishing this goal with written contracts, so there is little reason to believe that anyone can do it with code.

§ 2:8   Smart contract use cases—Financial Industry

The use cases that always come to mind first involve digital currency and other ways to store value on distributed ledgers. This is not surprising given that blockchain technology was developed to solve issues with digital currencies. Ironically, Bitcoin, which was often proclaimed to be the beginning of the end of banks, has triggered an explosion in investment by financial institutions in blockchain technology. Banks, insurance companies, securities exchanges, and other financial institutions are working towards unlocking the cost savings, efficiencies, and competitive advantages that distributed ledgers provide over outdated centralized systems. Use cases in the financial industry go well beyond payment methods.

In addition to its logical association with financial transactions, blockchain technology has also benefitted by the more general explosion in FinTech investment. Whether in New York or London, the financial capitals of the world are busy developing the next generation of technologies that will overhaul our financial systems and grant access to hundreds of millions of people who currently lack access to modern payment systems and banking services. The blockchain has attracted a significant amount of attention in the FinTech community because of its value proposition and borderless platform perfectly suited for international transactions and those countries lacking stable currencies.

NASDAQ has invested significant resources in developing a distributed exchange platform and has established a Blockchain Innovation group within the company. NASDAQ's most significant contribution to date is its Linq system, which allows companies to develop digitally represented shares that can be traded. These efforts dovetail nicely with an initiative announced by the State of Delaware in May 2016 which will focus on facilitating the issuance of blockchain based shares in corporations organized in Delaware. In addition to enjoying increased speed and reduced trading costs, shares traded on blockchains would also benefit from more efficient and transparent proxy voting and dissemination of information to shareholders.

In the banking sector, Barclays and Santander Innoventures have routinely been in the news for proof of concept prototypes and financial support for further blockchain research. According to CoinDesk's Banks and the Blockchain Report, published in 2015, UBS, BNY Mellon, Royal Bank of

Scotland, Citibank, Goldman Sachs, and several other banks were involved in either developing or supporting research in blockchain technology. The focus is broad-based, including both payment systems as well as trading settlement platforms, such as commercial paper trading. While the diversity of interest bodes well for blockchain technology, it does highlight one of the greatest challenges for its implementation in the financial sector: uniformity. Blockchain technology will never reach its full potential if the existing patchwork of systems that exist today are simply replaced with a patchwork of blockchain protocols. The need for collaboration bodes well for the R3 Consortium's efforts to work with the banking industry in a collective fashion. Ultimately, it's the core protocol that must be uniform in order to permit efficient interoperability between financial institutions (not just within the United States or any other banking system, but globally). Individual institutions are still free to develop diverse ecosystems for internal systems, and in fact, such innovation should be encouraged.

There is probably no other industry where the debate between permissioned and open distributed ledgers is more important. Concerns with open distributed ledgers are twofold with financial institutions. First, they deal with sensitive financial information of their customers and their own proprietary information (e.g., trading information). Second, anti-money laundering (AML) requirements make it nearly impossible for banks to rely on a payment or settlement platform where validation is done by anonymous individuals. Encryption could mitigate privacy concerns, but doesn't solve AML concerns. As a result, we can expect the financial industry's focus to remain on permissioned ledgers for some time.

§ 2:9 Smart contract use cases—Legal Industry

Smart contract use in the legal industry is closely related to contract automation, which has historically suffered from an abysmal adoption rate within law firms. For a host of reasons, various attempts to create templating engines that would assist in the automation of legal document generation have failed to catch on in any meaningful way. This past failure might be seen as an indication of the difficulties that lie ahead in the adoption of smart contracts in law firms. There are, however, several reasons to have hope that the experience with smart contracts will be different. First, economic factors have changed. Law firms are having increasingly difficult times boosting law firm profits in a legal marketplace where demand for services has been flat for many years and shows no signs of increasing any time soon. As such, products and services which promote cost cutting and efficiencies (which in turn reduce input costs) are more attractive than ever. Second, as clients begin to adopt blockchain technology, law firms will have little choice but to join in the adoption of the same tools. The analogy would be a law firm who decided not to adopt e-mail in the 1990s because it was certain facsimile technology was far superior. At some point, you can't risk being left behind.

While one would expect this section to be the most extensive given this book is written by a group of transactional lawyers, the reality is that all of the use cases set forth in this book impact the legal industry. Lawyers are involved to some degree in virtually all of the businesses and transactions described in this book, whether in the context of supply chain management, or corporate governance. As such, all of these categories could rightfully be included under the legal industry classification. How the legal industry approaches these changes is important, including how we draft contracts and evidence the logic of contractual relationships between two or more parties. There will be significant changes in how lawyers accomplish these things, and we will talk about this topic in great depth in section 2:20 below.

Historically, lawyers have been slow to adopt new technology, let alone be at the forefront of developing it. Blockchain seems to be different. Perhaps the infringement of smart contracts and engineers[1] on turf that has historically been dominated by lawyers has led to greater interest. The profession's interest has been broad based, including those from academics, such as Aaron Wright, a professor at Cardozo School of Law, who has been active in leading the discussion on policy and blockchain technology and developing smart contract technology. In the legal profession itself, many lawyers who once coded as hobbyists only have now turned the focus of their hobby on smart contract technology[2]—

[Section 2:9]

[1]Leading to the development of the term "legal engineers."

[2]This author maintains http://contractcode.io, a site dedicated to advancing the concept of developing legal contracts with software engineering principles.

which provides the perfect intersection between legal theory and policy, on the one hand, and technology and software engineering on the other hand. Blockchain and smart contracts have become a lawyer-nerd's dream.

In addition to academics and practitioners, technologists and software engineers all over the world are working collaboratively to advance smart contract technology and to fuse smart contract components with real world legal contracts. For example, David Roon[3] has been working on software libraries that allow smart contract components (those parts of an agreement that can be self-implementing on a blockchain) together with traditional legal contracts. Legalese[4] is working on an ambitious approach to drafting contracts that would permit lawyers or non-lawyers to draft contracts in a far more efficient manner through the use of domain-specific programming languages. Once legal contracts are reduced to machine readable code, many of the tools software engineers use to develop code can be equally applied to legal contracts, including testing and a code reuse, which have the potential to speed up the generation of contracts while reducing errors and ambiguities (at least unintentional ones).

Again, we will spend more time in section 2:20 discussing specific issues and concepts for implementing legal contracts developed with engineering principles, but as a preliminary matter, it's important for the reader to appreciate that the change that is occurring is far more radical than the change from type writers to computer word processors. There is a more fundamental paradigm shift at play, not simply a replacement of one tool (i.e., a typewriter) with another (Microsoft Word). That's not to say that lawyers won't use word processors in the future, but rather the compilation of legal contracts after a lawyer user inputs certain transaction parameters will be very different than today—see Figure 2 below.

---

[3]http://www.davidroon.com/.

[4]http://legalese.com/.

Figure 2. The future of contract drafting?

```
1   package main
2
3   import "fmt"
4   import "github.com/jndewey/cctools"
5   import "net/http"
6
7   func main() {
8       var governingLaw cctools.Clause
9       governingLaw.Name = "Governing Law"
10      governingLaw.Text = "This agreement is governed by Florida law"
11      var venue cctools.Clause
12      venue.Name = "Venue"
13      venue.Text = "Venue will be in Miami-Dade County"
14      var contractTest cctools.Document
15      contractTest.Clauses = []cctools.Clause {venue, governingLaw}
16      var output = cctools.Text(venue)
17      fmt.Println(output)
18      var converted = cctools.ClauseToJSON(venue)
19      fmt.Printf("%s\n", converted)
20      jdata := []byte(`{"name": "Venue", "text": "Venue will be in Palm Beach County"}`)
21      var structOutput = cctools.JSONtoClause(jdata)
22      fmt.Println(structOutput.Text)
23      num := cctools.Length(contractTest)
24      fmt.Println(num)
25      venue.SetName("Venue and Jurisdiction")
```

§ 2:10 Smart contract use cases—Accounting Industry

From an auditing perspective, blockchain technology makes possible real-time "triple-entry" accounting. Triple-entry accounting builds upon double-entry accounting by introducing cryptography to the notion of traditional accounting ledgers. More specifically, the blockchain allows entries to be added to an accounting ledger by other parties using cryptographic keys. These ledgers can track transactions between different parties and update each party's ledger after each transaction. This allows for the easy detection of discrepancies between debits on one ledger and credits on another ledger. Because of the immutable nature of the blockchain, it is impossible to go back after the fact and try to "cook the books." In addition, because only authorized transacting parties have the private keys necessary to enter into a transaction, outside auditors or government officials can have faith in the authenticity of the transactions reflected on the ledgers. Without a common blockchain accounting ledger, it is practically impossible to compare the books and records of multiple companies who have transacted business to determine whether the books and records, in total, are consistent. This is only possible with a trustless, distributed ledger that is capable of implanting cryptographic solutions—i.e., a blockchain.

These capabilities will ultimately lead to greater efficiencies as individuals (e.g., investors, rating agencies) and governments (e.g., taxing authorities and regulatory agencies) will have greater confidence in the authenticity and accuracy of financial records that are maintained using these technologies. This should translate into a reduction in transactional costs associated with regulatory compliance as well as debt and equity transactions in both private and public markets. These savings will easily pay for the implementation of blockchain technology in this area. It's important to note that these systems can be implemented on quasi-permissioned systems (where the general public may submit transactions, but the validators (or nodes) of the blockchain are approved and known persons), but may also be implemented on public blockchains because sensitive financial information that can't be made public can be encrypted so that only those persons with access to the private key can unlock the information. Again, it is not necessary for the validating nodes (including miners in a proof-of-work consensus model) to see the encrypted data in order to reach consensus and accurately update the distributed ledger.

§ 2:11   Smart contract use cases—Predictive and Commodity Markets (Auger)

Another area that can be improved by distributed ledgers is prediction markets. Using marketplaces or exchange-like platforms to predict future outcomes is nothing new. In fact, prediction markets have been used in one form or another for many years. Regulatory concerns, however, have hampered private innovation in this area. Currently, most prediction markets that operate in, or allow participants from, the United States are affiliated with colleges or university research programs or are otherwise government sanctioned. Private prediction market, Intrade, was a popular prediction market that allowed participants to purchase "interests" (akin to a futures contract) in all sorts of outcomes, including presidential elections. Ultimately, however, Intrade was forced to cease operations because of an action brought by the U.S. Commodity Futures Trading Commission (CFTC) for the trading of options off a registered exchange in violation of U.S. law. Because licensing and compliance under the CFTC is expensive and cumbersome, private innovation in this area has been limited.

Unlike centralized systems like Intrade, decentralized prediction markets do not operate in any particular jurisdiction, and once established, almost run independent of any particular central authority—which makes enforcement actions difficult as you can't shut the system down and you can't identify any single person responsible for its operations. The most prominent player in this space today is Augur.[1] One of the unique prospects of Augur, which hasn't fully launched as of the publication of this book, is the ability of individuals to create their own prediction markets for outcomes in which they are interested. For example, if you are interested in who will win the 2018 Super Bowl, you could create your own option contracts marketplace with Augur and other people could purchase "options" with cryptocurrency based digital currency—so that there is a real payout in the event people correctly predict the outcome. Real monetary payouts are an important aspect of prediction markets because how

---

[Section 2:11]

[1]https://www.augur.net/.

people predict outcomes differs depending on whether there is financial risk associated with being right or wrong.

§ 2:12 Smart contract use cases—Supply Chain Management

After finance, supply chain management may be the next area most susceptible to disruption by blockchain technology. Historically, supply chains have been a mash up of paperwork, official and unofficial certifications and customs and regulations—often spanning numerous jurisdictions, each with their own rules. If one includes trade finance into the mix, the situation becomes even more cumbersome with many transactions still involving paper, merchant letters of credit and bills of lading or other written documents of ownership. Blockchain technology has the capability to replace all of these antiquated systems with more efficient and robust platforms. When combined with other technologies, such as Internet of Things, the possibilities are quite staggering.

One can easily imagine payment mechanisms being automatically triggered when a cargo crate (which is embedded with a unique identifier on an RFID, NFC, or microprocessor) are detected entering its destination warehouse. If driverless car technology is implemented for sea-going vessels, the day when products cross oceans and are unloaded and brought to warehouses without human involvement may be fast approaching. This is made possible by the ability to reliably track products throughout the supply chain coupled with the ability to have automatic payments in a digital currency that knows no geographic boundaries.

The application of blockchain technology to supply chains is happening today. Skuchain has developed products such as Data LC, Blockchain Based Obligation (BBO), Deep Tier Financing, and Cash Flow Strips.[1] All of these products mirror the traditional tools of trade finance (e.g., letters of credit, banker's acceptances), but operate on the blockchain; and thus, benefit from the near instant and trustless execution environment. It is possible to implement all of these tools with smart contracts drafted in Solidity on Ethereum or with Bitcoin's scripting language through nominal transac-

---

[Section 2:12]

[1]http://skuchain.wpengine.com/how-it-works/.

tions using the OP_RETURN function to embed data into the Bitcoin ledger.

Everledger[2] is another example of a company already using blockchain technology to address supply chain issues. Rather than trade finance, Everledger seeks to ensure that conflict diamonds do not enter the supply chain at all. By using the blockchain to log unique identifiers associated with diamonds, Everledger is reducing the number of conflict diamonds by eliminating malicious actors from producing counterfeit certificates for diamonds moving through the supply chain. Everledger can also serve as a way to reduce theft in the diamond market. Everledger and Skuchain are just a sample of the companies already entering the supply chain arena with innovative blockchain applications.

Provenance is another blockchain start-up that is focused on transparency in the supply chain. According to Provenance's white paper,[3] it uses blockchain technology "to enable secure traceability of certifications and other salient information in supply chains." This in turn helps consumers have greater trust in the authenticity of the goods being purchased. Provenance's white paper, citing a BBC report, states that 50,000 tons of beef sold was later determined to contain horse DNA.[4] The blockchain permits virtually anything to be digitally tagged (including a unique identifier), which can then be tracked by securely including information about the items as they move through the supply chain. For example, if a consumer is purchasing a high end purse, that purse will often contain some sort of paper certification or other evidence of authenticity. Unfortunately, with the current system, it is easy to forge these certificates of authenticity. If, instead of a paper certificate, a unique identification (UID) has been created and tracked on a blockchain ledger, then a customer can verify the UID against the information on the blockchain to confirm the authenticity of the good being purchased.

§ 2:13   Smart contract use cases—Real Estate Industry

Some of the most ambitious blockchain applications involve real estate. Distributed ledgers are particularly good

---

[2]http://www.everledger.io/.

[3]https://www.provenance.org/whitepaper.

[4]https://www.provenance.org/whitepaper.

at maintaining ownership records for assets easily tokenized. This makes the blockchain the perfect vehicle to maintain real estate records. Real estate ownership and the laws that govern and establish priorities of interests in land vary greatly across the globe. Most of the world uses either a Torrens-based system which involves government involvement in each transfer and the issuance of a quasi-judicial certificate evidencing ownership or the common law system utilized by the United States where there is no government involvement in the transfer process. There exists a third category, which is whoever controls the military determines ownership of land—usually the most precious resource in countries relying on this system of governance (if it can be called that). Setting this system aside for a moment, the other two both have pros and cons. Government involvement reduces incidents of fraud but increases transactional costs. The U.S. system ostensibly reduces costs by eliminating any government proceeding as a part of the transaction, but much if not all of these savings are lost because the purchaser must obtain title insurance in order to make sure that the status of title is as represented by the seller.

It's obvious that a blockchain solution would reduce incidents of fraud (such as forgery) and transactional costs. The biggest impediment to implementation, however, is the historical use of these systems for hundreds of years in many developed nations. This makes even slight changes in the process difficult to accomplish. Ironically, it may be the third category of countries that leads the way in this area. Countries like Honduras, Estonia, and the Republic of Georgia have all been cited as exploring the use of blockchains in maintaining real estate records. Honduras, for example, has long suffered from poor record keeping with respect to real estate ownership. These conditions make them ripe for innovation, especially when the benefits of a distributed ledger would be felt immediately. Companies, like Factom,[1] are ready to fill the void with blockchain-based solutions.

If distributed ledgers are successfully implemented in less developed countries, they could serve as an example for developed countries. It may also be possible to phase in the use of blockchains in countries like the U.S. with the need for minimal legislative changes. For instance, specially-

---

[Section 2:13]

[1]http://factom.org.

created trust vehicles (SPV) could be created to hold title to individual parcels of real estate. Once a parcel of property is transferred into the SPV, beneficial ownership interests in the SPV can be exchanged on a distributed ledger. In addition to ownership, the blockchain can easily handle encumbrances on real estate, such as mortgages and easements, and any other information that is currently maintained in public land registries. Once on the blockchain, a parcel of real estate could be transferred with the same level of simplicity as ordering a pizza on a smart phone. Like supply chain solutions, a real estate blockchain could be implemented on the Bitcoin blockchain, a smart contract on Ethereum, or a specially created ledger created using tools like Hyperledger.

§ 2:14 Smart contract use cases—Healthcare

As evidenced by the mandate in the Affordable Care Act, public policy is served by transitioning medical records from a paper-based system to digital records. Evidence shows that better outcomes are achieved when health records are maintained in digital formats. While this is a step in the right direction, the current status of medical records is by no means an optimal one. For one, patients have very little access and control over their own medical records. Similarly, getting medical records from one medical provider to another remains far more difficult than it should be.

Because of its cryptographic genesis, blockchain technology is particularly well suited for handling private records. Even on a public blockchain, patients and doctors can easily pass medical records back and forth without anyone else on the blockchain being able to access the actual information being transmitted. For example, patients could generate unique private keys that can unlock specific medical records (such as a set of x-rays). These private keys could then be securely delivered to a medical provider who could then use the key to unlock the information needed to provide treatment and care. These private keys could also have expiration dates so that the keys would only work for a set period of time thereby reducing the risk that private keys could be stolen or hacked since they would only be operable for a limited period of time.

Another exciting possibility of health records on the blockchain is the ability to run algorithmic or artificially intelligent (AI) solutions against your entire medical history.

The ability of an AI platform to see a person's entire medical history would unlock the possibility of diagnosing illnesses years earlier. These solutions are made possible by the potential to tag medical records to unique digital IDs that could exist on the blockchain. For example, a public key could be printed on your health insurance card and scanned by each medical provider you visit. All medical records generated by that provider would be kept in digital form and encrypted using your public key and then uploaded to the blockchain. Only the holder of the private key (you) would then be able to search for, and, more importantly, decrypt, those records.

§ 2:15 Smart contract use cases—Private Wealth and Estate Planning

In the U.S. and many other counties, testamentary transfers are based on centuries old principles and custom. The highly technical requirements for the execution of a valid testamentary instrument has caused numerous legal challenges over the rightful heirs to estate assets of deceased persons. Because of blockchain's immutable nature, it makes a fantastic tool for recording important information. In addition, the security afforded by cryptography integrated into blockchains also provide for a secure environment for estate planning. Cryptographic signatures are more secure than traditional "wet" signatures because forgery is more difficult.

Maybe more significant is that more and more of the assets that we own at death are digital in nature. This creates problems for our traditional estates and trusts laws which were developed before the proliferation of digital assets, such as digital photos, cryptocurrency holdings, and other data and information stored in cloud solutions like Dropbox. Often there are great difficulties in even locating the existence of these assets, and even if identified, there is the issue of having the information necessary to login and obtain control of these digital assets. Once again, blockchain technology is a perfect solution for these problems inasmuch as smart contracts can be created which automatically release this information to the individuals that the deceased identifies—but only upon the death of the decedent. As discussed in the context of oracles, it is possible to allow interaction between a smart contract and extrinsic information, such as vital statistics information when someone dies.

Over time, these tools will become more refined and their

usefulness more obvious. Hopefully, our laws will also evolve to permit the full utilization of this technology, which as of the publication of this book, has not occurred. Unfortunately, testamentary transfers remain subject to traditional "wet" signature requirements and are exempt from more progressive legislation like ESIGN and the UETA. The blockchain has the ability to reduce long probate periods and expensive estate administrations with near instant transfers and a greater certainty that the deceased's final wishes were truly implemented. This can all be accomplished while still keeping in place safeguards to protect against undue influence or individuals who lacked capacity when making testamentary decisions.

§ 2:16 Smart contract use cases—Governmental Matters

Blockchain technology has the potential to be used in several different aspects of government, including regulatory enforcement and creating efficiencies in providing services to its citizens. In each case, there are opportunities for cost reductions and improvement in services—an unusual dynamic in government. Adoption of blockchain technologies will face the same difficulties as in the private sector, but with the added challenge of trying to implement solutions with smaller budgets. For example, most municipal IT departments are already understaffed and operating with generations-old technology. Implementing blockchain solutions will require significantly more than incremental upgrades—especially in local governments where equipment is generally more aged than at the Federal level.

The long-term savings, however, will likely result in a rather short period of time to recapture the investment in technology. Areas of innovation, such as energy efficient grids, will also help implement important policy goals, such as less carbon emissions. Benefits in the energy sector could be particularly important in developing countries. An example of innovative, blockchain-based solutions in this area include a prototype of a distributed energy network that could more efficiently link various electricity generating plants and household generators. The project relied on the

Hyperledger blockchain platform and IBM's Bluemix cloud service.[1]

Ultimately, as governments, both large and small, look for ways to improve services while controlling costs, blockchain technology is likely to figure into many solutions. Hopefully, governments will foster innovation in this area and help blockchain technology grow. It may be more important for governments that blockchain technology succeed than any other particular industry. Whether they will heed the calls to balance regulation so as to avoid undue interference is yet to be seen; and as is usually the case with innovation, it is likely that some jurisdictions will benefit more than others by simply providing a more fostering environment.

§ 2:17   Smart contract use cases—Internet of Things

The Internet of Things (IoT) is one of the other technological advances often cited as a pillar of the Fourth Industrial Revolution. In fact, famed venture capitalist Marc Andreessen has been quoted as saying "The end state is fairly obvious—every light, every doorknob will be connected to the internet. Just like with the web itself, there will be thousands of use cases." IoT refers to the simple concept that more and more physical devices are becoming connected to the Internet (i.e., networked). Only a few years ago, computers were the predominate hardware connected to the Internet. Then smartphones and similar devices became connected to the Internet through WiFi and/or cellular data communications. But today, the types of devices being connected to the Internet is growing exponentially—both in terms of consumer and industrial products. For example, there are a number of health tracking devices that people can wear to track their exercise and vital signs. Most of these devices are now networked so that they automatically transmit the information from their sensors to the Internet. In the industrial context, many production systems, including solar production facilities, are connected to the Internet so that metrics can be more effectively monitored.

This trend is expected to continue over the next several years, such that virtually all physical objects in the world will be (or at least have the capability to be) connected to the

---

[Section 2:16]

[1]http://www.coindesk.com/consensus-2016-building-blocks-hackathon-winner/.

internet. These connections will work both ways. Physical objects will transmit information about their internal state and/or information about environmental factors (e.g., temperature, humidity). Many objects will also have physical actuators (i.e., things that interact with physical world such as motors, servers, LEDs). Together with sensors, this means that many physical objects will be able to transmit information over the Internet to applications that can analyze that data and send commands back to physical devices to interact with the physical world. For example, if a motor's internal temperature is too hot, that data will trigger an application monitoring that information over the Internet to send a signal back to the motor so slow down its RPMs in order that it may cool down.

IoT also has significant implications for the sharing economy. IoT makes it possible for virtually any physical device whose utility is capable of being locked to be the subject of the sharing economy. Imagine a warehouse full of 3D printers and other equipment useful for fabricating parts. Rather than having to interact with a human to secure the use of the 3D printer and pay for such use in a traditional manner, the user will be able to go on an app on her smartphone and obtain a digital key that will unlock the 3D printer for a specific period of time or based on a certain amount of filament. Imagine a fleet of smart cars just randomly left around town, each capable of being used in a similar manner through an app on your smartphone. It's almost mind-boggling to consider where this will evolve in the context of driverless cars.

Blockchain technology will augment IoT in several positive ways. First, blockchains' built-in cryptocurrency payment rails are perfect for interacting with such sharing economies, especially in the context of microservices. Second, and probably more importantly, the blockchain can add a level of security that no other existing technology can. The distributed ledger is perfect for ensuring that use rights are adequately tracked. In addition, the generation of public/private keys is perfect for ensuring that only an authorized user is able to rent a shared car. These benefits hold equally true in the industrial context, including the energy sector. For example, suppose you have a source of renewable energy that generates credits to persons involved in the generation of that renewable energy. The blockchain would allow for immutable record keeping and ensure that such credits are not double spent nor the overall regime abused.

The natural synergies between IoT and the blockchain are just now being explored, but several start-ups are already racing ahead in this space, most notably the German start-up, Slock.it. If your business or firm is already investing in IoT technology or you are studying its potential impact on your business in the coming years, you would be remiss not to consider the implications of blockchain technology in this area. Undoubtedly, over the next few years, more and more research will be directed towards the intersection of IoT and blockchain technology.

Further proof that IoT and blockchain technologies are growing in importance and relationship was the announcement in June 2016 that the Department of Homeland Security had awarded Factom, Inc. a $199,000 grant to work on digital identity solutions for IoT devices. Factom is a well-known blockchain start-up that plans on using blockchain software to prove the integrity of data processed or transmitted by networked devices. Digital identity is one of the more exciting aspects of blockchain technology and its ability to secure information from potentially billions of networked devices would be a significant contribution without regard to any payment functionality. This is impressive given that the underlying technology was developed as a solution to digital cash.

§ 2:18 Smart contracts and legal issues

The interplay between smart contracts and our incumbent legal system is far from established. Fundamental questions, such as whether "code is law" are yet to be answered and/or explored in depth by the judiciary and legislative bodies of government. Nevertheless, it is important to anticipate this interplay (as we attempt to do in the sections below) in efforts to help shape the technology in a manner that will allow for easier adoption and implementation.

§ 2:19 Smart contracts and legal issues—Choice of law and cross-border considerations

Smart (coded) contracts raise important jurisdictional questions. Many of these same issues were raised when the Internet began to develop and the World adjusted to a new digital age. Blockchain technology adds an entirely new layer of complexity because of its distributed nature. Unlike a traditional web-based service, there is no central server on which the company does business. Smart contracts work by changing the state of a distributed ledger on every node on the network. In other words, a smart contract is effectively executed on every node across the network (which in the case of Bitcoin or Ethereum means execution across the globe). This means that parties all over the world can easily contract on blockchains running seamlessly in virtually every country. Given this global reach, it is especially important for the parties to the transaction to specify in the smart contract what laws will govern the transaction, and to be confident that any court likely to hear any dispute arising out of the contract will honor the choice of law chosen by the parties.

Some smart contract enthusiasts may respond to this advice with an admonishment because they believe there is no need for a choice of law since there will be no need for a court. This camp argues the code is the code, or more aptly, the code is law. Unfortunately for this camp, code is not law. First, given the current limitations on human cognitive abilities and the state of artificial intelligence, it is simply impossible to create code that is deterministic of every possible outcome that could result from the relationship between two or more parties once you attempt to codify a transaction of any complexity. Lawyers are unable to capture all possible outcomes in paper contracts, so it is unreasonable to think a coder can code conditional logic statements for every possible outcome. This is, of course, fine. Over thousands of years, our legal systems have adapted to these gaps and legal doctrines developed to fill them. In addition, no matter how much of an idealist one might be, without the coercive power of the state, it is difficult to convert software into the final determiner of the outcome of legal arrangements between two or more people.

§ 2:20   Smart contracts and legal issues—Is code law?

The above is not meant to discourage the development of smart contracts that facilitate legal contracting. To the contrary, I am one of the biggest proponents of what has been dubbed "legal engineering" and I believe with deep conviction that lawyers should approach drafting legal contracts like software engineers approach developing code—that is, drafting in a precise and technical manner that leaves no ambiguity in interpretation and, therefore, performance.

During the last few years, there has been a growing chorus of individuals, mostly in the academic setting, advancing various theories of computational law.[1]

This is an attractive approach to building legal contracts. At their most basic level, contracts are after all simply the embodiment of agreed upon logic between two or more people. If X happens (you tender title to your car to me), then Y happens (I will pay you $10,000). Conceptually, software applications are no different. If X happens (the user presses the return key), then Y happens (a line break occurs). Ultimately, computers understand only a series of 1s and 0s or two states, "on" and "off." As a result, applications created for computers are nothing more than logic rules articulated in a language more easily understood by humans. It should therefore not be surprising that many of the concepts from software engineering are equally applicable to traditional contract drafting or at least effective contract drafting (see below discussion on object oriented programming). As noted, above, however, there are limitations on our ability to code highly deterministic outcomes when dealing with complex legal relationships. *The DAO* implosion arguably provides the best example of this to date. Not only is it difficult to anticipate every issue that might arise in a complex legal relationship, some settings may implicate game theory and complex microeconomic theory that are difficult to work through with code). Historically, we've addressed these complexities by developing release valves (i.e., courts of law). No such accepted mechanisms were in place when *The DAO* suffered a major catastrophe.

Within the coding world, there are many different types of programming languages, some of which are considered "procedural" languages and others considered "object oriented." Many of the concepts that underpin the notion of "coding contracts" are rooted in themes derived from object oriented programming (OOP). For those who are not familiar with object oriented programming, the term refers to a programming language that follows a design pattern that is built with objects, which objects can store properties (often referred to as "attributes") and that can be manipulated by the use of methods that can be called upon those properties.

[Section 2:20]

[1]See: https://law.stanford.edu/2015/05/08/justice-holmes-meet-dr-turing-law-is-computation/.

Objects could range from a digital representation of a car, a credit card, or a human being. One of the primary benefits of OOP is that objects can easily be recycled throughout a program (by simple reference to an existing object); thereby, reducing the overall amount of code. Some Basic Characteristics of Objects:

(1) Data attributes and properties. Objects hold information in variables called attributes or properties. For example, a car object could have attributes such as make, model, and year manufactured. Or a credit card could be represented by an object having the following attributes: cardholder name, card number, expiration date, and CSV code. Users generally have the ability to "set" values for each of these attributes and to also "get" or retrieve the values programmatically.

(2) Executing Functions or Methods on Objects. In addition to properties, objects can have functions or methods that can act on the object, including manipulating its properties. For example, our car object could have "setter" and "getter" methods in order to set and retrieve the make of each car object and print the result to the user's console.

(3) An incredibly useful aspect of object oriented programming is the ability to create "prototype" or "classes" of objects from which we can create new objects. This saves considerable time in coding by reducing the amount of code that must be drafted in order to achieve the same level of functionality. This ability to "inherit" attributes and methods from a prototype or parent class is similar to incorporating all of the terms and conditions of a credit agreement into a promissory note, where the promissory note is a new object that inherits all of the properties of its parent class, the credit agreement.

Like objects in programming, clauses or other snippets of contract language can be abstracted into properties and methods. For example, a promise to pay (the heart of a promissory note) could be constructed as the following object in JavaScript:

```
var promisePay= {
text: 'hereby promises to pay to the order of',
call: function (maker, payee) {
```

```
var reply = maker + + + + this.text + + + + payee;
return reply;
   }
};
```

This basic object in JavaScript has one property and one function that takes two arguments, a maker and a payee. If you call the function and provide a maker and a payee, the object will return the text "{Maker} promises to pay to the order of {Payee}". So, the following line of code: 'promisePay.call('Bob', 'John');' will return the following to the user: "Bob hereby promises to pay to the order of John". This is a very simple pattern, but the same pattern can be duplicated for more complicated contract clauses. Objects can manipulate their internal state and can act on and pass information to other objects. These basic characteristics enable object oriented patterns to be incredibly powerful for creating contracts.

While Solidity is the most popular programming language for drafting smart contract in Ethereum, some have suggested that JavaScript would make for a better language for smart contracts. First, as the language of the web, it is easy to link web-based forms to back-end models. Second, JavaScript is a fairly easy language to learn for beginner programmers and will be fairly easy to follow for novices. It is also easy to read and even non-programmers can follow along without too much difficulty. While low-level languages, like C, have many advantages in terms of speed and efficiency, those benefits are not particularly useful for drafting smart contracts. In addition, low level languages are often more daunting for beginner programmers.

At its core, code based contracts are objects that hold all of the material logic of a contractual relationship—a definition within which a traditional contract could fit. A code based contract, however, is distilled to the core logic and coded in one or more predefined patterns and syntaxes. Unfortunately, our current system of transactional practice has very few universally accepted syntax for drafting contracts. As any veteran transactional lawyer knows, there are almost an infinite number of ways to draft certain types of contracts. Some ways are better than others and some ways are more appropriate depending on the circumstances—but, ultimately, outside of a few areas of practice (such as derivatives contracts), there is little consensus among practitioners.

Maybe the most obvious benefit of code based contracts is the transactional efficiency of being able to automatically generate contracts based on agreed-upon patterns and syntax. Not only does this reduce overall drafting time and negotiation, but it's the first step towards a world in which many routine legal documents could be autonomously created with little, or in some cases, no human involvement. For example, we already have examples of high-frequency trading platforms that operate virtually computer-to-computer in managing a large portion of the securities settlements every day. Current systems, however, still rely on one or more layers of third party intermediaries (i.e., trusted parties) to ultimately settle each transaction. The blockchain has the potential to eliminate the "trusted parties" and allow computers to execute these transactions autonomously without much human interaction.

Maybe even more beneficial than the efficiencies gained by automation, code-based legal documents would be capable of debugging themselves. In other words, a code-based legal document platform would spot errors and inconsistencies within a legal document through machine logic. For example, if a contract contains an object of logic which provides that the contract is between two parties, but the contract's execution contemplates the signature of more than two parties, an exception would be thrown by the program and the coder alerted to the inconsistency. That's an obvious example that even the least capable drafter would certainly spot. More difficult issues, however, would also be capable of prevention. The platform could spot more nuanced inconsistencies—such as an object requiring one party to provide insurance, while another object provides for something inconsistent with that logic (e.g., the risk of loss being borne by the party not maintaining the insurance). As discussed below, advances in artificial intelligence will soon allow machines to understand more and more complex logic, and ultimately, be capable of alerting a coder to inconsistencies that often go unnoticed by human drafters. In addition, the speed at which these errors could be spotted by a computer are exponentially faster than that of a human lawyer. What would take three hours of human time could be done by a computer in one second. Even if you take a very conservative approach in insisting that any legal document be reviewed by an actual human lawyer (which is currently a good idea), applying a second machine review will undoubtedly catch errors missed by humans— and thus, the ultimate product provided to the client improved.

Another benefit would be the ability to code regulatory and other compliance logic into the platform. For example, if a coder is generating a promissory note where the governing law is a state whose maximum permitted rate of interest is 25%, then if the coder attempts to add an interest object with an interest rate of 26%, an error will be thrown. The ability to have a machine apply this sort of compliance logic would save certain industries an almost immeasurable amount of money and resources, including the financial and securities sectors and other highly regulated industries. For example, most U.S. banks spend a considerable amount of resources on compliance departments whose job it is to try and ensure that each transaction entered into by the bank is in full compliance with all state and Federal laws. This is a very labor-intensive process and costs associated with these compliance requirements ultimately reduce overall profitability and increase consumer pricing. There is no reason that all of these compliance requirements cannot be distilled into machine logic which can be easily applied to legal documents—provided those legal documents are in a format that can be easily understood by the machine (i.e., code).

Currently, large numbers of people do not have effective access to the legal system because they cannot afford the services of a private lawyer. While government programs and pro bono efforts help mitigate this problem, these efforts fall short of providing universal access to the legal profession. By significantly reducing the cost of providing legal services, code-based contracts would allow large swaths of the population to have access to quality legal advice that they would otherwise not be able to afford. While other companies, like LegalZoom, have done an admirable job making available certain legal documents (such as wills) to a broader population at a price that most can afford, such applications have limits in terms of the nature, and thereby complexity, of legal needs they can serve.

Another efficiency to code-based legal documents (i.e., smart contracts versus traditional contracts) is that they will incentivize the profession to uniformity in contract logic. This alone would be an amazing accomplishment that would save economies hundreds of millions or even billions of dollars in wasted transactional costs. There is likely no other profession or industry that reinvents the wheel more often than the legal profession—whose professionals are constantly drafting slightly different renditions of effectively the same agreement. On the blockchain, there will be pressure to reduce the amount of data that must be maintained in order to effectuate smart documents. As a blockchain grows in size, efficiency dictates that the less information that must be stored directly on the blockchain the better.[2]

As a result, many smart documents might take the form of a designated form or template (for example, an ISDA swap confirmation form), coupled with a coded object that contains the data necessary to complete the ISDA form into a completed confirmation. With this approach, you do not need to waste space on the blockchain by storing the text of the ISDA form on the blockchain each time an ISDA swap confirmation is effectuated on the blockchain. Instead, the final smart document embodying this transaction will include a reference to the ISDA swap confirmation form (and not the form itself), together with the code object that, when added to the form, will produce a completed trade confirmation.

We've already touched on some of the applications for artificial intelligence (including machine learning) in the context of legal documents. Artificial intelligence is still in its infancy, but progress is growing exponentially. We can expect that AI-technology will touch on a much broader range of subjects and tasks—with increasing capacity for more and more sophisticated logic and human like learning. Set forth below is just a brief outline of possibilities—each of which could be the basis of entire bodies of research. For example, an algorithm that can search existing databases of contracts (such as EDGAR) and determine when there are changes in "market" provisions found in certain types of contracts. The machine can then implement those changes in a company's own form contracts. The machine learning code would need to be able to distinguish between different types of contracts (e.g., this is a credit agreement) and learn from human corrections that override its automated changes. For example, if the machine believes that a certain type of provision is being added to credit agreements and recommends adding the same provision to the company's form, then the machine would learn from the human operator when it tells the machine that it is not appropriate to add in this case because that clause was in response to a law not in

---

[2]Remember, every node carries a full, or partial, copy of an entire blockchain for which it verifies transactions. The speed in which transactions can be verified will be dictated, to a large part, by how large (in data size) a particular blockchain is.

effect in the jurisdiction within which the company does business. Ultimately, the machine could even learn how the various provisions in a contract work together, so that if a change is made to one provision, the machine could alert the drafter to changes that should be made to other provisions on the contract.

With legal contracts distilled to electronic logic, enterprises that may have hundreds, thousands, or hundreds of thousands of executory contracts (think of Apple, Amazon, ExxonMobil) would be able to establish automated systems plugged into their database of electronic contracts. In other words, they would no longer need to have hundreds or thousands of individuals responsible for managing these contracts. In addition to massive cost savings, the quality of management would likely increase due to the lack of human error.

It is important to appreciate that the benefits described above are, to a large degree, only made possible by the conversion of traditionally drafted contracts into code-based legal documents (which would not have to be in any particular coding language) that are machine readable and subject to machine learning. These technologies are unique and extend far beyond the capabilities of simple language recognition technology and other similar advancements. With code-based legal documents, we will for the first time be able to communicate with our contracts.

Due to superior security and identity verification (which is improving every day), industries are steadily adopting electronic signatures (especially those based on PKI).[3] Innovative platforms like uPort (built for the Ethereum blockchain) are making it possible for individuals to have digital identities that will drastically reduce identity theft, while empowering individuals with greater control over their identities than ever before; while at the same time, improving our ability to implement KYC (know your customer) and AML (anti-money laundering) requirements. The improvements possible in this area will increase efficiency, while reducing overall transaction costs.

While many large financial institutions and others are investing significant resources into developing blockchain based technology, the reality is that the ability to implement

---

[3]PKI is a method of cryptography and stands for public key infrastructure—see Chapter 5 for an in-depth discussion of this technology and its application to blockchain technology.

this technology in most industries is very limited today. First, most IT, security, and compliance departments do not have a sufficient understanding of the underlying technology, which is to be expected at this stage of development. Second, most companies, including law firms, do not have the resources available to invest in personnel who do sufficiently understand this technology so as to be able to implement it in most enterprise settings. Third, the technology itself is still being refined, and as such, it is prudent for most companies to wait longer before expending significant resources in any particular blockchain infrastructure. Finally, there is not enough real world feedback yet to truly establish "best practices" and there are certain areas, such as key management (i.e., controlling access to specific blockchain accounts), in the enterprise setting that still need much consideration.

For the above reasons, our approach initially would be to implement a barebones platform as described above, which will also provide users with the ability to "parallel close" transactions, meaning that the documents will exist both in their more traditional written form using natural language, but also exist in parallel on the blockchain. While some might find this inefficient, we believe that this approach will ultimately lead to greater and faster adoption of this technology in the long road. The most important benefit of this approach is that it allows developers, law firms and companies (e.g., banks) to be immediately exposed to the benefits of blockchain technology. The sooner everyone in a law firm and a bank understand what a blockchain is, the sooner they can start taking steps to implement the technology in more meaningful ways. In addition, even these limited implementations can provide immediate, meaningful benefits to clients. For example, a bank who implements this platform with parallel closings will benefit from even the most basic error checking and compliance modules (e.g., Regulation B logic) and reduce the effectiveness of later claims by a borrower that a document was forged or that it was tampered with after execution. At the same time, however, because the more traditional written documentation will also exist, the level of push back based on the fear of the unknown is dramatically lower. Simply put, this approach will allow us to begin implementing this platform with companies, such as banks, and law firms immediately.

§ 2:21 Smart contracts and legal issues—Legal issues regarding electronic signatures and notarization

Even today, more than 15 years after Congress and most states decided to promote electronic transactions as a matter of public policy, some people are still hesitant to rely on digital signatures in lieu of traditional "wet" signatures. In most cases, there is no rational basis for this hesitancy, but rather it arises solely as an effect of tradition. There are, however, a handful of traps for the unwary. As such, it is important to understand the three most important pieces of legislation that add legitimacy and effect to most digital signatures and transactions.

§ 2:22 Smart contracts and legal issues—Legal issues regarding electronic signatures and notarization—The Electronic Signatures in Global and National Commerce Act

Whether implemented on a blockchain or a conventional centralized platform, in order for any electronic document to be enforceable, the law must recognize the ability of a person to the obligations set forth in the document. The authority for this recognition under federal law was established by the Electronic Signatures in Global and National Commerce Act and passed into law in 2000 ("ESIGN").[1]

ESIGN implemented a public policy that signatures and contracts should not be denied legal effect, validity, or enforceability because they exist only in electronic form. As a result of this legislation, the law must give effect to electronic signatures to the same extent it does to traditional "wet" signatures. This applies to notary acknowledgments and affidavits made under oath. Even in a real estate transaction, ESIGN permits all signatures to real estate documents, whether by an obligor, mortgagor, notary or witness, to be accomplished by electronic means.[2]

ESIGN also created the concept of a "transferable record," which is an electronic record that (i) would constitute a note

---

[Section 2:22]

[1]https://www.law.washington.edu/Directory/docs/Winn/Electronic%20 Records%20and%20Signatures.htm.

[2]http://www.uniformlaws.org/ActSummary.aspx?title=Real%20Prope rty%20Electronic%20Recording%20Act.

under Article 3 of the Uniform Commercial Code, (ii) the issuer thereof has expressly agreed that it constitutes a transferable record, and (iii) relates to a loan secured by real property.[3]

Accordingly, a transferable record is an electronic promissory note (sometimes referred to as an eNote). Unlike a paper document, an electronic promissory note is not capable of possession. As such, the traditional requirement of possession is replaced with a requirement that the holder have control of a transferable record. Under ESIGN, a person has control of a transferable record "if a system employed for evidencing the transfer of interests in the transferable record reliably establishes that person as the person to which the transferable record was issued or transferred." To determine control, ESIGN uses six factors, which if met, results in a person having control. The six items are as follows: (1) a single authoritative copy of the transferable record exists which is unique, identifiable, and, except as otherwise provided in paragraphs (4), (5), and (6), unalterable; (2) the authoritative copy identifies the person asserting control as—(A) the person to which the transferable record was issued; or (B) if the authoritative copy indicates that the transferable record has been transferred, the person to which the transferable record was most recently transferred; (3) the authoritative copy is communicated to and maintained by the person asserting control or its designated custodian; (4) copies or revisions that add or change an identified assignee of the authoritative copy can be made only with the consent of the person asserting control; (5) each copy of the authoritative copy and any copy of a copy is readily identifiable as a copy that is not the authoritative copy; and (6) any revisions of the authoritative copy is readily identifiable as authorized or unauthorized. A person deemed to have control of a transferable record is considered the holder of the transferable record and afforded the same rights and defenses as a holder of an instrument under Article 3 of the Uniform Commercial Code. ESIGN requires that a person seeking to enforce a transferable record provide reasonable proof that it is the person in control of the transferable record.

---

[3]https://www.law.washington.edu/Directory/docs/Winn/Electronic%20 Records%20and%20Signatures.htm.

§ 2:23 Smart contracts and legal issues—Legal issues regarding electronic signatures and notarization—Uniform Electronic Transaction Act

In addition to ESIGN, most states have adopted the Uniform Electronic Transaction Act ("UETA").[1] The few non-adopting states have nevertheless adopted a statute that deals with electronic records. UETA seeks to implement the same public policy as ESIGN by affording electronic signatures the same effect as traditional signatures, but without changing substantive law.[2]

Like ESIGN, UETA's goal was to remove barriers to contracting through digital means. There are some important aspects of UETA that parties must keep in mind. First, UETA only applies to transactions between parties who have agreed to conduct a transaction by electronic means, which may be determined by the context and surrounding circumstances. Because blockchain-based transactions are digitally signed, it is prudent to include a statement of consent to digital signatures in the contract—although it would almost certainly be inferred in any event. To the extent the parties have agreed to conduct a transaction by electronic means, the UETA determines whether an electronic record or signature has legal. Like ESIGN, the UETA establishes the fundamental rule that a record or signature may not be denied legal effect or enforceability solely because the record or signature is in electronic form.

Not all transactions fall within the scope of the UETA. More specially, the UETA does not apply to (1) wills, codicils and testamentary trusts; (2) the Uniform Commercial Code (other than Sections 1-107 and 1-206, Article 2, and Article 2A); and (3) the Uniform Computer Information Transactions Act. Real estate transactions, however, fall squarely within the scope of the UETA. Real estate finance involves both Article 3 and Article 9 of the Uniform Commercial Code. While Article 3 (negotiable instruments, such as promissory notes and checks) is exempt from the scope of this legislation, the reason is because electronic payment instruments

---

[Section 2:23]

[1]http://www.uniformlaws.org/ActSummary.aspx?title=Electronic%20 Transactions%20Act.

[2]http://www.uniformlaws.org/ActSummary.aspx?title=Electronic%20 Transactions%20Act.

are addressed by the creation of the transferable records concept (which the UETA also adopts), and the exclusion of Article 9 is necessary because it has already been revised to address issues unique to electronic records, including the creation of the concept of electronic chattel paper.

Courts are supposed to use a liberal standard for determining a person's intent to be bound by an electronic signature. Basically, if a person takes steps to complete an electronic signature, then that electronic signature will be effective against that person. Notwithstanding this liberal standard, we still suggest that express acknowledgements about electronic signatures be included in any platform designed to accept them. This avoids any risk that you will need to engage in fact based litigation on this point. The UETA also establishes the concept of a transferable record, adopting most of the same language found in ESIGN. UETA's definition of a transferable record is broader in scope in two respects. First, a transferable record can also include an electronic record that would otherwise constitute a document under Article 7 of the Uniform Commercial Code if it were in writing. Article 7 of the UCC governs documents of title for personal property. As we will see below in the context of supply chain management, this is important in the context of smart contracts that replace traditional merchant financing that often involve written bills of lading and other forms of documents of title. Again, UETA was adopted well before the development of blockchain technology—but nevertheless provides an amazing foundation for legally validating smart contracts and the underlying technology itself. Second, a transferable record under the UETA does not need to be secured by an interest in real property. So UETA also encompasses unsecured obligations, obligations secured by personal property and documents of title.

§ 2:24   Smart contracts and legal issues—Legal issues regarding electronic signatures and notarization—Uniform Real Property Electronic Recording Act

Historically, the offices that maintain our public land records required original documents with wet ink signatures in order to catalogue them in their grantor-grantee indexed records. This antiquated system was inefficient and costly. Ultimately, this led to the adoption of the Uniform Real Property Electronic Recording Act (the "URPERA"). As of this writing, over half of all U.S. states (plus the District of Columbia and the U.S. Virgin Islands) have enacted a form of URPERA.[1]

For those states that have adopted URPERA or similar legislation, there no longer exists any impediment to the execution *and recording* of instruments affected real property that are executed, witnessed (where required), and acknowledged by a notary public by electronic means. So even real estate transactions can now be implemented by blockchain based platforms. So much for the traditional real estate joke among "dirt" lawyers that the abolishment of the English common law doctrine known as the "Rule of Shelley's Case," which was established in 1581, was the last important change to real estate doctrine.

§ 2:25 Smart contracts, regulations, and policies

As the sections below discuss, smart contracts have the potential to significantly improve our regulatory landscape, but not before running into direct conflict with many of the regulatory structures currently in place. Some states, including New York, have begun to introduce their own virtual currency regulations, however, effective regulation will require time for the market and (often soon after) regulators to define the new policy concerns that smart contracts help bring to light.

§ 2:26 Smart contracts, regulations, and policies—Money transfer licensing

Pursuant to FinCEN guidance, any person who is an "exchanger" or an "administrator" is considered a money transmitter under FinCEN's regulations.[1] The significance of this classification is that all money transmitters are required

---

[Section 2:24]

[1]http://www.uniformlaws.org/ActSummary.aspx?title=Real%20Prope rty%20Electronic%20Recording%20Act.

[Section 2:26]

[1]https://urldefense.proofpoint.com/v2/url?u=https-3A__www.fincen.go v_resources_statutes-2Dregulations_administrative-2Drulings_request-2D administrative-2Druling-2Dapplication-2D0&d=CwIGaQ&c=4ZIZThykDL coWk-GVjSLm9hvvvzvGv0FLoWSRuCSs5Q&r=SAe0sFVgf84X_6Al-gxaQ RUSBPOiYLQq1KjAnwmvzDTJfwsXmYhuO5BqLYu6QSOO&m=16tsl3V3 Lp_YwbphxuHffC7vnrV9LYccKXy9Lb50oPw&s=4YFMmhs9J5r-ITuFZoe4 zE3CBx7e2RCoVgrGPT5koqc&e.

to register with FinCEN as a money service business. FinCEN guidance defines an "exchanger" as any person "engaged as a business in the exchange of virtual currency for real currency, funds, or other virtual currency" and an "administrator" as any person "engaged as a business in issuing (putting into circulation) a virtual currency, and who has the authority to redeem (to withdraw from circulation) such virtual currency."[2] Asked on FinCEN's guidance, it is clear that individuals who routinely exchange fiat currency for Bitcoin or other cryptocurrency or vice-versa are engaging in conduct subject to FinCEN's regulation and oversight. As a result of the regulation intensive environment created by being labeled a money transmitter, obtaining banking services for all but the largest and well-funded startups is incredibly difficulty. I've experienced this first hand by being the subject of inquiry from the national bank with whom I bank. Because of the fact that my research involves different blockchain platforms, I'm often using an account tied to that bank account to purchase Bitcoin, which can then be converted into difference virtual currencies, such as Ether. The pattern of purchasing relatively small amounts of Bitcoin was enough for my bank to initiate an investigation in order to verify that I was not engaged in activities that might constitute money transmission.

In the realm of state regulations, the State of New York took the lead with the enactment of BitLicense. Promulgated by the New York State Department of Financial Services ("NYSDFS"),[3] BitLicense was intended to regulate the conduct of business involving virtual currency. The legislation has been hailed by some as regulation necessary to legitimize Bitcoin and panned by others as more bureaucratic red tape destined to force innovative companies out of New York into neighboring states.[4]

As of the publication of this book, there are only a handful

---

[2]https://urldefense.proofpoint.com/v2/url?u=https-3A__www.fincen.go v_resources_statutes-2Dregulations_administrative-2Drulings_request-2D administrative-2Druling-2Dapplication-2D0&d=CwIGaQ&c=4ZIZThykDL coWk-GVjSLm9hvvvzvGv0FLoWSRuCSs5Q&r=SAe0sFVgf84X_6Al-gxaQ RUSBPOiYLQq1KjAnwmvzDTJfwsXmYhuO5BqLYu6QSOO&m=16tsl3V3 Lp_YwbphxuHffC7vnrV9LYccKXy9Lb50oPw&s=4YFMmhs9J5r-ITuFZoe4 zE3CBx7e2RCoVgrGPT5koqc&e.

[3]URL: http://www.dfs.ny.gov/legal/regulations/adoptions/dfsp200t. pdf.

[4]http://www.coindesk.com/months-bitlicense-bitcoin-still-startups-aw ait-approval-new-york/.

of licenses issued. While the ultimate impact of BitLicense and similar regulations sure to follow will not be known for some time, the initial impact has been neither a boom or bust for investment and innovation in blockchain technology. The gist of BitLicense requires any person engaged in "Virtual Currency Business Activity" to obtain a license from the superintendent from the NYSDFS. The NYSDFS defines such activities as the conduct of any of the following types of activities involving New York for a New York resident:[5]

(1) receiving Virtual Currency for Transmission or Transmitting Virtual Currency, except where the transaction is undertaken for non-financial purposes and does not involve the transfer of more than a nominal amount of Virtual Currency;

(2) storing, holding, or maintaining custody or control of Virtual Currency on behalf of others;

(3) buying and selling Virtual Currency as a customer business;

(4) performing Exchange Services as a customer business; or

(5) controlling, administering, or issuing a Virtual Currency.

The development and dissemination of software in and of itself does not constitute Virtual Currency Business Activity. The term "Virtual Currency" is defined to mean "any type of digital unit that is used as a medium of exchange or a form of digitally stored value. Virtual Currency shall be broadly construed to include digital units of exchange that (i) have a centralized repository or administrator; (ii) are decentralized and have no centralized repository or administrator; or (ii) may be created or obtained by computing or manufacturing effort."[6] The definition has several exclusions to make clear items like prepaid merchant gift cards and other items not normally associated with cryptocurrency.

Even today, many banks are afraid of doing business with companies who are involved in the cryptocurrency industry. The primary fear of most banking institutions is that a deposit holder is engaged in money transmitter services without proper licensing. This leads to fears that the bank could be implicated in fostering violations of AML and other

---

[5]http://www.dfs.ny.gov/legal/regulations/adoptions/dfsp200t.pdf.

[6]https://www.andrewskurth.com/insights-1134.html.

regulatory requirements. This fear, whether justified or not, results in a barrier to entry in some ways similar to what marijuana companies have faced in those states where the production of marijuana is legal under state laws. Regardless of the U.S. Department of Justice's position on the ability of banks to do business with marijuana growers in states like Colorado and Washington, most simply avoid them at all costs.

§ 2:27   Smart contracts, regulations, and policies— Anti-Money Laundering (AML) and Know Your Customer (KYC) considerations

FinCEN, BitLicense, and other money-related regulations generally seek to implement policy in two areas—consumer protection and anti-money laundering (AML). Our focus will be on the AML aspect of these regulatory regimes. In its current state, cryptocurrencies have raised money laundering concerns inasmuch as Bitcoin is pseudoanonymous, and has the potential to be completely anonymous. The ability to exchange Bitcoin for fiat currency and vice versa, coupled with the ability to move Bitcoin from person to person around the globe makes it an ideal vehicle to launder money. Concerns over Bitcoin's role in money laundering are only bolstered by its continued use as the currency of choice for those engaged in the sale of illicit drugs in online marketplaces.

Combating these concerns has been primarily accomplished by requiring licensing and aggressive enforcement actions against those who fail to obtain a license and institute adequate institutional AML controls. All of these efforts primarily focus on a narrow subset of transactions— the exchange of Bitcoin and fiat currencies. The effectiveness of this approach may be diminishing as the number of vendors accepting Bitcoin for goods and services increase. Online shops like Open Bazaar[1] allow people to buy goods and services for Bitcoin in an eBay-like marketplace. As time goes on, even more traditional brick and mortar stores accept Bitcoin for payment. As Bitcoin addresses its scaling issues, it seems likely that the proliferation of Bitcoin as an everyday currency will continue and grow. The ability to spend Bitcoin in exchange for goods and services eliminates

---

[Section 2:27]

    [1]URL: https://openbazaar.org.

the need to exchange it into a fiat currency—a transaction that triggers AML techniques. Only time will tell how prevalent Bitcoin or other cryptocurrencies become, but there is no doubt that the number of retailers accepting it will increase as time goes on.

§ 2:28 Smart contracts, regulations, and policies—A tool to combat fraud and corruption

Ironically, for all the fear of Bitcoin's use in illicit activities, the blockchain has the potential to become one of the most effective tools in fighting money laundering and AML compliance, among other regulatory regimes that will benefit. Closely related to the work being done with digital identities on the blockchain, this technology has the ability to allow different financial institutions to coordinate their AML efforts in ways that are simply not possible today. Today, transactions come from one institution to another and from that institution to another institution, but analysis of a transaction beyond the two institutions is not practical. Blockchain technology can change this by allowing transactions to be reported to a common ledger accessible to all financial institutions, who can use this ledger (similar to how the triple accounting works) to verify that related transactions are congruent with the stated intentions and information provided by customers. Intertwined transactions involving cash moving through numerous institutions for the purpose of obscuring the true nature of the transactions will no longer be isolated, but subject to financial institutions being able to see the "big picture." This also opens up the possibility of applying constantly improving AI and machine learning software to identify patterns that can be used to catch money launderers.

§ 2:29 Smart contracts, regulations, and policies— Scope of CFTC's jurisdiction over prediction markets

One of the first online prediction markets that saw success was Intrade. Intrade was a unique prediction market that allowed people to place investments (wagers) on the outcome of events like U.S. Presidential elections. While Intrade was not a U.S. company, it did solicit investments from U.S. Residents. Ultimately, the CFTC asserted jurisdiction over their activities based on the claim that what they sold were in essence futures contracts.[1] In the end, Intrade dropped its fight with the CFTC and closed operations. That left the only prediction markets in operation to be academically run marketplaces that had obtained exemption letters from the CFTC. The Ethereum blockchain is once again testing the limits of the CFTC's regulatory authority. Prediction markets like Augur[2] are proposing to bring back robust prediction markets. Unlike Intrade, Augur utilizes the Ethereum decentralized network. Ultimately, however, the basic principles are the same. Augur, like Intrade, is a prediction market that allows individuals, including U.S. residents, to wager real value on future outcomes. With respect to Augur, the CFTC seems to be taking a wait and see approach.

§ 2:30　Smart contracts: Where we stand today

As time goes on, the underlying technology will mature and become better understood by people. In addition, through limited implementation today in the real world, we will immediately begin to receive feedback that will be helpful in truly determining in which capacities these technologies offer the greatest efficiencies, and hopefully, lead us to discovering use cases not even considered today. This sort of real-time feedback from applications being put to use in the outside world provides useful information that can't be replicated in the lab setting.

While we will continue this discussion in Chapter 4 in the context of decentralized autonomous organizations (which can be considered smart contracts on steroids), it's important to note that the efforts of computational legal studies, "legal engineering," and other attempts to leverage technology in the context of contract drafting and law more generally should not be viewed as an attempt to replace the law with computer code. Social media is filled with slogans like "code is law" and other talk of replacing our current legal system and contracts with computer code. This approach misses the mark dramatically. The World's developed legal systems are the result of thousands of years of human interaction and experiment. They are influenced by culture, economic theories, religion, and other traditions. Some aspects of the resulting legal framework are less desirable than others, but

---

[Section 2:29]

　[1]http://www.cftc.gov/PressRoom/PressReleases/pr6423-12.

　[2]URL: https://www.augur.net.

the idea that these systems can be replaced whole cloth by software is not only wrong, it's counterproductive. For code's most encouraging prospects for advancing legal practice is as a supplement and tool for lawyers. Lawyers who can build legal contracts with software engineering tools and philosophies will be able to build better more accurate contracts. This will allow lawyers to focus on those tasks where they can provide better value to their clients, such as strategic planning.

Make no mistake, the opportunities in this area are significant and the manner in which legal contracts are built, and in some cases, enforced, will be dramatically different than today. The blockchain will complement this new regime of contract construction by facilitating the ability of machines to contract with other machines and the ability to efficiently process payments for microservices and other automated commerce. I suspect that there will even be creative dispute resolution ideas that will enable even greater efficiency in commerce. Ultimately, however, all of this innovation should dovetail with our existing legal system—not replace it. For a long time to come, courts will be necessary for those to seek redress when a "smart contract" does not operate as intended, just like courts must hear disputes about traditional contracts that did not meet one or more of the parties' intentions. This should not be confused with any sort of ringing endorsement for our existing judicial system, which suffers from issues of access, delays, and other inefficiencies. Rather, we believe that by leveraging this technology we can retain the best aspects of our system while improving those that have long suffered.

For lawyers, the implications can be seen as a mixed bag, but on whole, should be viewed in a positive light. While machines will displace a certain number of tasks historically performed by lawyers (as they have in countless other industries), demand will continue to exist for those who can provide strategic counsel, especially those who understand the capabilities (and limitations) of new technology.

Chapter 3

Blockchain Protocols

§ 3:1   Summary of important points:

- There are numerous blockchain protocols, each of which exhibits the key characteristics of a blockchain, but through different techniques.
- Bitcoin is the oldest and most prevalent blockchain in use today.
- There are other blockchains, such as Ethereum and Hyperledger, that have active development communities and show tremendous promise for future use.
- There will likely be numerous blockchains in use in the future, each having characteristics favorable for certain uses. This technology won't likely end in a VHS vs. Beta winner take all adoption, but rather a Windows/MacOS/Linux environment, each with its own active development community.

§ 3:2   Existing protocols

As discussed in Chapter 1, the term "blockchain" does not

refer to a single software application or even a single type of software system. To the contrary, blockchains manifest themselves in various forms, some of which bear little resemblance to the original Bitcoin blockchain. While all blockchains have certain fundamental characteristics, such as being distributed in nature and having some mechanism for reaching consensus, there is no single way to "do blockchains." While blockchain protocols are evolving every day, the remainder of this chapter discusses some of the most prominent systems in use or under development as of the writing of this book.

§ 3:3   Existing protocols—Bitcoin

Bitcoin was the first implementation of blockchain technology (in fact, for years, it remained the only implementation) and continues to be the most well-known and used protocol at the time of this writing. Over the years, new cryptocurrencies emerged (often referred to as "alt coins"), including Litecoin and Dogecoin. The vast majority of these alt coins added little improvement, if any, to blockchain technology; and in some cases, they simply represent a "hard fork"[1] of Bitcoin and the creation of a new genesis block. While many of these alt coins maintain an almost cult- like following, their application to future blockchain use cases remains uncertain, at best. Bitcoin, on the other hand, shows no signs of giving up its status as the most influential blockchain protocol in the world.

Bitcoin maintains a large following of active developers who contribute to both the maintenance and (new) use cases for the protocol. The majority of the Bitcoin Core protocol developers (those who maintain the core protocol actually run by nodes and miners) are now a part of MIT Media Lab's Digital Currency Initiative. This includes Gavin Andresen, Wladimir van dear Laan, and Cory Fields. It's important to remember, however, that Bitcoin is open source software, which no individual or company owns. Ultimately, the Bitcoin protocol is determined by those who install the protocol as part of running nodes and mining for Bitcoin.

──────────

[Section 3:3]

[1]The term "hard fork" simply refers to the concept of copying the source code from one project, making one or more changes to the protocol and then releasing that source code as a new project (or new version of an existing project).

While there are many benefits to decentralization, it is not without its challenges. As this book is being written, there is a critical debate raging in the Bitcoin community over the size of blocks in the current Bitcoin protocol. As demand for Bitcoin continues to increase, the time it takes to confirm transactions has been increasing. Transactions that used to take a few minutes to confirm can now take over an hour— these delays in processing must be overcome in order for the Bitcoin network to scale up to the level necessary to serve as a global backbone for global payments.

Some in the Bitcoin community have proposed increasing the size of the Bitcoin block from 1MB (the original and still current size limit) to a larger size (e.g., 8 MB)[2] in order to allow more transactions to be processed in each block, thereby increasing processing times. Many in the community are hesitant to change any of the code in the core protocol for fear of inadvertently breaking it or unknowingly causing a security breach or attack vector. Many in the community rightfully point out that no one has been able to breach the Bitcoin protocol in any material respect since its inception— notwithstanding that it has (as of the date of this book) a market capitalization of over $10 billion U.S., which is one heck of a "bug bounty." Few software platforms can boast of such a feat. So the fear of tinkering with the protocol is not unjustified, but the inability of the core protocol to scale will ultimately leave Bitcoin unable to compete with alternative blockchain solutions that can scale and meet global demand. To put things in perspective, PayPal can process several million transactions per day, while Bitcoin processes several hundred transactions per day. If Bitcoin is to become a mainstream payment vehicle, it must overcome its scaling issue.

Another important technology in the payment channel arena is the open source software library (available in Python as of the writing of this book) developed by Bitcoin 21. Bitcoin 21 is a well-funded company that envisions virtually all networked devices being on the Bitcoin network. In order to make this vision a reality, Bitcoin 21 has developed a payment system that easily implements what Bitcoin 21 calls the "machine payable web." More specifically, Bitcoin 21 allows for the implementation of Bitcoin based payments

---

[2]For a good discussion of the pros and cons of increasing the block size and the various proposals under consideration, see URL: https://en.bitcoin.it/wiki/Block_size_limit_controversy.

into web applications with the inclusion of just a handful of additional lines of code. This system is particularly useful for microservices. Services rendered for small amounts, say a penny, generally don't make sense for inclusion on the Bitcoin blockchain, or frankly, any other payment processor (including credit card processors). Bitcoin 21 solves these issues and allows for people to sell any type of software service (e.g., translation, data storage, geolocation conversion) for payment in Bitcoin. In addition to developing a simple-to-use code base, users of Bitcoin 21 are connected by a unique Bitcoin 21 marketplace network that allows them to transact business "off-chain" and settle up on the blockchain after transactions are processed. Bitcoin 21 aptly analogizes these payment channels to running a bar tab. The bartender does not charge your credit card every time you order a drink. Instead, the vendor keeps track of the drinks you ordered and when you are done for the night, your card is charged for the total amount owed.

§ 3:4   Existing protocols—Ethereum

After Bitcoin, Ethereum represents the second most well-known and robust blockchain community (many would argue that there is more enthusiasm and focus by developers on Ethereum versus Bitcoin) and protocol. Ethereum is often credited with setting the stage for "Blockchain 2.0." Blockchain developers utilizing Ethereum are no longer subject to the boundaries resulting from Bitcoin's fairly limited scripting language. Instead, the Ethereum protocol includes the Ethereum Virtual Machine (EVM) that can run code ultimately written in Turing-complete[1] high level languages, such as Solidity (similar to the JavaScript programming language) and Serpent (similar to the Python programming language). With the advent of the EVM, blockchain developers are now able to write smart contracts with almost no limits on what they can implement on the blockchain. Rather than a distributed protocol being used solely for purposes of maintaining a ledger of Bitcoin transactions, the EVM can

---

[Section 3:4]

[1]Turing-complete languages (named after Alan Turing, an English mathematician and early computer scientist) is the name given to programming languages that allow its users to write applications that have no limitations in terms of the logic that can be implemented. In other words, they are general purpose programming languages rather than limited scripting languages like Bitcoin utilizes.

run full applications in a distributed manner—these applications are known as distributed applications or simply Dapps.

Like Bitcoin, the Ethereum protocol is open source and maintained by its community of users. The Ethereum Foundation, a nonprofit foundation, promotes the Ethereum protocol and includes the work of Vitalik Buterin, the creator of the Ethereum protocol. Like the core developers of Bitcoin, the Ethereum foundation supports and encourages development of the Ethereum platform, but ultimately, because of its open source nature, the community of users are important contributors to the Ethereum blockchain. While the same is also true of Bitcoin in some sense, it is more obvious how important third party developers are to the Ethereum protocol. While Bitcoin developers have focused primarily on improving wallets, developers have been at work developing a number of novel blockchain based applications on the Ethereum blockchain, including prediction markets, corporate governance models and even decentralized poker games!

While the active developers of the Ethereum protocol ultimately plan on moving Ethereum from a proof-of-work to a proof-of-stake consensus model, the protocol is likely to continue using a proof-of-work system for some time. Unlike Bitcoin, however, miners generally use regular computers or graphics cards to mine Ether (the native cryptocurrency of Ethereum). Like on the Bitcoin protocol, miners on the Ethereum network must solve an algorithm to mine a block, however the algorithm used by the Ethereum protocol is memory intensive, which means Ethereum is resistant to ASIC mining. This was a conscious choice by the core developers to help avoid the massive concentration of hashing power to which ASIC-based mining has arguably led. As a result, many Ethereum miners today use the same GPU mining rigs that Bitcoin miners used several years ago before the proliferation of ASIC miners.

The recent controversy regarding the massive theft of Ether-based tokens in connection with *The DAO* (see Chapter 4) raised significant issues about the viability of the Ethereum blockchain network for business use. The incident gave rise to a major debate within the community on whether to use a hard fork to recover the stolen tokens. As of the writing of this book, the community has not yet made a decision, but the mere fact that the debate is taking place has caused some stir among businesses and commentators. Many blockchain detractors have pointed to the prospect of miners agreeing to unwind or invalidate a prior transaction is proof that a public ledger can't be used to store permanent records. Ironically, this is one area where Bitcoin's limited scripting language is a positive attribute as it limits the possibility of unintended consequences.

Ultimately, however, the debate is somewhat confused by all sides. First, the proposed hard fork is not intended to invalidate or alter any transactions on the public ledger, except for a single account that maliciously obtained tens of millions of dollars in Ether-based tokens because of a coding error in the smart contract that was implemented to govern *The DAO*. As such, it is difficult to argue that the hard fork is in any way malicious or disruptive. Second, even under traditional legal doctrine, the individual who took the tokens would almost certainly be compelled to return them and would likely be subject to criminal prosecution. So the hard fork is only implementing what would be done in a traditional judicial setting in any event. Proponents of the hard fork, however, overlook legitimate concerns raised by the hard fork. One problem is that it is difficult to deny at least the appearance of a "bail out." In other words, the creator of *The DAO* (Slock.it) implemented it with shoddy code and is now looking for the broader Ethereum community to rescue it from its mistake. Proponents also overlook the fact that while hard forks are necessary from time to time to upgrade networks, just like any software applications, none have ever been implemented to reverse or target a single or series of transactions.

Notwithstanding the negative publicity of *The DAO* implosion, the future for the Ethereum protocol is bright. The active developer community has a number of brilliant individuals from all aspects of the blockchain technology contributing to its future success, including mathematicians, cryptographers, and computer programmers. In addition to the core development team, there are numerous private offshoots who are actively developing decentralized applications for Ethereum, including Consensys.net, founded by Joseph Lubin (one of the original pioneers of Ethereum). Consensys has formed several strategic alliances within the technology community, including Microsoft, whereby Consensys brought Ethereum to Microsoft's cloud system, Azure. This began a trend in the industry of BaaS, or blockchain as a service.

After the manuscript for this book was completed, but before publication, the Ethereum hard fork took place. Something interesting enough took place that we felt it was necessary to update the book to address it. While the hard fork was implemented and a majority of miners and nodes updated their software to integrate the changes made by the core development team, a significant number chose not to upgrade. In furtherance of their challenge, they even coined the term "Ethereum Classic" (symbol: ETC) as the name of their protocol, which is the Ethereum protocol minus the hard fork and established an organization to maintain it.[2] What had expected to happen was that the hard fork would be implemented by enough miners and nodes that those not upgrading would be small and eventually crowded out into oblivion. At least as of now, this has not happened. To the contrary, several exchanges have expressed support for Ethereum Classic and plan to allow trading in ETC along with ETH. This marks the first time in crypto-currency history that a major blockchain has split like this into two identical ledgers (except for one ledger's erasing *The DAO* theft from its records).

It's still unclear whether both ETH and ETC will coexist for any significant period of time or whether one will eventually prevail over the other. But regardless of the ultimate fate of Ethereum Classic, the entire episode will be studied for years to come and will be a constant reminder to blockchain communities about the possible implications of hard forking in order to implement controversial changes, which in this case, was to alter what was thought, by some, to be a sacred, immutable ledger. The hard fork and splitting of Ethereum has also bolstered arguments of those in favor of permissioned ledgers for financial institutions and most other commercial use cases.

§ 3:5 Existing protocols—Ripple Consensus Network

A number of financial institutions have experimented or implemented blockchain-based solutions, using Ripple Lab's Consensus Network, which runs on the XRP cryptocurrency. XRP is in the top five of cryptocurrencies based on market share by value. Ripple is known to be very focused on compliance with U.S. law—albeit Ripple learned the hard way having been charged by FinCEN with violations of several requirements of the Bank Secrecy Act, which it ultimately settled in exchange for paying a $700,000.00 civil money

---

[2]https://ethereumclassic.github.io./.

penalty.[1] This early set back, however, has turned out to be a positive event inasmuch as it forced Ripple to become first in class with respect to compliance matters.

The Ripple Protocol Consensus Algorithm (RPCA) uses a modified form of proof-of-stake as its consensus formula. The details of its methodology are set out in detail in a paper published in 2014 by David Schwartz, Noah Young, and Arthur Britto, which is aptly entitled "The Ripple Protocol Consensus Algorithm." In short, the protocol uses known mathematical formulas to determine the maximum fault tolerance that is acceptable for a system to still reach accurate results (or more specifically, a trusted ledger) without the use of a proof-of-work algorithm. Instead of miners competing to create the next block, the RPCA utilizes "consensus rounds" whereby each node on the network has a "Unique Node List" with which that node will interact in broadcasting transactions and reaching consensus. Transactions only make it into a confirmed block (or what Ripple describes as the "Last-Closed Ledger") if a sufficient level of consensus is reached based on its mathematical fault tolerance requirements. The authors of the paper concluded that so long as these fault tolerances are met, the proof-of-stake system that makes up the RPCA is sufficient to overcome the "Byzantine Generals Problem" (see discussion in section 1:6).

§ 3:6   Existing protocols—Hyperledger

Hyperledger is an open source project sponsored by the Linux Foundation with aims of advancing blockchain technology by "identifying and addressing important features for a cross-industry open standard for distributed ledgers that can transform the way business transactions are conducted globally."[1] The project is a collaborative effort among some of the largest technology companies in the industry, including IBM and Intel, whom aim to break down barriers in the financial industry to enable individuals/companies/financial institutions to move value across the

---

[Section 3:5]

[1]See http://www.paymentlawadvisor.com/2015/05/12/fincen-and-depa rtment-of-justice-settle-anti-money-laundering-charges-against-crypto-cur rency-company-ripple-labs/.

[Section 3:6]

[1]See https://www.hyperledger.org/about.

world quickly and easily, similar to sending an e-mail.[2] Other companies involved in the project include the CME Group, Digital Asset, J.P. Morgan and Accenture. HyperLedger is still in the early stages of development. A sub-project of Hyperledger called "fabric" is said to still be in "incubation," but will ultimately serve as the foundation for the Hyperledger protocol. Architecturally, the Hyperledger protocol is a highly modular platform.

One of the contributors, Intel, has included its Sawtooth Lake technology as part of the project. Sawtooth Lake is a blockchain protocol based on a consensus algorithm called "Proof of Elapsed Time" or PoET. In the documentation for Sawtooth, Intel breaks down a distributed ledger into three components:

(1) a data model covering the current state of the distributed ledger;

(2) a language that can be used to change state of the distributed ledger;

(3) a protocol that includes a consensus algorithm to determine which transactions are accepted by the ledger.

While Intel provides an out-of-the-box solution for the first two elements, it is intended that many users will ultimately provide their own data models and languages—making Sawtooth highly modular. Regardless of the data model and language, users would be able to use the unique Sawtooth PoET consensus algorithm, which ultimately, is intended to execute within a trusted hardware environment—often referred to as a "Trusted Execution Environment (TEE)". Like other consensus algorithms, PoET seeks to create a process of building agreement among a group of untrusted participants. Intel, however, recognizes that while all consensus algorithms are designed to address Byzantine failures, other application requirements may influence what constitutes an optimal consensus model.

Given the different demands of different applications, Intel has separated the data models and transaction structuring from consensus. In addition, Sawtooth Lakes provides developers with two consensus models from which to choose. The first, PoET, is a lottery based protocol executed within a trusted environment. While PoET is conceptually similar to the consensus protocol used by Bitcoin, it requires the use of

---

[2]http://www.econotimes.com/A-Closer-Look-At-Hyperledger-136624.

far less resources than Bitcoin because of Intel's proprietary Software Guard Extensions (SGX) technology. More specifically, the system guarantees randomness in the election of a "leader" validator for each block, which process repeats itself for every block. While this method of consensus easily scales and is cost effective, it requires the use of proprietary Intel chips. The alternative consensus model, called Quantum Voting, is a permutation of the Ripple Consensus Algorithm that relies on Byzantine Fault Tolerance algorithms and uses multiple consensus rounds.

IBM's contribution to HyperLedger is currently focused on the fabric repository.[3] Like Microsoft, IBM had added blockchain capabilities to its cloud service, Bluemix. More specifically, developers can create blockchain test networks based on the fabric repository and develop test applications in the cloud. This service allows businesses to easily deploy test transactions to IBM's implementation of the blockchain. IBM's implementation of fabric is based on a permissioned system that also allows for transaction participants to engage in confidential transactions on the ledger so that only the parties to the transaction are able to see the details of the transaction—yet consensus is still reached through the use of permissioned nodes.

One component of the fabric blockchain implementation is the concept of a certificate authority that handles "Membership Services"; which is the term given to the protocol that is responsible for managing identities, network permissions, and if necessary, confidential transactions. The certificate authority accomplishes these responsibilities through the issuance of digital certificates, which thereby creates certainty as to the identity of the individuals operating a peer node on the blockchain. Now is a good time to stop and remind ourselves that this entire concept is foreign to the Bitcoin protocol, which has no barriers in terms of operating a mining or non-mining node on the Bitcoin network. There is also no capability to determine the identity of those individuals participating in the Bitcoin network. This highlights a key concept that is important to remember—different businesses have unique needs and those needs may require certain attributes that one blockchain protocol provides and that others do not. Blockchains are not inherently a one size fits all technology.

---

[3]A repository or "repo" is just coding jargon for a place where source code is stored for collaborative use. For example, the fabric repository can be found on GitHub. URL: https://github.com/hyperledger/fabric.

One of the primary advantages that cloud-based blockchain services give businesses and firms wishing to beginning testing blockchain applications is the ability to focus on application development (i.e., coding applications and preparing test transactions). Starting from scratch and creating your own blockchain test network requires a fair amount of work in order to properly prepare the testing environment. Without a highly experienced blockchain team, this chore can be time consuming and distracting. Given the fact that most IT departments do not have great familiarity with blockchain technology, these cloud-based services are worth serious consideration by most businesses and firms.

§ 3:7   Existing protocols—R3's Corda

Corda is a distributed ledger designed specifically for financial services, which is not surprising given that R3 is a consortium of financial institutions and other firms that support financial institutions. R3 has a broad base of U.S. and non-U.S. financial institutions and other diverse participants, such as Thompson Reuters (the publisher of this book). Corda is described by R3 as "a distributed ledger platform designed from the ground up to record, manage and synchronize financial agreements between regulated financial institutions."[1] Due to its target user, Corda is a closed, permissioned system, so access to the ledger is controlled. The design includes the ability to enable regulatory agencies to operate supervisory nodes that will allow them to monitor the institutions transacting business on the platform in real time. Unlike most traditional blockchains, Corda does not have any native crypto currency—as described below, the platform is primarily focused on the validation and authentication of regulated transactions rather than the transfer of crypto or virtual currency.

Richard Brown of R3 has described the "blockchain bundle" as containing five distinct (but related) concepts:[2]

(1) consensus
(2) validity
(3) uniqueness

[Section 3:7]

[1]http://www.coindesk.com/9-takeaways-r3s-new-distributed-ledger-tech/.

[2]"Introducing R3 Corda: A Distributed Ledger Designed for Financial Services," r3cev.com Blog Post, April 5, 2016, by Richard Gendal Brown.

(4) immutability

(5) authentication

Corda tackles the above concepts differently than other blockchains, reflecting its acknowledgment that its target users are financial institutions. For example, with respect to consensus, the Corda protocol is less concerned about reaching global consensus, but rather reaching consensus between the transacting parties. As Brown puts it, it is sufficient that "I know that you see the same details about a shared fact that I see."[3] Put another way, Corda allows its users to develop validation schemes (not to be confused with consensus algorithms) on a transaction by transaction basis based on their specific transaction needs—there is no benchmark algorithm under which the platform operates in order to validate a transaction. For example, two regulated banks to a transaction could establish a validation scheme whereby consensus must be reached by the two parties to the transaction and that this validation (and potentially other information) pertaining to this transaction also be available to one or more regulators having authority over those financial institutions. The ability to refine consensus and validation requirements at such a granular level could provide many industries, especially those that are regulated, with powerful tools enabling them to take advantage of efficiencies and thereby cost savings, while discarding those that provide no benefit or are otherwise contrary to their interests (e.g., public disclosure of private information).

While Corda's consensus requirements can be set-up to be radically different from those of traditional blockchains, once consensus is reached the immutability aspect and data structures utilized by the Corda platform follow the traditional principles that we've discussed above with respect to Bitcoin and other protocols. As such, Corda still uses many of the core components of blockchain technology that are seen in Bitcoin, but provides its users with the ability to tailor consensus requirements, and as a result, who on a network can access all or pieces of information related to an individual transaction. While Corda is still in the development stages as we write this book, it will likely become one of the more prominent "permissioned" blockchain protocols, especially within the financial industry.

---

[3]"Introducing R3 Corda: A Distributed Ledger Designed for Financial Services," r3cev.com Blog Post, April 5, 2016, by Richard Gendal Brown.

§ 3:8 Existing protocols—Symbiont Distributed Ledger

Symbiont's blockchain is a permissioned ledger system designed to handle smart contracts within the financial services sector. As a permissioned system, its consensus model does not require a cryptographic currency in order to operate. Symbiont's primary product is known as "Smart Security" which "allows for complex financial instruments to be modeled in an easy to understand programming language and fully digitized onto a distributed ledger." Like other blockchain protocols, Symbiont offers cost savings by largely automating formerly manual and back office tasks. In addition, instruments deployed on Symbiont's blockchain are cryptographically signed and tamper proof. It is also worthy to note that it's "Smart Security" platform can run on many blockchains. This is another example of a blockchain company focused on developing smart contracts that are protocol agnostic. Ultimately, this interoperability may well be an indication of the future where companies are able to run smart contracts of their choosing and interact with others notwithstanding that they may not operate on the same distributed ledger protocol.

§ 3:9 Existing Protocols—Tendermint

Tendermint has developed its blockchain protocol from the ground up, which is capable of being deployed on AWS, Google Cloud, Microsoft Azure or Digital Ocean. The Tendermint protocol is open source and uses a Byzantine Fault Tolerant consensus algorithm. One advantage to Tendermint's protocol is that it allows the deployment of smart contracts programmed in any programming language using Tendermint's TMSP (The Tendermint Socket Protocol).[1] Tendermint Core is the consensus engine, which interacts with the TMSP. TMSP handles the modes of communication between the nodes that make up the blockchain, while an application developed by a developer is responsible for maintaining the actual ledger and handling cryptographic signatures.

§ 3:10 Existing Protocols—Digital Asset Holdings

Digital Asset Holdings (DAH), headed by former JPMorgan

[Section 3:9]

[1]http://tendermint.com/blog/tendermint-socket-protocol/.

executive Blythe Masters, has been actively developing permissioned blockchain technology and smart contracts aimed at the financial services industry. DAH is one of the best funded smart contract start-ups having secured several million dollars in investment from ASX Limited.[1] DAH is also a major contributor to the Hyperledger open source project. In addition, DAH has been a major thought leader in the implementation of blockchain technology on Wall Street and is likely responsible for FinTech's significant investment in this area.

§ 3:11 Existing protocols—Rubix (Deloitte) and Eris Industries, Ltd.

Rubix is less of a blockchain protocol and more of a development shop specializing in tailoring blockchain solutions, including those based on Ethereum, for clients. Like Rubix, Eris Industries, Ltd. specializes in developing blockchain-based smart contract solutions for clients. Eris makes available a suite of open source components that enable companies to "roll their own" blockchain based on the components provided by Eris. Eris is a well-known thought leader at the intersection of law and blockchain technology, with many of its principals being lawyers. Eris has positioned itself well as the market leader of legal-based, smart contracts. Eris's philosophy is that smart contracts need to run parallel with traditional contracts—smart contracts should contain a copy of the traditional contracts and the traditional contract contain an online reference to the smart contract. This "dual-integration" approach, according to Eris, would allow a judge in the incumbent legal system to enforce the terms of a smart contract.[1]

[Section 3:10]

[1]https://urldefense.proofpoint.com/v2/url?u=http-3A__www.bloomber g.com_news_articles_2016-2D01-2D21_blythe-2Dmasters-2Dfirm-2Draise s-2Dcash-2Dwins-2Daustralian-2Dexchange-2Ddeal&d=CwIGaQ&c=4ZIZ ThykDLcoWk-GVjSLm9hvvvzvGv0FLoWSRuCSs5Q&r=SAe0sFVgf84X_6 Al-gxaQRUSBPOiYLQq1KjAnwmvzDTJfwsXmYhuO5BqLYu6QSOO&m= 16tsl3V3Lp_YwbphxuHffC7vnrV9LYccKXy9Lb50oPw&s=X_Mmi_jNvruxQ WAnmPBlQcBod52Luvu8r2qflof4X3w&e=

[Section 3:11]

[1]https://erisindustries.com/components/erislegal/.

§ 3:12 Determining how blockchain technology can help your business or firm

The first step to determining how blockchain technology can help your business or firm is to understand the technology (which you are doing by reading this book). It's only with a true understanding of blockchain technology that one can appreciate where blockchain technology can create efficiencies and add value (and recognize where it is simply hype). The authors of this book believe that blockchain technology is and will continue to be an important driver of innovation across the globe—otherwise, we would not have invested the time to write this book—but like many misunderstood technologies, it is subject to tremendous hype and misinformation. Blockchain technology can't solve all the world's problems—alternative and current centralized solutions may still be the best answer for existing challenges. Ultimately, the only way to be able to discern whether a blockchain proposition for your business is value-add or hype is to understand the technology itself.

Every business is unique and the issues that one industry confronts are often very different from others. This uniqueness means that within the broader scope of blockchain technology certain blockchain platforms or solutions will be better suited than others. So even after determining that blockchain technology can help your firm, you still need to make sure to deploy the right platform. For example, if your business is not heavily regulated and your firm is looking for an alternative payment vehicle, Bitcoin likely provides a solution (or at least a good starting point). On the other hand, if your company is looking for a secure way to license out Internet of Things devices, then Ethereum's ability to easily process smart contracts will probably work much better out of the box than a Bitcoin platform.

§ 3:13 Considerations for determining the blockchain protocol best for your business or firm

The principle drivers for selecting a platform are:

(1) the problem(s) you are trying to solve;
(2) the nature of your business;
(3) the regulatory regimes applicable to your business;
(4) overall resources; and
(5) IT resources.

The first step is to determine what problem you are trying to solve. Are you looking for a new payment service or a way to license out Internet of Things devices? Similarly, the nature of your business is also important. Are you a large enterprise with thousands of employees or a startup comprised of two cofounders? Ethereum may be the perfect platform for a startup with limited resources that is developing an IoT product. Ethereum provides a ready to go platform with several smart contract templates that make it easy to get up and running. Similarly, solutions that do not require vetted and identified validators, like Ethereum and Bitcoin, offer viable alternatives.

On the other hand, if you are a financial institution looking to incorporate a platform for purchasing and selling commercial paper to other financial institutions, then a permissioned ledger is probably a starting point. Additionally, both regulatory constraints and the ability to potentially reduce regulatory compliance costs from a system tailored to financial institutions may dictate a Hyperledger protocol with a Digital Asset Holdings smart contract solution. Having large IT resources (whether in-house or through outsourcing) equates into the ability to carefully tailor not only more narrowly tailored platforms, but the ability to combine components from several platforms to take the best aspects from different systems.

Whether or not your use case dictates a payment component, platforms that include a cryptocurrency may still be the best protocol for the job. For example, a company looking for an immutable record keeping system with each entry time stamped and tamper-proof may find that nominal Bitcoin transactions and OP_RETURN codes provide all the performance necessary to solve the problem. On the other hand, converting complex derivative products like interest rate swaps into programmatic, digital instruments that can be traded without the need for a third party intermediary will likely find Bitcoin a less than optimal solution—especially given the number of other options currently available.

§ 3:14 Developing a strategy to integrate blockchain technology into your business or firm

Understand that blockchain technology is still a work in progress. As such, expect the planning and implementation phase to be an extended process—one that is likely to require re-evaluation of solutions as technology continues to evolve.

In addition, training individuals may prove more difficult than your average enterprise solution because many of the core underpinnings of blockchain technology are novel and not readily understood by most in the work force. Even most IT professionals lack a comprehensive understanding of the technology.

The first step to any strategy should be education. It's especially important for IT personnel to understand the basic mechanics of blockchain technology and to stay up to date with developments on different blockchain protocols. Learning to distinguish between fairy tales and realistic capabilities is essential. Understanding real capabilities allows businesses to identify those problems or areas of its business that could be improved with blockchain technology. It makes little sense to focus on problems where blockchain technology is ill suited or provides little enhancement in performance. Such a strategy will likely result in wasted expenditures and disappointment.

Last, but certainly not least, plan on implementing blockchain solutions as redundant systems to your existing, conventional solutions. At first glance, you rightfully may find that approach to be the antithesis of creating efficiencies. This redundancy is temporary. As with any new technology, even systems marketed as "production ready" are rarely ready for prime time. This is especially true with blockchain technology. Most prudent businesses that are already incorporating blockchain solutions into their business model (which, as of the writing of this book, is most limited to companies that are actively engaged in this space) are doing so on top of existing systems. Eventually the training wheels will come off and the redundant systems will disappear. A conservative transition phase will help avoid catastrophic system failures that are inevitable if you rely solely on new technologies like blockchain.

Chapter 4

Decentralized Autonomous Organizations (DAOs)

§ 4:1   Summary of important points

- Decentralized autonomous organizations (DAOs) are a new take on corporate governance and finance that utilize code implemented on a blockchain in lieu of traditional bylaws and director and shareholder meetings.
- The code that implements a DAO must be highly deterministic as it must contemplate, and appropriately address, all of the material logic and decision making that goes into operating a common enterprise.
- It is unclear how regulatory agencies, like the SEC, will treat the tokens that evidence "ownership" of DAOs.
- The largest DAO to date, known as *"The DAO,"* had a market capitalization of approximately $130 million at one point, but ultimately failed when a flaw in the code was exploited and tens of millions of dollars in cryptocurrency was taken contrary to the intention of *The DAO*'s creators.

§ 4:2   Business organizations reinvented: The fundamentals of DAOs

There are many differences among the traditional types of organizations with which we are familiar—partnerships, limited liability companies, for-profit and not-for-profit corporations, trusts, and the like—but they also have common elements. Perhaps most fundamentally, almost all organizations are governed by a contract. Certificates of incorporation and bylaws function as contracts among the internal stakeholders of a corporation (i.e., its shareholder, directors, and officers); partners typically make written or verbal agreements; limited liability companies have operating agreements. To be sure, each type of traditional organization is authorized by statute, and these statutes (and regulations and case law related to them) sometime constrain contract terms crafted by stakeholders. Law also can supplement contract terms on issues not explicitly addressed by the stakeholders.

These traditional types of organizations, if well run, also record various types of transactions in various traditional (non-distributed/centralized) ledgers. Corporations record issuances and transfers of stock in a stock ledger. Disbursements and receipts of cash are recorded in an organization's general ledger. Contracts and their key terms (e.g., payment obligations and expiration dates) are logged in contract management software.

A decentralized autonomous organization, or DAO, is a new type of organization, but it shares these basic features of traditional organizations. It is a creature of contract and its activities are recorded in a ledger. A DAO, however, relies much more heavily and fundamentally upon automated processes than other types of organizations. Its contract is a smart contract, and its ledger is a blockchain. The terms of its governing contract are expressed and implemented algorithmically in computer code recorded on its blockchain. Transactions among *The DAO* and its stakeholders (e.g., investments in the organization and transfers of evidence of these investments), as well as transactions between *The DAO* and third parties, also are effectuated through and recorded on its blockchain.

Most organizations of any kind exist to address certain aspirations, needs, and concerns that call for collective action. This is true of traditional organizations, and it is true of DAOs. For a given organization, these interests may include some or all of the following:

- Aggregating capital, other resources (including human talent), and opportunities
- Investing resources in opportunities that may return a profit or produce other benefits
- Simplifying group decision making and action and

otherwise reducing burdens and costs associated with independent or less coordinated effort

- Making it possible for initial stakeholders to depart, and new stakeholders to enter, without disbanding the collective or disrupting its activities
- Shielding stakeholders from liability and otherwise reducing and/or sharing risk
- Minimizing tax obligations

Each type of traditional organization addresses some of these (and other) interests more effectively than the other types of organizations, which is why a palette of options has emerged over time.

A DAO can address many of these interests, as *The DAO*, one of the earliest and most visible DAOs, illustrates. *The DAO* was established on the Ethereum blockchain network to operate much like a venture capital fund.[1] It set an online fundraising (aka crowdfunding) record in early 2016. It raised ETH (Ether tokens, Ethereum's Bitcoin-like cryptocurrency) worth more than $130 million, proving that a DAO can serve as a vehicle for aggregating a large amount of capital. (Never mind that approximately a third of this amount soon was pilfered in an attack that exploited vulnerabilities in *The DAO's* software, sending *The DAO* into a tailspin. Other DAOs will deploy more secure software, and, as we know, traditional organizations' computer systems frequently are exploited.) Those who paid ETH to *The DAO* received one or more "DAO tokens" evidencing membership in *The DAO*. *The DAO* solicited proposals for investment of its funds in other blockchain based businesses—ventures that would require initial, and perhaps also ongoing, human involvement (from software developers, for instance).[2] *The DAO's* contract terms specify that investment decisions are to be made by majority vote of its members. Members wishing to exit or reduce their participation in *The DAO* could trade their DAO tokens on a cryptocurrency exchange, such as BTC Markets. Of course, the original hope was that the value of one's DAO tokens would appreciate substantially

---

[Section 4:2]

[1]http://fortune.com/2016/05/15/leaderless-blockchain-vc-fund/.

[2]Since a DAO largely exists and functions through software, it must enlist humans to do things that, at least for now, only humans can do, like develop a product. Individuals and other organizations a DAO enlists in this way are known as "contractors."

based upon the success of the blockchain based products and services financed by *The DAO*.

The DAO is just one example of a DAO; its particular structure and terms are not the only structure and terms those forming a DAO may choose. As we already can see, however, it is possible to create a DAO that answers many of the aspirations, needs, and concerns which have lead people to form one of the traditional types of organizations. Other examples of DAOs are discussed below. Like *The DAO*, all are generally based on a white paper published by Christopher Jentzsch at Slock.it.[3]

Putting aside technologists' perennial fascination with the seemingly unlimited potential of technology (and general fascination with all things shiny and new), the following are among the features that distinguish, or can distinguish, a DAO from other types of organizations, and which therefore might be among the reasons to form one:

- *Self-governance and automated operations.* A DAO automates, in a highly integrated way, many governance and operational functions of a traditional organization that typically require human judgment and effort (sometimes aided by software systems that may or may not be well integrated with one another). The organizational functions a DAO can automate range from admission of new stakeholders to contracting with third parties to taking other actions that normally require human deliberation. Automation may lower overhead and transaction costs; help eliminate or minimize errors in judgment and execution, and even the sort of self-dealing and other forms of intentional misconduct in which agents of an organization sometimes engage; and eliminate or reduce the need for human oversight of other humans. It is important to note that a DAO need not take humans out of the equation entirely. The governing terms of *The DAO*, for example, make provision for a two-week period of online discussion among members before a vote is called on a contractor's proposal to transact with *The DAO*, and an elected group of "curators" performs certain verification functions related to the integrity of proposals from and contracts with contractors.

- *Organizational Immutability.* Once the governing

---

[3]https://download.slock.it/public/DAO/WhitePaper.pdf.

principles of a DAO—its contract or bylaws—are expressed and implemented through software code recorded on a blockchain, they are very difficult to change. As Stephan Tual, a founder of the blockchain projects Ethereum and Slock.it, says, "A DAO is an organization that's self-governing and not influenced by outside forces: its software operates on its own, with its by-laws immutably written on the blockchain, not controlled by its creators."[4] It is theoretically possible, though most often practically infeasible, for a group of a DAO's token holders acting in concert to manipulate *The DAO's* ledger through a procedure known as a "51 percent attack." Even so, a successful attack would enable these token holders to interfere with transactions (such as the confirmation of proposals and the exchange of tokens) for a period of time, but not to fundamentally rewrite *The DAO's* contract.

- *Transparency.* A DAO's governing source code is accessible to anyone who cares—and knows how—to read it. While key organizational documents of many companies whose shares are listed on a major stock exchange, and also of many not-for-profit organizations, are publicly available, the governing documents of the vastly greater number of for-profit private companies are not. Even when an organization's primary governing documents are publicly accessible, one may not have access to other important documents affecting how the organization functions (e.g., an organization chart and company policies). Under applicable law, one ordinarily must be a significant shareholder to gain access to these documents, or else seek their production in litigation based upon some grievance with respect to which they are relevant. Furthermore, interest holders in traditional organizations typically have no right to attend, let along participate in, meetings of the organization's governing board and management. Compared to a DAO, the inner workings of most traditional organizations are relatively opaque.

- *Infallible Recordkeeping.* A blockchain ledger is distributed (i.e., exact copies exist on multiple computers with no central administration), making it effectively impervious to error and tampering, including outright fraud.

---

[4]https://blog.slock.it/a-primer-to-the-decentralized-autonomous-organization-dao-69fb125bd3cd#.c1d5l8sfj.

If one owns a share of a company one believes has issued 1,000 shares, but which has fraudulently issued 100,000 shares, one obviously has a much less valuable investment than one assumed (and not just merely because there are many more shares than one believed). There may be ways to defraud a DAO's stakeholders, but manipulation of its ledger is unlikely to be among them. This level of recordkeeping integrity may be particularly significant where there are many investors in a business venture and their involvement is passive.

- *Personal Anonymity.* In blockchain networks like Bitcoin and Ethereum, tokens are associated with public accounts corresponding to alpha-numeric public keys, not with individuals' names. While it is not necessarily impossible to trace ownership back to an individual in some cases, it is possible to avoid detection if a token holder leaves no evidentiary trail at the time he, she or it exchanges state issued currency for cryptocurrency. Even this trail can be obscured with enough sophistication; for example, by using TOR or a similar proxy service or the conversion and/or "tumbling" of crypto-coins (e.g., converting Bitcoin to ETH and back and forth or the use of services that effectively "clean" cryptocurrencies). This level of anonymity does not mean DAOs are destined to be used primarily for illegal or other shady purposes. There are many legitimate reasons for seeking a degree of anonymity in one's financial affairs, and it already is possible to do so using traditional types of organizations (i.e., setting up several layers of off-shore entities and trusts).

- *Liquidity.* It is often difficult for the owner of an interest in a private entity (and even in a public entity not listed on a stock exchange) to identify and transact with a buyer when the owner resolves to sell that interest. Ignoring for the moment legal restrictions on marketing and transferring ownership interests in business ventures, there are active online exchanges on which cryptocurrencies like Bitcoin and ETH, as well as DAO tokens premised upon these currencies, easily can be bought and sold.

These are some of the reasons people might choose to form a DAO. A traditional organization may be engineered to have some of these features, at least to some degree, but the highly automated, "hardwired" nature of a DAO affords it comparative advantages in these respects. It presently is hard to imagine creating a traditional organization that would have all of these features in equal measure. Of course, some of these seeming advantages also have potential downsides. An immutable organizational structure may prove to be unfortunate if the structure is flawed, as the stakeholders in *The DAO* discovered when hackers exploited structural vulnerabilities which enabled them to divert tens of millions of dollars in value previously controlled by *The DAO*. Even if a DAO's structure is perfectly engineered for all foreseen purposes and invincible from attack, business purposes tend to evolve over time, and most traditional organizations are flexible enough to adapt accordingly. Anonymous ownership is appropriate in some situations, but most stakeholders in most organizations—not to mention most third parties—will rightly prefer to know who else can influence and benefit from the organization's activities.

The preceding discussion ignores legal issues that inevitably will impinge upon the formation and operations of a DAO. Some of the more significant of these issues are addressed in the remaining sections of this chapter, which focus mainly on United States laws and certain cross-border transactional concerns. It remains to be seen whether *The DAO* organizational form will become as widely utilized as traditional types of organizations and, if so, the legitimate purposes for which people will consider it superior to other organizational forms. Even now, however, the organizers and members of a DAO, and those doing business with one, would be unwise to assume that this new form of organization operates in a "regulation free zone." It does not. Regulators in the United States and other countries are watching the development of *The DAO* form closely, and it seems likely that they eventually will introduce regulations tailored to it. In the meantime, public and private actors (e.g., aggrieved investors in or contractors with a DAO) will attempt to take action against DAOs and their members under existing legal principles when they believe they have cause to do so. The application of some existing principles to DAOs will prove clumsy or ineffective, but those with a present need to fit *The DAO* "peg" into some legal hole—whether a lawyer advising business founders who wish to form a DAO or members of *The DAO* searching for a way to recover diverted funds—have little choice for now, other than to work with legal norms established before *The DAO* organizational form appeared on the scene.

§ 4:3 Where do DAO token holders fit?

As with any new legal relationship, legal constructs must be developed to govern the issues that arise between, or with respect to, the participants in that relationship. For a multitude of reasons (efficiency being one of them), we like to classify people and things into abstract categories. For example, when your sink drain no longer functions and you call a plumber to fix it, the individual who shows up to do the work necessary to repair your sink possibly invokes several different legal abstractions. The individual is likely an *employee* of a *company* that has been created by statute (e.g., a corporation, limited liability company, limited partnership). Depending on the category (or type) of business organization chosen, the manner of taxation on the income from the company can vary as can the liability of the company in the event the plumber accidentally damages your car. Some of these categories, such as corporations, have existed in one derivation or another for several hundred years, and as such, the body of jurisprudence (i.e., legal guidance) is voluminous.

The idea of a DAO, on the other hand, is a relatively recent concept. In fact, its very existence relies on blockchain technology, which has only been with us for less than eight years. In reality, it's an even shorter period of time when you consider that DAOs really require a more robust blockchain environment like Ethereum that can run smart contracts natively. As lawyers, our natural instinct when confronted with something new is to try and analogize it to a similar, existing concept from which we can draw parallels. Likewise, we take note of differences and try to account for them in the legal doctrine we develop to govern the new concept. For example, when ATMs and debit cards arrived, lawmakers and lawyers did not start from scratch in developing the legal doctrines which govern them. Instead, they started with the well-established body of law that governed other payment instruments, such as checks, and modified the law to the extent necessary to take into account the unique nature of those then new forms of electronic payments.

At the heart of any DAO, however, is software code. *The DAO*'s code establishes how *The DAO* will conduct its business or other enterprise (say in the case of a philanthropic effort). By analogy, this code is not much different than the limited partnership agreement that governs an opportunity fund. The purpose of both is nearly identical in terms of governance—it's in the implementation that the two differ. One requires an extensive amount of human involvement in order to effectuate the requirements of the partnership agreement while the other needs far less human involvement, instead relying on token holders to simply vote yes, no or abstain from various proposals made to *The DAO*. Limited partnerships, like corporations, limited liability companies and business trusts are all creatures of statute.

Because no statute (at least not in the United States) authorizes the creation of a legally distinct entity in the form of a DAO, we can only abstract it as an unincorporated association of individuals with a common purpose, which, as others have suggested, is typically referred to as a general partnership or joint venture. To end the analysis there, however, would be an oversimplification; to the same extent as if we had simply said that a debit card is just a plastic reusable check, and as such, can be governed by the same laws that govern checks. The reality is that the way in which people come together to fund, participate, and interact with a DAO is significantly different than that of a traditional general partnership. As such, many of the principles applied to general partnerships and its partners seem misplaced in the context of a DAO.

One glaring concern is the liability of the participants (or more specifically, the token holders) for any damages or liability that might be asserted against *The DAO*. Under the law of general partnerships, each partner is responsible and liable for any damages or liability caused by its other partners arising out of the furtherance of partnership business. So hypothetically, let's say that *The DAO* votes in favor of a proposal to support and fund the manufacturing and sale of a particular piece of hardware. Unfortunately, there is a design flaw in the hardware, and as a result, several people are severely injured when the lithium batteries in their devices explode. Applying the law of general partnerships, each individual owning one or more tokens in *The DAO* could be liable to the injured individuals for any damages they sustained under product liability claims. Is that an economically efficient outcome that makes for good policy? Probably not.

In addition to the above being a sub-optimal outcome from a policy standpoint, there are practical impediments to identifying the actual holders of *The DAO* tokens. While it is not necessarily impossible to trace ownership back to an individual in some cases; it is possible to avoid detection if a token holder leaves no evidentiary trail at the time it converts from fiat currency to cryptocurrency. Even this trail can be covered up with enough sophistication, the use of TOR or similar proxy services and the conversion and/or "tumbling" of crypto-coins (e.g., converting Bitcoin to Ether and back and forth and the use of services that effectively "clean" cryptocurrencies). In addition, enforcing judgments against "distributions" to token holders is likewise futile. The software code that forms the governance documents for *The DAO* are immutable from outside forces (such as by court order). Again, because of its decentralized nature, there is no single point of failure—no server that the government can reprogram to conform to a court order or judgment.

So where does that leave the relationship of token holders of DAOs? Well, for those holding tokens in *The DAO*, I would not lose much sleep at night worrying about possible exposure for exploding batteries. It is also my suspicion that as policy makers begin to address these "unincorporated" organizations of like-minded individuals, that the law will analogize them to investors in a mutual fund, hedge fund or similar investment vehicle—and not as general partners. There are a number of other questions that will need to be answered about the nature of this relationship, including who has standing to sue on behalf of a DAO, whether a DAO has know your customer (KYC)/ anti-money laundering (AML) obligations and how DAOs should be treated from a tax perspective—which is an especially difficult question since DAOs are domiciled everywhere and yet nowhere. These questions represent the tip of the iceberg in terms of unresolved areas of the law.

Moving beyond the nature of *The DAO* and the legal relationship between its members, there are several interesting questions about the nature and treatment of the tokens issued by *The DAO*. For example, should the tokens be considered money or assets subject to appreciation and gain. The answer to this question has significant tax implications. Beyond taxability issues, even criminal cases could be impacted. The trial of Michell Espinoza, who had been accused of money laundering in Miami-Dade County, Florida, hinged on whether Bitcoin is considered money. The defendant's position, which was accepted by the judge in the context of this case, is that Bitcoin does not constitute money, and therefore, his trading in Bitcoins (even though linked to illicit activities) can't be considered a crime under Florida's anti-money laundering statute. It's important to note that what might be considered money in the context of a criminal case might be different than in another context, especially when the term money is used in the broader context of a store of value.

§ 4:4 Capitalization structures

As DAOs mature, more complicated capital structures are likely to develop. Rather than all token holders having equal rights, analogous to a corporation which has only one series of common stock, DAOs can issue different tokens that represent different economic interests in *The DAO*. This is no different than a corporation that may have Class A common stock, Class B common stock, and preferred shares, each with its own set of entitlements. Because DAOs operate solely based on their code, the distribution payable to each type of token holder would be automatically determined based on the code for *The DAO*. Ultimately, there is no reason a DAO cannot replicate any capitalization that rivals that of a traditional corporation.

§ 4:5 SEC and securities issues

While an in-depth discussion of securities act rules and regulations are outside the scope of this book, the issue must at a minimum be raised. The legal definition of a security is derived from the '33 Act, which provides a broad definition of the term.[1] This definition includes what most think of when they hear the word "security": stocks and bonds. However, this definition also includes "investment contract[s]," which are investments of money in a common enterprise with the expectation that profits will be derived solely from the efforts of others.

Investors in *The DAO* have likely entered into an investment contract, and tokens in *The DAO* are likely securities. With respect to what qualifies as an investment of money, some courts have found that crypto-currency is the equivalent of money while others have not—but almost all would agree it is an item of value. Investors in *The DAO* convert standard currency into ETH, which is the crypto-currency of the Ethereum blockchain. They invest in *The DAO* by exchanging their ETH for tokens. These investments of

---

[Section 4:5]

[1]https://www.sec.gov/about/laws/sa33.pdf.

crypto-currency are likely investments of money for the purposes of the '33 Act.

Courts of appeal for the United States have defined the term "common enterprise" differently.[2] However, most agree that the pooling of like interests amongst investors qualifies as a common enterprise.[3] *The DAO* is likely a common enterprise, as investors possess a like interest in *The DAO*. *The DAO* investors pool their ETH in *The DAO* and receive tokens that are uniform in their characteristics, including proportional voting rights. The only difference amongst holders of tokens is how many tokens they hold, which is proportional to their investment of ETH in *The DAO*. The more tokens a holder possess, the more votes they may cast and the higher their pro-rata share of return on *The DAO* expenditures.

The term "solely" has not been interpreted literally, and it is sufficient for profits to be derived predominantly from the efforts of others. It is also sufficient if the efforts of others are dedicated to essential managerial tasks which impact the success of failure of the enterprise. Investors in *The DAO* can vote their tokens to approve or deny any expenditure *The DAO* might make. *The DAO* makes expenditures to fund third-party projects, which promise a return on investment. Once an expenditure has been made, the essential managerial tasks which impact the success or failure of the projects are conducted by third-parties. For this reason, profits derived from *The DAO* are derived predominantly, if not solely, from the efforts of others. Tokens in *The DAO* are likely securities, which the Securities Exchange Commission (SEC) may exercise jurisdiction over.

The '33 Act requires the registration of public offerings, or sales of securities to the general public, with the SEC.[4] However, certain private offerings are exempt from registration.[5] For example, sales of securities to certain "accredited investors," which include sales to individuals who, jointly with their spouse, have a net worth exceeding $1 mil-

---

[2]See: http://blj.ucdavis.edu/archives/vol-5-no-2/why-the-common-enterprise-test.html.

[3]http://blj.ucdavis.edu/archives/vol-5-no-2/why-the-common-enterprise-test.html.

[4]https://www.law.cornell.edu/wex/securities_act_of_1933.

[5]https://www.sec.gov/answers/accred.htm.

lion, are exempt from registration.[6] In addition, sales of securities to up to 35 non-accredited, "sophisticated" investors, regardless of net worth, are also exempt from registration.[7] With private offerings, issuers cannot generally solicit or advertise the sale, including over the Internet. Securities sold in private offerings are "restricted securities" that cannot be resold. The sale of tokens in *The DAO* likely does not fit within the private offering exemption to the registration requirement of the '33 Act. First, token ownership with respect to *The DAO* was unrestricted up until its closing, meaning securities were available to individuals with a net worth of less than $1 million and individuals with little or no investment experience. Second, *The DAO* acquired investors via use of the Internet, which likely constitutes general solicitation.

A sale or offer of sale occurring outside of the United States to a non-United States person is also not subject to registration under the 33' Act, but where the "sale" of a token in *The DAO* occurs is difficult to determine.[8] *The DAO*, being a creature of blockchain technology, does not have a location. The blockchain is simply a code connecting a number of devices. *The DAO* has no centralized server. A sale cannot occur where *The DAO* is located because *The DAO* does not have a single location. However, if "sales" occur where the token purchaser is located, *The DAO* would only fall within this exemption if all token purchasers were non-United States persons purchasing tokens outside of the United States. This is unlikely, although the anonymity afforded to token holders makes determining the location and identity of token holders nearly impossible. *The DAO* likely engaged in a public offering of securities to the public, subjecting it to the registration requirements of the '33 Act.

Under the Securities Exchange Act of 1934 ('34 Act), all "exchanges" must be registered with the SEC.[9] An exchange is defined broadly and includes any "organization, association, or group of persons" which provides a market place for the trading of securities.[10] The '34 Act also imposes a

---

[6]http://www.ecfr.gov/cgi-bin/retrieveECFR?gp=&SID=8edfd12967d69 c024485029d968ee737&r=SECTION&n=17y3.0.1.1.12.0.46.176.

[7]https://www.sec.gov/answers/rule506.htm.

[8]https://www.law.cornell.edu/wex/securities_act_of_1933.

[9]https://www.sec.gov/about/laws/sea34.pdf.

[10]https://www.sec.gov/about/laws/sea34.pdf.

registration requirement on traded securities, whereas the '33 Act only imposes a registration requirement on offerings of securities.[11] The definition of security under both the '33 Act and '34 Act are treated as identical, despite minor drafting differences. Currently, *The DAO* tokens are trading on a number of websites which support the trading of *The DAO* tokens, including Coincheck, BTC Markets, and Bittrex. If *The DAO* tokens are securities (they likely are), then these websites are likely "exchanges" that must be registered with the SEC under the '34 Act.

The consequences of failure to abide by the registration requirements of both the '33 Act and the '34 Act can be dire. Under the '33 Act, an SEC enforcement proceeding can result in the issuance of an injunction or the imposition of civil penalties against an issuer of securities who violates the Act.[12] Further, the '33 Act and '34 Act grant private individuals (investors) rights of action for injuries suffered as a result of violations of SEC registration and reporting requirements.[13] Recently, *The DAO* was hacked by an individual who was able to withdraw $50 million in ETH from the fund. However, the Ethereum core developers, after much debate, agreed to move forward with a hard fork in attempt to recover the withdrawn ETH (See section 3:3 for an in-depth discussion about the Ethereum hard fork). Were a more serious looting of *The DAO* to occur, investors might seek remedies against the developers via the rights of action afforded to them under the securities laws. The SEC may become more involved with *The DAO* and the development of similar projects should *The DAO* suffer additional attacks on investor assets. The founders of future DAOs should be aware of the securities law issues they might face should the SEC decide to get more heavily involved with the regulation of crypto-currency. If that's the case, then individuals raising money or facilitating the raising of money should be cautious not to run afoul of the S.E.C. and state and Federal securities laws, which require that security offering either be registered with the S.E.C. or otherwise be sold to accredited investors or qualify for another exemption to registration.

Ultimately, the well-meaning nature of DAOs and their mission to explore alternative forms of governance and crowd

---

[11]https://www.sec.gov/about/laws/sea34.pdf.

[12]https://www.sec.gov/about/laws/sea34.pdf.

[13]https://www.sec.gov/about/laws/sea34.pdf.

funding are not sufficient to exclude them from regulation under Federal law. The pilfering and subsequent shut down of *The DAO* is almost certain to bring unwanted scrutiny, especially given that tens of millions of dollars were effectively stolen from *The DAO* because of bad code in its implementing smart contract. While *The DAO* and it token holders ultimately recovered the funds by implementing a hard fork, we suspect the damage is already done. Even assuming a desire to comply with applicable security laws, how do you determine what jurisdiction's laws with which *The DAO* must comply with? This is a difficult question to answer because DAO tokens can easily be purchased anywhere in the world and proxy relays, like TOR (see section 7:3 for more on TOR), make it difficult to restrict the sale of DAO tokens to people living in a particular jurisdiction.

While short lived, *The DAO* tokens were listed on several cryptocurrency exchanges, which meant that tokens for *The DAO* could be bought and sold for fiat currencies as well as being exchanged for BTC or ETH. While it will take some time for the wounds to heal from the fallout of *The DAO* hack, DAOs will return, and when they do, there will continue to be trading platforms. The question is whether the S.E.C. will require those platforms to be licensed securities exchanges. Only time will tell how the government ultimately reacts to these crowd funding platforms on steroids.

§ 4:6 Transactions secured by DAO tokens

Another host of transactions that have garnered little attention are secured transactions, or more specifically:

- The idea of pledging stuff (property, securities, contract rights, etc.) as collateral, and how it's typically done.
- Difficulties of doing this with DAO tokens.

With respect to shares in a corporation, we could determine the proper method to perfect a security interest in a loan secured by DAO tokens as collateral by reference to Article 8 and/or 9 of the Uniform Commercial Code as adopted in the State in which the debtor is secured. This is one of those areas, however, where the law needs implementing legislation to fix certain gaps.

Because DAO tokens do not likely fit the definition of a security under Article 8, they may be considered a general intangible of some sort under Article 9 of the UCC. If that's the case, then Article 9 says that you must file a UCC-1 Financing Statement with the state in which the debtor is organized (if an entity) or residing (if an individual).[1] Due to the liquidity of DAO tokens, this is akin to taking a security interest in cash. In other words, the secured party may be legally protected on paper, but be left holding the bag if the debtor transfers *The DAO* tokens to another party.

§ 4:7 Taxation

Certain entities are "disregarded entities" for the purposes of federal taxation. A disregarded entity is, as the name suggests, disregarded by the IRS. The owner and the entity are treated as one for the purposes of federal taxation, and taxes are paid through the filing of the owner's income tax return. Under a strict construction the Internal Revenue Code section concerning disregarded entities, only one type of business organization qualifies as a disregarded entity; the single member LLC.[1] However, a single member LLC, like all LLCs, may elect to be taxed as a C corporation or S corporation.[2] Multi-member LLCs are taxed as partnerships by default, but also may elect to be taxed as a C corporation or S corporation.[3]

Certain entities are known as "pass-through" entities, as income is "passed" to owners. These entities, like disregarded entities, are not taxed.[4] Pass-through entities include sole proprietorships, partnerships, LLCs (if not electing to be taxed as a C corporation), and S corporations.[5] Practically speaking, disregarded entities and pass-through entities are the same with respect to how the profits of the organization are ultimately taxed. The primary benefit of being a disregarded or pass-through entity is the avoidance of double taxation. Ordinary C corporations pay taxes on after-expense

---

[Section 4:6]

[1]https://www.law.cornell.edu/ucc/9/9-503.

[Section 4:7]

[1]https://www.irs.gov/businesses/small-businesses-self-employed/single-member-limited-liability-companies.

[2]https://www.irs.gov/businesses/small-businesses-self-employed/llc-filing-as-a-corporation-or-partnership.

[3]https://www.irs.gov/businesses/small-businesses-self-employed/llc-filing-as-a-corporation-or-partnership.

[4]https://www.irs.gov/uac/choosing-a-business-structure.

[5]https://www.irs.gov/uac/choosing-a-business-structure.

profits at a maximum rate of 35%.[6] Owners then pay taxes on dividends paid to them from the corporation at ordinary income rates. This is the "double taxation" that disregarded and pass-through entities avoid.

Would *The DAO*, or any DAO, be taxed on its profits? A DAO is not a legally recognized entity. Currently, no statute authorizes the creation of a DAO. Regarding existing and recognized entities, as discussed above, *The DAO* is most analogous to a partnership. A partnership is two or more individuals, acting as co-owners, engaged in business for a profit. With respect to *The DAO*, investors pool ETH, a cryptocurrency, into *The DAO* with the expectation that profits will be derived from returns on the funding of third-party projects. Token holders make decisions regarding distributions, acting as "co-owners" of the fund. If *The DAO* or DAOs of similar operation were to be treated as partnerships, they would be pass-through entities, and taxes would be imposed upon token holders. However, the IRC states that a business entity is presumed to be a corporation by default, and if this presumption is applied to DAOs, taxes would be imposed on DAO profits at corporate rates. Of course, there are a number of practical problems to taxing a DAO. Who would file its tax returns? How do you determine the jurisdiction of a DAO for tax purposes? The IRS may have an easier time taking token holders, and it does have a method of taxing tokens.

The characterization of income by the IRS can make a big difference in the amount of tax owed on an article of income. The IRS currently taxes crypto-currency (which it calls virtual currency) as it does any other capital asset, like stock in corporation. The IRS defines virtual currency as "a digital representation of value that functions as a medium of exchange, a unit of account, and/or a store of value."[7] Using *The DAO* as an example, an investment of ETH into *The DAO* produces tokens, which are freely tradable on supporting web-based exchanges. Tokens are likely a "medium of exchange" as, at the very least, they can be exchanged for real currencies. A "unit of account," according to InvestorWords.com, is a "basic function of money, providing a measurement for defining, recording, and comparing

---

[6]https://ct.wolterskluwer.com/resource-center/articles/how-are-c-corp orations-taxed.

[7]https://www.irs.gov/pub/irs-drop/n-14-21.pdf.

value."[8] By this definition, a token is likely a unit of account. A token is also likely a "store of value" as tokens are nothing more than a representation of value, just like any other real currency. Because tokens fit the definition of virtual currency, they are taxed under the IRC as capital assets, meaning gains made upon their sale or exchange are taxed as capital gains. For capital assets held for more than one year, a maximum capital gains rate of 15% applies, whereas a maximum rate of 39.6% (the maximum ordinary income rate) applies to capital assets held for less than a year.[9] If distributions of ETH are made to token holder of *The DAO*, like dividends paid from a corporation, they are taxed as ordinary income by the IRS. Recipients of the distributions must include the fair market value of ETH received in their ordinary income when filing their taxes.

The practical concern the IRS should have regarding taxation of token holders in *The DAO* is enforcement. There is no public ledger containing the names of token holders. The blockchain contains a ledger of all transactions occurring on it but that ledger reflects ownership of tokens by reference to an alphanumeric sequence rather than a name. While the IRS has a method of taxing the profits of *The DAO,* whether a single cent of tax will be paid to the IRS on those profits remains to be seen.

The DAO, or any DAO, doesn't necessarily have to invest in third-party projects with the expectation of monetary return on investment. The deliverable could be a product, and *The DAO* could hypothetically set up channels by which to sell that product. In that case, *The DAO,* or token holders in it, could be subject to value added, use, or sales tax. As mentioned before, given the jurisdiction questions raised by decentralized applications, policy makers will have their hands full when any significant amount of commerce is accomplished through the use of DAOs and other forms of decentralized applications.

§ 4:8　Other areas impacting DAOs

In addition to the above, there are entire areas of the law and matters of policy that have been largely unaddressed by anyone involved in the process. For example, imagine a

---

[8]http://www.investorwords.com/17812/unit_of_account.html.

[9]http://www.taxpolicycenter.org/briefing-book/how-are-capital-gains-t axed.

DAO—we'll use *The DAO* in this example—funds the development of a drug created to treat a previously untreatable illness. The drug is initially hailed as a triumph of modern science, but shortly after the drug is prescribed to hundreds of thousands of patients, those patients begin to suffer extreme side effects. Some patients die and many are left with permanent disabilities. The patients and their families want to sue *The DAO* because it is a deep pocket. The question is: how do you sue a DAO? Can you sue a DAO?

Corporations, for example, are legal persons that can be taken to court and sued. They have representatives who can be served with summons, and they have physical addresses which help in resolving matters of jurisdiction. A DAO is not an entity recognized under the law of any state. Being a decentralized entity, it has no fixed, physical location. This makes resolving matters of jurisdiction complicated. Even if bringing a suit were possible it would be nearly impossible for the blockchain code on which it is built to be modified in compliance with a court order. The DAO could not be forced to satisfy a judgment against it. Suing a DAO is likely to be prohibitively difficult, so a litigant may wish to go after the entity's owners. For example, someone suing *The DAO* might want to go after its investors; the token holders.

As noted above, in the context of an entity, *The DAO* is most analogous to a general partnership. A general partnership is an entity in which individuals join together to conduct a business. In a general partnership, each individual partner retains some control over the day-to-day operations of the business. Token holders of *The DAO*, by virtue of holding tokens and voting them, exercise some level of control over the business operations of *The DAO*. One of the risks associated with being a general partner is unlimited liability, which may not be an issue if you're a limited liability entity. However, if you're an individual, it can be financially disastrous. In a corporation or a limited partnership, shareholders or limited partners relinquish control over their investment in return for limited liability. If an owner has limited liability, he or she cannot be held personally responsible for the liabilities of the business entity in which he or she has an ownership stake. A litigant can receive in a judgment an amount no greater than the owner's investment in the entity. General partners do not have limited liability. Any token holder or holders of *The DAO*, if identified, could be held jointly or separately responsible for the liabilities of *The DAO*. Of course, a single investor, or even a small number of them, likely would not be able to satisfy a judgment. Meaning this option is also unsatisfactory for a would-be plaintiff.

Fortunately for token holders, obtaining their identities is incredibly difficult. While evidence of investment in *The DAO* could be acquired to prove an individual's status as a token-holder, there are methods by which tech-savvy investors can cover their tracks. If a litigant wanted to sue a token holder, they would have to identify the person, locate them, find a court that can exercise jurisdiction over them, file a suit, and serve them with process. This would be very difficult, and token holders likely do not have to be concerned with being dragged into court. The easiest target for a suit would be the creators of the DAO. Unlike token holders, these individuals might be more easily identified and served with process, but like token holders, their pockets may not be deep enough to satisfy a large judgment.

Another area that DAOs should address when funding projects is intellectual property. This is important for both the DAO and the person seeking funding from the DAO. If the project involves any intellectual property, including patents, trade secrets, and trademarks, ownership of the IP should be specifically addressed by the parties. There can be a significant difference in a person's rights to IP if it is determined to be the owner or the IP rather than someone hired to produce it for another. Similarly, ownership versus being a licensee of IP has material consequences on a person's ability to utilize the IP. Because these issues have not yet been dealt with by courts, it is especially important for parties to deal with them in detail by contract.

Chapter 5

Key Management for Businesses and Professional Firms

§ 5:1   Summary of important points

- At the heart of blockchain security is public key infrastructure cryptography (PKI).
- PKI works by randomly creating public and private key pairs with elliptical mathematics that make it possible to determine if someone possesses the private key that corresponds to a public key. It is not possible, however, to determine the private key from the public key.
- Most digital assets are "owned" by virtue of someone having the private key that corresponds to that asset's public key.
- PKI allows people to cryptographically sign with their private key without having to disclose the actual private key to any other person.
- One of the biggest challenges to enterprise level adoption of blockchain technology will be key management among potentially thousands of employees.

§ 5:2   Public Key Infrastructure

Bitcoin and most other blockchain protocols utilize public key infrastructure to control accounts. Generally, public key cryptography is based on the generation of two keys, one of which is called the "public" key and the other of which is called the "private" key. As previously noted, the public key generally serves double duty by also being the genesis of the "account" number that serves as the digital representation of the blockchain asset (e.g., a Bitcoin). Accordingly, public keys are shared with the community, and in fact, in the context of PGP (Pretty Good Privacy) or GPG (GNU Privacy Guard) cryptography, both of which are implementations of asymmetric public key cryptography, there are registries where you can associate your identity (including your email address) with a public key. This is useful if you want to be able to cryptographically sign something, such as an email, so that the recipient knows you were the real sender. For every public key, there is a corresponding private key. Private keys must be guarded and kept secure by the individual key holders.

Today, the generation of public and private key pairs is predominately based on elliptic curve multiplication. While a detailed discussion of elliptic curve multiplication is beyond the scope of this book, it is not important to understand its intricacies in order to grasp public key infrastructure (PKI). For our purposes, we can abstract the concept as follows— elliptic curve multiplication is a mathematical calculation that results in a pair of keys whose relationship is determinable only in one direction. In other words, if presented with the private key we can determine whether that private key corresponds to a given public key. The private key, however, cannot be derived from the public key. Simply put, the public key provides us with no clues as to the composition of the private key. It is this one-way relationship that makes modern PKI virtually impossible to crack—not even a brute force attack with the world's most powerful computers can feasibly unlock blockchain accounts.

§ 5:3   Signing a transaction

While possession of the corresponding private key is necessary to control a blockchain account, the keys themselves are not a part of the blockchain network. It is for this reason that blockchain protocols are incredibly secure. If private keys were stored on the network, then the database in which they were maintained would be susceptible to a breach—and as a result, the dissemination of private keys to malicious actors. Instead, private keys remain in the possession of the user, where they are locally stored on the user's computer or in a local database, known as a "wallet," on a physical device, such as a computer, smartphone or hardware wallet (a cold storage device, which is discussed in more detail below). In fact, public-private key generation can be accomplished without any connection to the blockchain network or Internet. As described above, public key cryptography is based on mathematical principles that can be implemented without input from the network.

If you have ever owned Bitcoin or another cryptocurrency, you may have stored your cryptocurrency in a "wallet." A cryptocurrency wallet is a software application that is intended to securely store your private keys. Using a wallet, most users may not have ever seen their private keys because the wallet takes care of the generation of the keys and stores them without, in many cases, displaying the private key. Instead, the wallet requires the user to enter a passphrase (which should be a lengthy phrase rather than a short password). It's this passphrase that then becomes critical because the passphrase is what will give the user access to the private keys stored in the wallet. See section 1:9 for a detailed discussion of "wallets."

At this point, you may be wondering how private keys are kept safe when a user attempts a transaction that requires it to prove to the network that it actually possesses the private key. Obviously, disclosure of the private key to the network as a means of proof would defeat the purpose. Fortunately, the user never needs to disclose the private key to the network. Instead, the user can use the private key to "sign" a transaction and broadcast the transaction to the network without the private key itself. The basic principle being to prove through the signature that you know a secret (the private key) without ever revealing it.

§ 5:4   Multi-sig systems for enhanced protection

Most blockchain protocols, including Bitcoin's scripting language, allow for accounts or unspent transaction outputs (UTXO) to be encumbered by a requirement that more than one private key be presented in order for that account or UTXO to be accessed or spent by the recipient. This requirement is referred to as a multi-sig or multi-signature arrangement. Multi-sig transactions are particularly well-suited for escrow type transactions. In fact, multi-sig transactions are often used in substitution for a third party intermediary who would otherwise hold funds or an asset in escrow for two or more other transacting parties. Instead, the funds or assets are encumbered by a requirement that two or more persons cryptographically sign in order for the funds or assets to be released. For example, if I owned a digital asset represented by a token on a blockchain and I wished to sell it to you for cryptocurrency, together we could construct a smart contract that was comprised of a multi-sig transaction. The contract would automatically transfer the asset token to you and transfer your cryptocurrency to me once we both cryptographically signed the transaction. With this multi-sig arrangement, neither you nor I can cheat the other out of its asset or funds by failing to perform.

§ 5:5 Storing private keys (cold versus online storage)

It is critically important that private keys be kept safe and stored securely. It is equally important that private keys be backed-up. A user who does not back-up her private keys risks losing them in the event of physical damage to, or failure of, the storage medium where the private keys reside. If you lose the private key, then the asset in the corresponding account is gone forever. There is no way to regenerate the private key based on the information made available by the public key information. So, unlike your passwords to your email account and other online services, losing a private key is far less forgiving—there simply is no "forgot private key" button.

§ 5:6 Managing access to private keys within an enterprise

While public key cryptography is an incredibly powerful form of encryption, its strength can create complications at the enterprise level. If it is difficult for any individual to manage her personal private keys, imagine the level of difficulty in managing thousands of private keys within an organization of tens of thousands of people. The puzzle becomes even more complicated when you consider that every employee's need to have access to certain things unlocked by private keys is different than the other employees. In addition, employees come and go every day in large organizations. That means a large company must have the ability to grant and revoke access to private keys in a manageable fashion.

It's useful to compare the dilemma posed by private keys versus access issues that companies routinely address today. Most companies have sensitive information and data that some employees must access, while others do not. With conventional information systems, this information is generally stored in one or more centralized databases and access is controlled by requiring the employee to input a username and corresponding password. When a new employee is hired, she is given a unique username and she selects a password. An individual with administrative privileges to those databases then adds the user to the database and grants some level of rights to view information in those databases. When an employee quits or is fired, the administrative user removes the user from the databases and access is effectively eliminated. In addition to managing users within a database, highly sensitive information may also require the employee to have a physical access card or chip which uses near field communication (NFC) or radio-frequency identification (RFID) that has been embedded with a unique identification number.

The difficulty with private key based access is that once the private key is disclosed, you can't undisclosed it. If disclosed, then the only way to protect against its misuse if an employee is fired or quits is to eliminate (in the sense of no longer using) the corresponding public address and creating a new public/private key pair. If a company has thousands or perhaps millions of public/private key pairs, then this constant regeneration of key pairs may become overly cumbersome. As a result, a better system is to grant access to the private key to employees without actually disclosing the private key to them. This is when you may be thinking— "say what?" It is, however, possible to give access to a private key without disclosing it.

In order to accomplish access without disclosure, the safest solutions will most likely involve hardware. Companies like Ledger, who manufacture a large number of physical Bitcoin and Ethereum wallets (called hardware wallets), will almost certainly lead the charge into secure hardware devices that can safeguard private keys within a secure environment. These secured keys could still be used by the person in possession of the hardware device so long as the device's unique identification was still shown as active by the enterprise's systems. The keys themselves would be protected in such a way that they could not be extracted from the device at all. If the employee is terminated and refuses to return the device, then under those circumstances the company could regenerate key pairs for the information or assets in question, or alternatively, deactivate the hardware rendering it unusable by the employee or other malicious actors that might come into possession of it.

Hardware can be expensive, however, if it must be provided to potentially thousands of employees. The value of keeping sensitive company information private is probably

113

far more valuable. Additionally, some data and access privileges are more sensitive than others; and accordingly, not all information will need to be protected with the same level of security. Likewise, not all employees will need access to information or blockchain data that requires public/private key pair information. Public key hardware is also becoming less expensive as electronic components, including integrated circuits, continue to fall in price. Ultimately, it's also likely that other solutions will be developed within the next few years to address these issues in cost effective ways. The important message for companies today is to start thinking about these issues in particular when you consider ways that you might adopt blockchain technology into your company. Sooner or later, anyone who adopts these technologies will be confronted with the challenges discussed above.

Chapter 6

Digital Identification on the Blockchain

§ 6:1   Summary of important points
§ 6:2   Digital blockchain based identification and
         reputation models
§ 6:3   Leveraging digital identification to reduce
         regulatory compliance costs
§ 6:4   Control over identification
§ 6:5   Interoperability
§ 6:6   Certifications and digital assets
§ 6:7   Challenges

§ 6:1   Summary of important points

- There are many blockchain developers focusing on the development of digital identities based on blockchain protocols, primarily because of the security afforded by public key infrastructure.
- Digital identities could be useful for regulatory and compliance purposes.
- Digital identities will also facilitate individuals being able to give access to specific information to specific individuals (e.g., allowing surgeon access to x-rays by providing a time restricted private key).

§ 6:2   Digital blockchain based identification and reputation models

Several blockchain developers are working on digital identification solutions that are based on blockchain technology. ConsenSys is working on a solution it calls uPort.[1] Decentralized applications, like uPort, allow the user to regain control of their digital identification. Each person will be assigned a unique identification number. In addition, information can be locked and unlocked by individuals based

---

[Section 6:2]

[1]https://consensys.net/ventures/core-components/.

on public/private key pairs. Another startup, ShoCard,[2] is also implementing its digital identification system on the blockchain, stating "[t]he ShoCard Identity Platform is built on a public blockchain data layer, so as a company we're not storing any data or keys that could be compromised. All identity data is encrypted and hashed then stored in the blockchain, where it can't be tampered with." Another player in this space is Onename[3] which is built on top of the Blockstack blockchain.

Some of the difficulties with identity verification today are the lack of a central database and the consistency in what documentation must be provided. These difficulties are compounded when identification is in the context of an international transaction. Blockchains have the potential, however, to function as an identification repository for everyone. There are added benefits to industries adopting common forms of blockchain based identification. For one, it might reduce the redundancy that exists today. Every time an individual begins a new relationship with a financial institution, that institution must verify the individual again. Sometimes individuals must be vetted several times by the same institution.

In addition to just pure identification, because of its secure environment of public key cryptography and tamper proof ledger, blockchain technology makes for a fantastic repository for reputation related matters. Imagine eBay-like scores but on a macro-level scale and with safeguards to prevent fraudulent or malicious attacks on individual's reputations. Traditional reputation systems have struggled to accomplish these goals. Their failure is likely the result of a handful of factors, including limited resources and inconsistent methodologies. The blockchain can overcome these hurdles by allowing for collective resources to be applied towards a solution. Public blockchains, like Bitcoin and Ethereum, have an astounding amount of computational power that can be utilized for digital identification purposes. There is also no reason to believe that the different approaches won't eventually coalesce around some basic standards—something that has yet to be done.

---

[2]https://shocard.com/.

[3]https://onename.com/.

§ 6:3 Leveraging digital identification to reduce regulatory compliance costs

This is a use case that has the potential to significantly reduce compliance costs at financial institutions while increasing capabilities at the same time. The key to maximizing success is for financial institutions to utilize a common blockchain if possible. With a shared distributed ledger that all banks can use, each bank could then rely on the clearance already given by another institution because each bank would know that everyone is operating off the same information found in the distributed ledger, and presumably, the same standards established by applicable regulation.

Because distributed ledgers can hold virtually any type of data, in addition to identification and reputation, information about a person's income and assets can also be included, which could be used to verify things such as accredited investor status for securities offerings. Not only can this save consumers money, but investment funds and others responsible for securities compliance can have greater confidence in the accredited investor status of potential investors.

§ 6:4 Control over identification

In addition to providing the above benefits, the blockchain allows individuals to ultimately regain control over their identification, and more importantly what people want and do not want to share with others. Public key cryptography ensures that information is safe and immune from even brute force attack. Yet, at the same time, a person can easily share information necessary to open a checking account with her bank by simply interfacing with an application on a smart phone. That sort of power and ability to control the details of our identity does not exist outside of the potential of blockchain technology.

A legitimate question at this point would be, "What specifically about blockchain technology makes it better suited to address identity issues?" The answer is intertwined with smart contracts and the immutable nature of the blockchain. Immutability provides confidence in the information far greater than what can be achieved with existing centralized databases, which can be subject to undetected manipulation. It's important to recognize that manipulation of information (even for malicious purposes) isn't necessarily problematic, so long as the manipulation is detectable. As such, the blockchain doesn't need to limit people's ability to alter records or change the state of information on the blockchain, it just needs to ensure that any alterations or changes in state are visible to others—and that's what the blockchain does perfectly. It is this visibility of changes in state that provide a much higher level of confidence in an identification system built on the blockchain.

Beyond confidence, smart contracts allow for digital identification systems to give control over access to information at an incredibly granular level. Rather than giving someone access to your "financial records," you could give them access to "receipts for business expenses incurred on January 1, 2016 between 1:30 p.m. and 2:30 p.m. eastern time." The access being granted can also be finely controlled in terms of who can see specific items of information. Smart contracts can be coded that allow for the issuance of a private key (which could have an expiration date and time) that matches a public key tied to a specific item of information. For example, if you were applying to college and an admissions office needed your high school transcripts, then you could provide the admissions office with a private key (good for six months), during which time that office could access your transcripts. Alternatively, smart contracts could allow you to issue private keys that are good until you decide to generate a new public/private key pair.

§ 6:5 Interoperability

Another inherent flaw in our existing systems of identification is the fragmented nature of how the information about us is stored. This is especially true in a geographic sense. If you are a resident of the United States, then there is a vast amount of information about you in numerous centralized databases throughout the United States—but what about France or China? Information about people is subject to geographic barriers, and more specifically, the failure of these systems to be interoperable with each other. While these issues may not be cause for concern for most individuals who spend the vast majority of their time interacting with others within their own country, they have dire consequences for those within the intelligence community and law enforcement. These agencies are engaged in a constant struggle against terrorist and crime organizations who operate across geographic and sovereign boundaries with far greater ease than their good guy counterparts. Blockchain technology has the potential to overcome these geographic and sovereign barriers and allow for an unprecedented sharing of information within the international intelligence community and those law enforcement agencies charged with fighting international crime syndicates.

§ 6:6 Certifications and digital assets

One area of digital identification that could be very useful in the future is with respect to individual certifications. For example, a person has to be certified by one of a handful of recognized scuba diving certification organizations in order to rent or purchase scuba tanks. Without having the minimum education necessary to obtain certification, scuba diving is a far more hazardous sport. The current method of tracking certification is by the issuance of a paper or plastic certification card (or "c card"). Not only is a certification card easily fabricated, but many vacationers have created lasting memories (myself included) after forgetting their certification card when traveling to an ideal diving location half way around the globe. Both of these issues are easily addressed by the blockchain. Once you have established a digital identification that is unique to you, the certifying organization can cryptographically sign a digital certificate that is digitally appended to your digital identification. Now the certification can't be forged and you never need to worry about forgetting your c card again! Unlike their physical counterparts, digital certifications and other rights and assets that can be represented digitally, and can't be lost or stolen. Anyone who has lost or had stolen a wallet or purse knows the amount of work it takes to cancel and/or replace all of the cards and other pieces of information—which is usually far worse than the monetary value of what was actually lost or stolen.

§ 6:7 Challenges

While there is great promise in the application of the blockchain to digital identification matters, it is not without challenges. For instance, many people still do not have access to the Internet in undeveloped nations. Even some people in developed countries have limited to no access to the tools necessary to use digital identifications. In addition, the information on the blockchain still has to be put there by humans, which means that the information is subject to errors or inaccuracies. Some people will simply refuse to partake of a technology that involves any personal information being disclosed on a public network—whether encrypted or not.

It is still very early in the development of solutions around digital identifications. While there is tremendous potential for blockchain in this area, we are still in the earliest stages of the evolution of real world products. So, while interest rate swap contracts are already fully functional on the blockchain as smart contracts, there does not exist any widely recognized digital identification protocol and it is unlikely that one will exist in the near future. There are also still a number of countries that lack a reliable system of paper identification. Without such a basic system in place, it is virtually impossible to bring individuals into a blockchain based system and have any high level of confidence in the accuracy of the identification. Even in developed counties, this initial transition from paper to digital will take time to solve and to create a uniform system. Maybe the biggest issue that will have to be overcome is the divergent interests of governments, individuals, and business interests. Individuals generally want to limit the information about them that is available to others; while governments want all the information; and business interests want to re-sell all that information to others for marketing.

Chapter 7

Related Technologies that Complement Blockchain Technology

§ 7:1   Summary of important points

- There are several technologies that are complementary to blockchain protocols, such as distributed file storage systems like interplanetary file system (IPFS).
- TOR technology, coupled with cryptographic technology, can allow relatively anonymous use of the Internet, including commerce when Bitcoin or other digital currencies are used.
- Most of the major cloud providers, such as IBM, Microsoft and AWS, are developing blockchain tools that can be used in the cloud.

§ 7:2   Interplanetary file system (IPFS) and file storage

IPFS is a decentralized file storage system and operates in ways similar to a blockchain protocol. Rather than maintaining a digital ledger, however, data and files are stored in a totally decentralized manner across all of the nodes participating in the IPFS network. Others, such as StorJ,[1] have also entered the decentralized storage marketplace. IPFS and other decentralized storage providers may play an

---

[Section 7:2]

[1]https://storj.io.

important role in the development of smart contracts. Many have proposed that executed documents could be stored on IPFS or similar decentralized storage applications and the cryptographic hash of the stored document then written to a blockchain (e.g., the Bitcoin ledger). If anyone wants to find the authoritative copy of the executed document, they can check the Bitcoin address where the hash was stored, gather the hash information and then pull up the document using the IPFS hash. This prevents any person from tampering with or altering a document after it has been signed, hashed and stored on IPFS.

For those worried about security, encryption can be used to encrypt sensitive information before it is stored on IPFS or other centralized protocols. In addition, developers are implementing a technique known as "sharding," which breaks up individual files into numerous subparts and saves those subparts in random places across the storage network that makes up the decentralized storage protocol. Using this technique, even if someone is able to access data residing on a particular storage device, they would only have access to a presumably useless shard without the benefit of the remainder of the shards that made up the file. This is an especially powerful technique when coupled with encryption techniques. Data stored in this manner is likely more secure than most data stored on even the most "secure" centralized databases.

§ 7:3   The Onion Relay (TOR)

The Onion Relay (TOR) began as a government program and still receives funding from government agencies.[1] TOR allows users to surf the Internet anonymously.[2] While the relationship between TOR and Bitcoin has been primarily for illicit activities, such as the sale of narcotics on the darknet, TOR makes it possible for people to conduct business with blockchain assets in a very anonymous way, which can also be used for non-illicit purposes, including supporting political dissidents or U.S. Intelligence officers getting sensitive information from hostile territories back to the U.S.

[Section 7:3]

[1]http://www.bloomberg.com/news/articles/2014-01-23/tor-anonymity-software-vs-dot-the-national-security-agency.

[2]http://www.bloomberg.com/news/articles/2014-01-23/tor-anonymity-software-vs-dot-the-national-security-agency.

There have been reports, however, of U.S. agencies using sophisticated techniques to observe, at a minimum, patterns in the traffic of data packets through the TOR protocol network.

§ 7:4 New microservices with built-in micropayment rails

One of the difficulties with microservices[1] on the Internet is the disproportionate amount of transaction costs incurred in connection with these services. Bitcoin and other cryptocurrencies now make it possible to provide and charge for these services on as-used basis with immediate payment and only nominal transaction costs in the form of transaction fees paid to miners. Bitcoin 21 is one of the most developed payment channels allowing for the development of microservices. In addition to providing a built-in Bitcoin payment library for software developers, Bitcoin 21 allows for parties to open up "off-chain" payment channels (similar in concept to the Lighting Network) and continually transaction business for some period of time before closing the channel and finally submitting the aggregate payment amount due to the blockchain as one transaction.

Microservices are becoming a more prominent fixture of the Internet, and with the payment barriers being eroded by blockchain technology, it will only grow. These services can also be chained together, whether provided by one provider or several providers, and smart contracts (even with Bitcoin's scripting language) can accommodate directing the appropriate payment amounts to the respective microservice provider. This should all lead to more innovation in microservices by creating better incentives. While there is no shortage of software engineers willing to develop microservices as open source projects, enabling them to obtain compensation by charging micropayments will no doubt lead to the creation of even more innovative and useful microservices.

§ 7:5 The cloud: Blockchain-as-a-service

Many businesses and firms are hesitant to make a significant investment in blockchain technology, especially given

---

[Section 7:4]

[1]The term "microservice" generally refers to discrete services that do a specific task for a relatively small amount of consideration. For example, a service where you submit a street address to a service which returns a geolocation data set (i.e., longitude and latitude) is a classic microservice.

that the technology is still in its early stages and it is unclear which protocols will ultimate become market standard. Fortunately for those businesses and firms, several well-known enterprise grade services are providing blockchain-as-a-service in the cloud. These enterprise cloud providers include Microsoft, IBM, and AWS. Considering that these three providers make up the backbone of enterprise-level cloud computing, virtually anyone should be able to find a BaaS solution if they want to begin prototyping potential blockchain systems and use cases. Again, this sort of cloud based prototyping requires very little upfront expenditures and requires no investment in specific hardware since you are relying on the BaaS services to provide the infrastructure regardless of the architecture you are trying to implement. It's also worth noting that each of these providers is also actively developing IoT cloud platforms and aggressively competing for business in this area. Given the future relationship between blockchain technology and IoT, these cloud base solutions will likely provide one stop shopping in the future enabling businesses to take advantage of blockchain controlled IoT solutions within making heavy investments in equipment.

§ 7:6   The cloud: Blockchain-as-a-service—Microsoft Azure

Microsoft was an early adopter of blockchain services on its Azure cloud platform. Microsoft offers a handful of blockchain options.[1] BlockApps, developed by Consensys, is available for use as a service on Azure. BlockApps runs the Ethereum protocol, which allows users to draft smart contracts in solidity or serpent and then compile them into bytecode which can be processed by the Ethereum Virtual Machine (EVM). In addition to BlockApps, Eris Industries' blockchain template is also available on Azure. Further evidencing Microsoft's commitment to blockchain and BaaS, in 2016, Microsoft added solidity to its popular development environment, Visual Studio. In addition, Microsoft has developed DevTest Labs for Blockchain as a Service.[2] This service allows businesses and firms to quickly create for deployment blockchain applications that can be used for

---

[Section 7:6]

[1]https://azure.microsoft.com/en-us/solutions/blockchain/.

[2]https://azure.microsoft.com/en-us/services/devtest-lab/.

testing. Microsoft's service supports both open and permissioned blockchains.

§ 7:7 The cloud: Blockchain-as-a-service—IBM Bluemix

As described in Chapter 3, IBM Bluemix offers an implementation of Hyperledger's fabric blockchain protocol. As of the writing of this book, the fabric implementation was solely for prototyping and testing. The benefit of Bluemix's implementation is that it is very modular and granular. For those with more sophisticated blockchain development teams who are looking to develop very tailored, industry specific blockchains, IBM's Bluemix implementation looks very promising. Without ample resources, however, Bluemix may overwhelm businesses and firms who are just now dipping their toe into the blockchain water. That said, it is a far better environment to begin than attempting to set-up internal blockchain architecture without a sufficiently trained IT team.

§ 7:8 The cloud: Blockchain-as-a-service—Amazon Web Services (AWS)

Amazon's AWS also provides cloud based blockchain services. Currently, Eris Industries, Ltd.'s blockchain application is also available on AWS. In addition, AWS has entered into a collaboration with Digital Currency Group[1] to provide a platform for both potential consumers and providers of blockchain solutions. DCG has several blockchain subsidiaries and portfolio companies that utilize AWS's blockchain platform in order to foster innovation.

[Section 7:8]

[1]http://dcg.co/.

Chapter 8

General Policy Considerations for Future Regulations

§ 8:1   Summary of important points

- Regulation, or lack thereof, is a double edge sword. Too little regulation and users may lack confidence in the space, while too much regulation can stifle innovation and development.
- Blockchain development is still in its infancy, but is developing at a fast pace. Legislators and regulators will be challenged to keep up.
- One of the most challenging tasks confronting policy makers is developing regulations that can distinguish between legitimate use cases (which should be allowed to flourish without overbearing regulations) and the use of blockchain technology for illicit purposes such as the sale of illegal drugs on darknets.

§ 8:2   Implementing and enabling legislation

The most important focus for the future of blockchain technology is identifying current laws, regulations and policies that constitute road blocks to implementation. This is analogous to the advent of digital signatures when there was uncertainty about the validity of a digital signature and whether courts would give them the same effect as traditional signatures. ESIGN and UETA are great examples of enabling legislation that addressed these issues and paved the way for the widespread use of digital signatures. While ESIGN and UETA were passed well before blockchain technology had been developed, both pieces of legislation are useful for blockchain technology and actually provide a perfect foundation upon which future legislation can be built.

The first step in this process is to identify those areas of the law where there are deficiencies in terms of the law giv-

ing effect to blockchain technology. While the universe of
these areas is constantly evolving and new issues will pop
up every day, there are already a few identifiable problems.
One area talked about before is in the context of testamentary instruments, which are not covered by ESIGN and
UETA. Unfortunately, the result of this is to prevent
blockchain technology from being used to its full potential in
this area because wills and testamentary trusts must still be
executed on paper with old fashion ink signatures. Another
area that needs improvement is how a security interest or
pledge can be granted in assets evidenced on the blockchain.
Pledging an address that evidenced Bitcoin was not contemplated when Article 9 of the UCC was drafted or during any
of its updates to date. The problem is that Bitcoin is likely
considered a general intangible, which means that the proper
method of perfecting a security interest in it is to file a
UCC-1 Financing Statement.[1] Bitcoin, however, is more analogous to cash than to a traditional general intangible. As
such, filing a Financing Statement does little to prevent a
debtor from transferring the Bitcoin to someone else, and after a handful of transfers, it may become impossible to track
down where the Bitcoin went.

§ 8:3   Balancing regulation

There is no doubt that certain aspects of blockchain
technology are appropriate for regulation. When Bitcoin is
used in the same manner as a traditional fiat currency it
makes little sense to treat it differently than fiat currency.
For example, if a person is in the business of exchanging
Bitcoin for U.S. dollars and vice versa, this is economically
the same thing as if the person were exchanging U.S. dollars
for other currencies or facilitating international transfers if
the cash is taken and Bitcoin sent to an individual overseas.
If left totally unregulated, these activities will become a
breeding ground for money laundering and other illicit
activities. What is critical is that regulation is drafted with
enough precision that it can distinction between these types
of activities and those where the existence and use of a
cryptocurrency is tangential to a greater purpose. For
example, if a company is using OP_RETURN functions with
Bitcoin to establish the date a record of something was

[Section 8:2]

[1]http://apps.americanbar.org/buslaw/blt/2005-01-02/soukup.shtml.

established, this is a wildly different activity. Loosely worded regulations, however, can often pick up both types of activities, which in turn, creates a barrier to entry for the second use that serves no policy objective.

One reason for concern is the recent inability of our elected officials to make such nuanced distinctions. This seemingly results from a failure by many in government to truly understand these technologies—especially in the area of cryptography. The recent (and still ongoing) debate about the use of cryptography by social media providers like Facebook shows a complete lack of understanding on how this technology works. Never mentioned in the debate is that, setting aside whether a backdoor given to the government by Facebook is a good idea, the government's access to Facebook, Google, or Apple messaging will do little in the fight against terrorism. Why? Because there exists numerous open source based PKI encryption technologies—all of which are easily used by malicious actors. We can't afford uneducated decision making to cloud regulation with respect to this technology. The burden will fall quite heavily on those developing these technologies to educate policy makers.

This also means that stakeholders in the technology can't afford to take hard-line ideological based positions, such as there can be no regulation whatsoever. Alternatively, the position that all blockchain technology should be regulated is as equally untenable. Both positions fail to distinguish between the significant differences that exist between various use cases and the protocols themselves. Again, one size fits all regulations will not work. They will ultimately quash innovation in this area by created unnecessary transaction costs and barriers to entry. People do, however, need faith that those uses which involve currency or what amount to securities are governed by similar policies that govern fiat currency and traditional securities. As *The DAO* implosion shows us, risks exist in decentralized autonomous organizations just like any other investment fund. There is no reason that one should be highly regulated and another lack any oversight whatsoever.

Regulation that is overburdening risks alienating an entire class of individuals working in the blockchain area. In addition to stifling innovation, over regulation will lead many individuals to simply ignore regulation. For better or worse, to some extent, compliance is a matter of voluntary decisions. While regulation traditionally has the backing of a coercive state to enforce compliance, the combination of the decentral-

129

ized nature of the blockchain with public key cryptography allows individuals to operate in the shadows and operate decentralized systems that can't be unplugged like a centralized server. There is also no shortage of jurisdictions that will not extradite individuals for violations of regulations of this nature—even those that otherwise maintain friendly relations with the United States. As such, it's important that policy makers get buy-off from the vast majority of individuals contributing to the development of these systems. It is far better to limit those unwilling to comply to a handful of outliers rather than for their approach to become the norm.

On the other end of the spectrum, an absolute wild west approach risks leading to continued Mt. Gox like failures, which ultimately taint the legitimacy of the technology and operate to make blockchain solutions less attractive to the business community. Legitimate concerns are raised when DAOs are permitted to solicit financial investments from individuals within the United States and other countries without any oversight, registration or property disclosure. For many individuals, myself included, the failure of *The DAO* was of no financial significance (as I only purchase enough to play around with the technology in order to better understand it.) I suspect many others fell into this category (perhaps with the exception of those most adamantly supporting the Ethereum hard fork in order to obtain the return of most of *The DAO* funds). In any case, a delicate balance must be achieved and the two extremes avoided.

Fortunately, institutions and stakeholders include enough individuals capable of navigating the public policy realm. In addition, organizations like the Chamber of Digital Commerce[1] are also helping organize the industry's efforts and becoming active participants in the policy making process. As these efforts grow, we can expect to see better, more thought out legislation and regulation. While there will always be those individuals who believe that blockchain technology is outside the reach of policy makers because of its distributed nature, they will be overshadowed by the massive majority of stake holders who want sensible and balanced legislation to help bring more customers and consumers into the blockchain marketplace. We are confident that, eventually, a proper balance can be found.

[Section 8:3]

[1]http://www.digitalchamber.org/.

Finally, as time goes on, more and more traditional systems will be replaced by blockchain-based solutions. In some cases, a blockchain solution will represent simply a different or supplemental tool used to accomplish traditional goals. In other cases, blockchain solutions will represent radically different ways of doing business. Policy makers will need to be able to discern between the two. The first category lends itself to simply applying existing regulations with only those modifications as are necessary to implement the technology. For the more divergent cases, policy makers will have to rethink their existing regulations in order to confirm they remain appropriate for blockchain solutions.

Chapter 9

Conclusion and Thoughts about the Future

§ 9:1   Summary of important points
§ 9:2   Don't panic, but start planning
§ 9:3   Where does all this leave businesses and
         professions

§ 9:1   Summary of important points

- There is no need to panic about implementing block-chain technology, but now is the time to begin under-standing what blockchain technology does well and what it doesn't do well.
- For some industries, such as financial services and the supply chain industry, blockchain based solutions will likely appear sooner than many other industries.
- For blockchain technology to be fully utilized, it is nec-essary to educate people on the nature of the technology.
- Developers and companies working on blockchain solu-tions need to actively engage policy makers in order to ensure proper regulation and useful legislation.

§ 9:2   Don't panic, but start planning

When discussing blockchain technology with clients and others, one of the most commonly asked questions is "when will the actual use of this technology become widespread?" It's a good question because it gets to the real concern the person asking has—when do I need to worry about this stuff. In some respects, the technology is already in widespread use. There is no denying that Bitcoin is a real force in payments. With a market cap of several billion dollars and numerous well-funded exchanges, the question of whether Bitcoin will be successful has already been answered. Even if Bitcoin is ultimately replaced, it will have been a success. To conclude otherwise, is to suggest that Ford's Model T was a failure because they are no longer in production.

Of course, most businesses and industries can continue to be successful without incorporating Bitcoin into their business model. Besides, much of this book is devoted to use cases that go beyond a payment service or digital currency. So when people ask the above question, they are really concerned about those blockchain 2.0 implementations. Their concern is that competitors will implement these technologies more rapidly and leave them at a competitive disadvantage. On the other hand, no one wants to spend resources on something that turns out to be nothing more than empty promises. In light of the companies now devoting significant resources to these technologies, such as IBM, Microsoft, and Intel, it's hard to believe there "isn't something to this."

The biggest question then is not if, but when, blockchain resources will move from the development and testing phase to production ready, enterprise level solutions. Unfortunately, any predictions on that front on our part would be pure speculation. What we can provide are some predictions about which we have a higher level of confidence, all of which we think are useful to consider. First, blockchain solutions will consist of more than one blockchain. This is not a race where one competitor or technology will prevail. Different industries need different tools, and it is all but certain that there will never be a one size fits all blockchain protocol. As such, certain solutions will need public and open blockchain solutions based on protocols like Bitcoin and/or Ethereum. Other solutions will require permissioned ledgers like Hyperledger. In some industries, the solution will require a payment component and a corresponding digital currency like Bitcoin. Other industries, however, will use blockchain solutions as a secure way to maintain records in an immutable fashion. Many of these solutions don't require any digital currency, so they don't require a Bitcoin like protocol.

Second, investment in research and development of blockchain technologies will continue to grow in the coming years. This is likely to speed up the pace of implementation. To date, most of this investment has come from private investment, which should continue to grow. Hopefully, government investment in blockchain technology will also increase over the coming years, which together with increasing private investment, will lead to even more innovation and use cases not even considered today.

§ 9:3 Where does all this leave businesses and professions

The most important steps businesses can take today is to

stay informed on the status and development of this technology. This includes the process of making sure IT personnel are not only aware of the technology, but begin to become conversant in the technology and truly understand it. This includes understanding what blockchain technology can realistically do and what is not feasible. As with any new technology, it can often be difficult to differentiate between legitimate capabilities versus pie in the sky claims. Again, education is the key to staying informed about realistic capabilities.

Another important step for those who can benefit from blockchain solutions is to lobby elected and government officials for balanced and appropriate legislation and regulations as discussed in the previous chapter. The first step for governments is to identify what legislation is necessary in order to permit businesses and individuals to take full advantage of the technology. The other task for government is to balance regulations that will add confidence to the technology versus those that will create barriers to entry and ultimately reduce innovation. A proper balance is not only achievable, but vitally necessary for the future of this technology.

For academics, developers and practitioners, the burden is on us to continue to educate the public, including business leaders, on the promise of blockchain technology. This requires an honest assessment of those things that blockchain technology does well and candid disclosure when existing, conventional solutions are more appropriate. We must also recognize that blockchain technology is an interdisciplinary study—implicating finance, microeconomics, game theory, and legal theory to name a few. These are in addition to the more obvious fields of mathematics, cryptography, electrical engineering, and computer science. Ultimately, the most compelling case for the future of blockchain technology is that many of the brightest and most entrepreneurial individuals in each of these fields have converged on one technology—blockchain.

APPENDICES

GLOSSARY

Blockchain Terminology

Address: a string of alphanumeric characters used to receive and send transactions on a blockchain.

Altchain: a blockchain that is alternative to the Bitcoin blockchain.

Bitcoin: a type of digital currency in which encryption techniques are used to regulate the generation of units of currency and verify the transfer of funds, operating independently of a central bank.

Block: a collection of transactions that have occurred on a particular blockchain during a period of time.

Blockchain: a data structure that makes it possible to create a digital ledger of transactions and share it among a distributed network of computers.

BTC: short for the Bitcoin currency.

Bitcoin network: a decentralized system where nodes form peer-to-peer relationships with other nodes, which in turn have other relationships with other nodes and so on.

Cryptocurrency: a form of digital currency based on mathematics in which encryption techniques are used to regulate the generation of units of currency and verify the transfer of funds.

Cryptography: the use of mathematics to secure/protect information.

Decentralized: without a central authority or controlling party.

Decentralized Autonomous Organization: an organization that exists only as shareholders without any central management.

Distributed Ledger: distributed ledgers are a type of database that are spread across multiple sites, countries or institutions.

Encryption: the use of cryptography to encode a message or transaction such that only the intended recipient(s) can decode it.

Ethereum: a smart contract network and altchain that is known for facilitating decentralized applications with a token called ether.

Ether: a token used on the Ethereum network, but not considered a virtual currency.

Genesis Block: the very first block in a blockchain.

Miner: a computer or group of computers that add new transactions to blocks and verify blocks created by other miners.

Mining: the process by which transactions are verified and added to a blockchain, which process includes solving cryptographic problems using computing hardware.

Multi Signature: a mechanism that requires multiple parties to require more than one key to authorize a transaction.

Node: a participant in a blockchain, which shares a copy of the blockchain and relays new transactions to other nodes.

Permissioned Ledger: a permissioned ledger is a ledger where actors must have permission to access the ledger.

Peer to Peer: a type of network where participants communicate directly with each other rather than through a centralized server.

Private Key: a private key is a string of data that shows you have access to virtual currency in a specific wallet; can be thought of as a password.

Proof-of-Stake: an alternative to the proof-of-work system, in which your existing stake in a cryptocurrency (the amount of that currency that you hold) is used to calculate the amount of that currency that you can mine.

Protocol: the official rules that dictate how participants on a network must communicate.

Proof-of-Work: a system that ties mining capability to computational power.

Public Key: a string of letters and numbers that is derived from a private key, which is given to others in order for them to send you virtual currency.

Signature: a mechanism used at a certain point in a blockchain transaction that proves that the owner of the private key has approved the transaction.

Smart Contracts: contracts whose terms are pronounced in a computer language instead of legal language and whose terms can be automatically executed by a computing system, such as a suitable distributed ledger system (blockchain).

APPENDIX A

Uniform Electronic Transactions Act (1999)

Drafted by the

NATIONAL CONFERENCE OF COMMISSIONERS ON
UNIFORM STATE LAWS

and by it

APPROVED AND RECOMMENDED FOR ENACTMENT
IN ALL THE STATES

at its

ANNUAL CONFERENCE

MEETING IN ITS ONE-HUNDRED-AND-EIGHTH YEAR
IN DENVER, COLORADO

JULY 23—30, 1999

WITH PREFATORY NOTE AND COMMENTS

Copyright© 1999 By

NATIONAL CONFERENCE OF COMMISSIONERS ON
UNIFORM STATE LAWS

Approved by the American Bar Association Dallas, Texas,
February 14, 2000

The Committee that acted for the National Conference of

Commissioners on Uniform State Laws in preparing the Uniform Electronic Transactions Act (1999) was as follows:

PATRICIA BRUMFIELD FRY, University of North Dakota, School of Law, P.O. Box 9003, Grand Forks, ND 58201, *Chair*

STEPHEN Y. CHOW, 30th Floor, One Beacon St., Boston, MA 02108

KENNETH W. ELLIOTT, City Place Building, 22nd Floor, 204 N. Robinson Avenue, Oklahoma City, OK 73102

HENRY DEEB GABRIEL, JR., Loyola University, School of Law, 526 Pine Street, New Orleans, LA 70118

BION M. GREGORY, Office of Legislative Counsel, State Capitol, Suite 3021, Sacramento, CA 95814-4996

JOSEPH P. MAZUREK, Office of the Attorney General, P.O. Box 201401, 215 N. Sanders, Helena, MT 59620

PAMELA MEADE SARGENT, P.O. Box 846, Abingdon, VA 24212

D. BENJAMIN BEARD, University of Idaho, College of Law, 6th and Rayburn, Moscow, ID 83844-2321, *Reporter*

EX OFFICIO

GENE N. LEBRUN, P.O. Box 8250, 9th Floor, 909 St. Joseph Street, Rapid City, SD 57709, *President*

HENRY M. KITTLESON, P.O. Box 32092, 92 Lake Wire Drive, Lakeland, FL 33802, *Division Chair*

AMERICAN BAR ASSOCIATION ADVISORS

C. ROBERT BEATTIE, Plaza VII, 45 S. 7th Street, Suite 3400, Minneapolis, MN 55402-1609, *Business Law Section*

AMELIA H. BOSS, Temple University, School of Law, 1719 N. Broad Street, Philadelphia, PA 19122, *Advisor*

THOMAS J. SMEDINGHOFF, 130 E. Randolph Drive, Suite 3500, Chicago, IL 60601, *Science and Technology Section*

EXECUTIVE DIRECTOR

FRED H. MILLER, University of Oklahoma, College of Law, 300 Timberdell Road, Norman, OK 73019, *Executive Director*

WILLIAM J. PIERCE, 1505 Roxbury Road, Ann Arbor, MI 48104, *Executive Director Emeritus*

Copies of this Act may be obtained from:

NATIONAL CONFERENCE OF COMMISSIONERS ON UNIFORM STATE LAWS

211 E. Ontario Street, Suite 1300 Chicago, Illinois 60611

312/915-0195

TABLE OF CONTENTS

143

PREFATORY NOTE

With the advent of electronic means of communication and information transfer, business models and methods for doing business have evolved to take advantage of the speed, efficiencies, and cost benefits of electronic technologies. These developments have occurred in the face of existing legal barriers to the legal efficacy of records and documents which exist solely in electronic media. Whether the legal requirement that information or an agreement or contract must be contained or set forth in a pen and paper writing derives from a statute of frauds affecting the enforceability of an agreement, or from a record retention statute that calls for keeping the paper record of a transaction, such legal requirements raise real barriers to the effective use of electronic media.

One striking example of electronic barriers involves so called check retention statutes in every State. A study conducted by the Federal Reserve Bank of Boston identified more than 2500 different state laws which require the retention of canceled checks by the issuers of those checks. These requirements not only impose burdens on the issuers, but also effectively restrain the ability of banks handling the checks to automate the process. Although check truncation is validated under the Uniform Commercial Code, if the bank's customer must store the canceled paper check, the bank will not be able to deal with the item through electronic transmission of the information. By establishing the equivalence of an electronic record of the information, the Uniform Electronic Transactions Act (UETA) removes these barriers without affecting the underlying legal rules and requirements.

It is important to understand that the purpose of the UETA is to remove barriers to electronic commerce by validating and effectuating electronic records and signatures. It is NOT a general contracting statute—the substantive rules of contracts remain unaffected by UETA. Nor is it a digital signature statute. To the extent that a State has a Digital Signature Law, the UETA is designed to support and compliment that statute.

A. **Scope of the Act and Procedural Approach.** The scope of this Act provides coverage which sets forth a clear framework for covered transactions, and also avoids unwarranted surprises for unsophisticated parties dealing in this relatively new media. The clarity and certainty of the scope of the Act have been obtained while still providing a solid legal framework that allows for the continued development of innovative technology to facilitate electronic transactions.

With regard to the general scope of the Act, the Act's coverage is inherently limited by the definition of "transaction." The Act does not apply to *all* writings and signatures, but only to electronic records and signatures relating to a transaction, defined as those interactions between people relating to business, commercial and governmental affairs. In general, there are few writing or signature requirements imposed by law on many of the "standard" transactions that had been considered for exclusion. A good example relates to trusts, where the general rule on creation of a trust imposes no formal writing requirement. Further, the writing requirements in other contexts derived from governmental filing issues. For example, real estate transactions were considered potentially troublesome because of the need to file a deed or other instrument for protection against third parties.

Since the efficacy of a real estate purchase contract, or even a deed, between the parties is not affected by any sort of filing, the question was raised why these transactions should not be validated by this Act if done via an electronic medium. No sound reason was found. Filing requirements fall within Sections 17-19 on governmental records. An exclusion of all real estate transactions would be particularly unwarranted in the event that a State chose to convert to an electronic recording system, as many have for Article 9 financing statement filings under the Uniform Commercial Code.

The exclusion of specific Articles of the Uniform Commercial Code reflects the recognition that, particularly in the case of Articles 5, 8 and revised Article 9, electronic transac-

145

tions were addressed in the specific contexts of those revision processes. In the context of Articles 2 and 2A the UETA provides the vehicle for assuring that such transactions may be accomplished and effected via an electronic medium. At such time as Articles 2 and 2A are revised the extent of coverage in those Articles/Acts may make application of this Act as a gap-filling law desirable. Similar considerations apply to the recently promulgated Uniform Computer Information Transactions Act ("UCITA").

The need for certainty as to the scope and applicability of this Act is critical, and makes any sort of a broad, general exception based on notions of inconsistency with existing writing and signature requirements unwise at best. The uncertainty inherent in leaving the applicability of the Act to judicial construction of this Act with other laws is unacceptable if electronic transactions are to be facilitated.

Finally, recognition that the paradigm for the Act involves two willing parties conducting a transaction electronically, makes it necessary to expressly provide that some form of acquiescence or intent on the part of a person to conduct transactions electronically is necessary before the Act can be invoked.

Accordingly, Section 5 specifically provides that the Act only applies between parties that have agreed to conduct transactions electronically. In this context, the construction of the term agreement must be broad in order to assure that the Act applies whenever the circumstances show the parties intention to transact electronically, regardless of whether the intent rises to the level of a formal agreement.

B. **Procedural Approach.** Another fundamental premise of the Act is that it be minimalist and procedural. The general efficacy of existing law in an electronic context, so long as biases and barriers to the medium are removed, validates this approach. The Act defers to existing substantive law. Specific areas of deference to other law in this Act include: (1) the meaning and effect of "sign" under existing law, (2) the method and manner of displaying, transmitting and formatting information in Section 8, (3) rules of attribution in Section 9, and (4) the law of mistake in Section 10.

The Act's treatment of records and signatures demonstrates best the minimalist approach that has been adopted. Whether a record is attributed to a person is left to law outside this Act. Whether an electronic signature has any effect is left to the surrounding circumstances and other law. These provisions are salutary directives to assure that records and signatures will be treated in the same manner, under currently existing law, as written records and manual signatures.

The deference of the Act to other substantive law does not negate the necessity of setting forth rules and standards for using electronic media. The Act expressly validates electronic records, signatures and contracts. It provides for the use of electronic records and information for retention purposes, providing certainty in an area with great potential in cost savings and efficiency. The Act makes clear that the actions of machines ("electronic agents") programmed and used by people will bind the user of the machine, regardless of whether human review of a particular transaction has occurred. It specifies the standards for sending and receipt of electronic records, and it allows for innovation in financial services through the implementation of transferable records. In these ways the Act permits electronic transactions to be accomplished with certainty under existing substantive rules of law.

SECTION 1. SHORT TITLE. This [Act] may be cited as the Uniform Electronic Transactions Act.

SECTION 2. DEFINITIONS. In this [Act]:

(1) "Agreement" means the bargain of the parties in fact, as found in their language or inferred from other circumstances and from rules, regulations, and procedures given the effect of agreements under laws otherwise applicable to a particular transaction.

(2) "Automated transaction" means a transaction conducted or performed, in whole or in part, by electronic means or electronic records, in which the acts or records of one or both parties are not reviewed by an individual in the ordinary course in forming a contract, performing under an existing contract, or fulfilling an obligation required by the transaction.

(3) "Computer program" means a set of statements or instructions to be used directly or indirectly in an information processing system in order to bring about a certain result.

(4) "Contract" means the total legal obligation resulting from the parties' agreement as affected by this [Act] and other applicable law.

(5) "Electronic" means relating to technology having electrical, digital, magnetic, wireless, optical, electromagnetic, or similar capabilities.

147

(6) "Electronic agent" means a computer program or an electronic or other automated means used independently to initiate an action or respond to electronic records or performances in whole or in part, without review or action by an individual.

(7) "Electronic record" means a record created, generated, sent, communicated, received, or stored by electronic means.

(8) "Electronic signature" means an electronic sound, symbol, or process attached to or logically associated with a record and executed or adopted by a person with the intent to sign the record.

(9) "Governmental agency" means an executive, legislative, or judicial agency, department, board, commission, authority, institution, or instrumentality of the federal government or of a State or of a county, municipality, or other political subdivision of a State.

(10) "Information" means data, text, images, sounds, codes, computer programs, software, databases, or the like.

(11) "Information processing system" means an electronic system for creating, generating, sending, receiving, storing, displaying, or processing information.

(12) "Person" means an individual, corporation, business trust, estate, trust, partnership, limited liability company, association, joint venture, governmental agency, public corporation, or any other legal or commercial entity.

(13) "Record" means information that is inscribed on a tangible medium or that is stored in an electronic or other medium and is retrievable in perceivable form.

(14) "Security procedure" means a procedure employed for the purpose of verifying that an electronic signature, record, or performance is that of a specific person or for detecting changes or errors in the information in an electronic record. The term includes a procedure that requires the use of algorithms or other codes, identifying words or numbers, encryption, or callback or other acknowledgment procedures.

(15) "State" means a State of the United States, the District of Columbia, Puerto Rico, the United States Virgin Islands, or any territory or insular possession subject to the jurisdiction of the United States. The term includes an Indian tribe or band, or Alaskan native village, which is recognized by federal law or formally acknowledged by a State.

(16) "Transaction" means an action or set of actions occurring between two or more persons relating to the conduct of business, commercial, or governmental affairs.

Sources: UNICTRAL Model Law on Electronic Commerce; Uniform Commercial Code; Uniform Computer Information Transactions Act; Restatement 2d Contracts.

Comment

1. **"Agreement."**

Whether the parties have reached an agreement is determined by their express language and all surrounding circumstances. The Restatement 2d Contracts § 3 provides that, "An agreement is a manifestation of mutual assent on the part of two or more persons." See also Restatement 2d Contracts, Section 2, Comment b. The Uniform Commercial Code specifically includes in the circumstances from which an agreement may be inferred "course of performance, course of dealing and usage of trade . . ." as defined in the UCC. Although the definition of agreement in this Act does not make specific reference to usage of trade and other party conduct, this definition is not intended to affect the construction of the parties' agreement under the substantive law applicable to a particular transaction. Where that law takes account of usage and conduct in informing the terms of the parties' agreement, the usage or conduct would be relevant as "other circumstances" included in the definition under this Act.

Where the law applicable to a given transaction provides that system rules and the like constitute part of the agreement of the parties, such rules will have the same effect in determining the parties agreement under this Act. For example, UCC Article 4 (Section 4-103(b)) provides that Federal Reserve regulations and operating circulars and clearinghouse rules have the effect of agreements. Such agreements by law properly would be included in the definition of agreement in this Act.

The parties' agreement is relevant in determining whether the provisions of this Act have been varied by agreement. In addition, the parties' agreement may establish the parameters of the parties' use of electronic records and signatures, security procedures and similar aspects of the transaction. See Model Trading Partner Agreement, 45 Business Lawyer Supp. Issue (June 1990). See Section 5(b) and Comments thereto.

2. **"Automated Transaction."**

An automated transaction is a transaction performed or conducted by electronic means in which machines are used without human intervention to form contracts and perform obligations under existing contracts. Such broad coverage is necessary because of the diversity of transactions to which this Act may apply.

As with electronic agents, this definition addresses the circumstance where electronic records may result in action or performance by a party although no human review of the electronic records is anticipated. Section 14 provides specific rules to assure that where one or both parties do not review the electronic records, the resulting agreement will be effective.

The critical element in this definition is the lack of a human actor on one or both sides of a transaction. For example, if one orders books from Bookseller.com through Bookseller's website, the transaction would be an automated transaction because Bookseller took and confirmed the order via its machine. Similarly, if

Automaker and supplier do business through Electronic Data Interchange, Automaker's computer, upon receiving information within certain pre-programmed parameters, will send an electronic order to supplier's computer. If Supplier's computer confirms the order and processes the shipment because the order falls within pre-programmed parameters in Supplier's computer, this would be a fully automated transaction. If, instead, the Supplier relies on a human employee to review, accept, and process the Buyer's order, then only the Automaker's side of the transaction would be automated. In either case, the entire transaction falls within this definition.

3. **"Computer program."** This definition refers to the functional and operating aspects of an electronic, digital system. It relates to operating instructions used in an electronic system such as an electronic agent. (See definition of "Electronic Agent.")

4. **"Electronic."** The basic nature of most current technologies and the need for a recognized, single term warrants the use of "electronic" as the defined term. The definition is intended to assure that the Act will be applied broadly as new technologies develop. The term must be construed broadly in light of developing technologies in order to fulfill the purpose of this Act to validate commercial transactions regardless of the medium used by the parties. Current legal requirements for "writings" can be satisfied by almost any tangible media, whether paper, other fibers, or even stone. The purpose and applicability of this Act covers intangible media which are technologically capable of storing, transmitting and reproducing information in human perceivable form, but which lack the tangible aspect of paper, papyrus or stone.

While not all technologies listed are technically "electronic" in nature (e.g., optical fiber technology), the term "electronic" is the most descriptive term available to describe the majority of current technologies. For example, the development of biological and chemical processes for communication and storage of data, while not specifically mentioned in the definition, are included within the technical definition because such processes operate on electromagnetic impulses. However, whether a particular technology may be characterized as technically "electronic," i.e., operates on electromagnetic impulses, should not be determinative of whether records and signatures created, used and stored by means of a particular technology are covered by this Act. This Act is intended to apply to all records and signatures created, used and stored by any medium which permits the information to be retrieved in perceivable form.

5. **"Electronic agent."** This definition establishes that an electronic agent is a machine. As the term "electronic agent" has come to be recognized, it is limited to a tool function. The effect on the party using the agent is addressed in the operative provisions of the Act (e.g., Section 14)

An electronic agent, such as a computer program or other automated means employed by a person, is a tool of that person. As a general rule, the employer of a tool is responsible for the results obtained by the use of that tool since the tool has no independent volition of its own. However, an electronic agent, by definition, is capable within the parameters of its programming, of initiating, responding or interacting with other parties or their electronic agents once it has been activated by a party, without further attention of that party.

While this Act proceeds on the paradigm that an electronic agent is capable of performing only within the technical strictures of its preset programming, it is conceivable that, within the useful life of this Act, electronic agents may be created with the ability to act autonomously, and not just automatically. That is, through developments in artificial intelligence, a computer may be able to "learn through experience, modify the instructions in their own programs, and even devise new instructions." Allen and Widdison, "Can Computers Make Contracts?" *9 Harv. J.L.&Tech* 25 (Winter, 1996). If such developments occur, courts may construe the definition of electronic agent accordingly, in order to recognize such new capabilities.

The examples involving Bookseller.com and Automaker in the Comment to the definition of Automated Transaction are equally applicable here. Bookseller acts through an electronic agent in processing an order for books. Automaker and the supplier each act through electronic agents in facilitating and effectuating the just-in-time inventory process through EDI.

6. **"Electronic record."** An electronic record is a subset of the broader defined term "record." It is any record created, used or stored in a medium other than paper (see definition of electronic). The defined term is also used in this Act as a limiting definition in those provisions in which it is used.

Information processing systems, computer equipment and programs, electronic data interchange, electronic mail, voice mail, facsimile, telex, telecopying, scanning, and similar technologies all qualify as electronic under this Act. Accordingly information stored on a computer hard drive or floppy disc, facsimiles, voice mail messages, messages on a telephone answering machine, audio and video tape recordings, among other records, all would be electronic records under this Act.

7. **"Electronic signature."**

The idea of a signature is broad and not specifically defined. Whether any particular record is "signed" is a question of fact. Proof of that fact must be made under other applicable law. This Act simply assures that the signature may be accomplished through electronic means. No specific technology need be used in order to create a valid signature. One's voice on an answering machine may suffice if the requisite intention is present. Similarly, including one's name as part of an electronic mail communication also may suffice, as may the firm name on a facsimile. It also may be shown that the requisite intent was not present and accordingly the symbol, sound or process did not amount to a signature. One may use a digital signature with the requisite intention, or one may use the private key solely as an access device with no intention to sign, or otherwise accomplish a legally binding act. In any case the critical element is the intention to execute or adopt the sound or symbol or process for the purpose of signing the related record.

The definition requires that the signer execute or adopt the sound, symbol, or process with the intent to sign the record. The act of applying a sound, symbol or process to an electronic record could have differing meanings and effects. The consequence of the act and the effect of the act as a signature are determined under other applicable law. However, the essential attribute of a signature involves applying a sound, symbol or process with an intent to do a legally significant act. It is that intention that is understood in the law as a part of the word "sign", without the need for a definition.

This Act establishes, to the greatest extent possible, the equivalency of electronic signatures and manual signatures. Therefore the term "signature" has been used to connote and convey that equivalency. The purpose is to overcome unwarranted biases against electronic methods of signing and authenticating records. The term "authentication," used in other laws, often has a narrower meaning and purpose than an electronic signature as used in this Act. However, an authentication under any of those other laws constitutes an electronic signature under this Act.

The precise effect of an electronic signature will be determined based on the surrounding circumstances under Section 9(b).

This definition includes as an electronic signature the standard webpage click through process. For example, when a person orders goods or services through a vendor's website, the person will be required to provide information as part of a process which will result in receipt of the goods or services. When the customer ultimately gets to the last step and clicks "I agree," the person has adopted the process and has done so with the intent to associate the person with the record

of that process. The actual effect of the electronic signature will be determined from all the surrounding circumstances, however, the person adopted a process which the circumstances indicate s/he intended to have the effect of getting the goods/services and being bound to pay for them. The adoption of the process carried the intent to do a legally significant act, the hallmark of a signature.

Another important aspect of this definition lies in the necessity that the electronic signature be linked or logically associated with the record. In the paper world, it is assumed that the symbol adopted by a party is attached to or located somewhere in the same paper that is intended to be authenticated, e.g., an allonge firmly attached to a promissory note, or the classic signature at the end of a long contract. These tangible manifestations do not exist in the electronic environment, and accordingly, this definition expressly provides that the symbol must in some way be linked to, or connected with, the electronic record being signed. This linkage is consistent with the regulations promulgated by the Food and Drug Administration. 21 CFR Part 11 (March 20, 1997).

A digital signature using public key encryption technology would qualify as an electronic signature, as would the mere inclusion of one's name as a part of an e-mail message—so long as in each case the signer executed or adopted the symbol with the intent to sign.

8. **"Governmental agency."** This definition is important in the context of optional Sections 17-19.

9. **"Information processing system."** This definition is consistent with the UNCITRAL Model Law on Electronic Commerce. The term includes computers and other information systems. It is principally used in Section 15 in connection with the sending and receiving of information. In that context, the key aspect is that the information enter a system from which a person can access it.

10. **"Record."** This is a standard definition designed to embrace all means of communicating or storing information except human memory. It includes any method for storing or communicating information, including "writings." A record need not be indestructible or permanent, but the term does not include oral or other communications which are not stored or preserved by some means. Information that has not been retained other than through human memory does not qualify as a record. As in the case of the terms "writing" or "written," the term "record" does not establish the purposes, permitted uses or legal effect which a record may have under any particular provision of substantive law. ABA Report on Use of the Term "Record," October 1, 1996.

11. **"Security procedure."**

A security procedure may be applied to verify an electronic signature, verify the identity of the sender, or assure the informational integrity of an electronic record. The definition does not identify any particular technology. This permits the use of procedures which the parties select or which are established by law. It permits the greatest flexibility among the parties and allows for future technological development.

The definition in this Act is broad and is used to illustrate one way of establishing attribution or content integrity of an electronic record or signature. The use of a security procedure is not accorded operative legal effect, through the use of presumptions or otherwise, by this Act. In this Act, the use of security procedures is simply one method for proving the source or content of an electronic record or signature.

A security procedure may be technologically very sophisticated, such as an asymetric cryptographic system. At the other extreme the security procedure may be as simple as a telephone call to confirm the identity of the sender through another channel of communication. It may include the use of a mother's maiden name or a personal identification number (PIN). Each of these examples is a method for confirming the identity of a person or accuracy of a message.

12. **"Transaction."** The definition has been limited to actions between people taken in the context of business, commercial or governmental activities. The term includes all interactions between people for business, commercial, including specifically consumer, or governmental purposes. However, the term does not include unilateral or non-transactional actions. As such it provides a structural limitation on the scope of the Act as stated in the next section.

It is essential that the term commerce and business be understood and construed broadly to include commercial and business transactions involving individuals who may qualify as "consumers" under other applicable law. If Alice and Bob agree to the sale of Alice's car to Bob for $2000 using an internet auction site, that transaction is fully covered by this Act. Even if Alice and Bob each qualify as typical "consumers" under other applicable law, their interaction is a transaction in commerce. Accordingly their actions would be related to commercial affairs, and fully qualify as a transaction governed by this Act.

Other transaction types include:

1. A single purchase by an individual from a retail merchant, which may be accomplished by an order from a printed catalog sent by facsimile, or by exchange of electronic mail.

2. Recurring orders on a weekly or monthly basis between large companies which have entered into a master trading partner agreement to govern the methods and manner of their transaction parameters.

3. A purchase by an individual from an online internet retail vendor. Such an arrangement may develop into an ongoing series of individual purchases, with security procedures and the like, as a part of doing ongoing business.

4. The closing of a business purchase transaction via facsimile transmission of documents or even electronic mail. In such a transaction, all parties may participate through electronic conferencing technologies. At the appointed time all electronic records are executed electronically and transmitted to the other party. In such a case, the electronic records and electronic signatures are validated under this Act, obviating the need for "in person" closings.

A transaction must include interaction between two or more persons. Consequently, to the extent that the execution of a will, trust, or a health care power of attorney or similar health care designation does not involve another person and is a unilateral act, it would not be covered by this Act because not occurring as a part of a transaction as defined in this Act. However, this Act *does* apply to all electronic records and signatures *related* to a transaction, and so does cover, for example, internal auditing and accounting records related to a transaction.

SECTION 3. SCOPE.

(a) Except as otherwise provided in subsection (b), this [Act] applies to electronic records and electronic signatures relating to a transaction.

(b) This [Act] does not apply to a transaction to the extent it is governed by:

(1) a law governing the creation and execution of wills, codicils, or testamentary trusts;

(2) [The Uniform Commercial Code other than Sections 1-107 and 1-206, Article 2, and Article 2A];

(3) [the Uniform Computer Information Transactions Act]; and

(4) [other laws, if any, identified by State].

(c) This [Act] applies to an electronic record or electronic signature otherwise excluded from the application of this [Act] under subsection (b) to the extent it is governed by a law other than those specified in subsection (b).

(d) A transaction subject to this [Act] is also subject to other applicable substantive law.

See Legislative Note below—Following Comments.

Comment

1. The scope of this Act is inherently limited by the fact that it only applies to transactions related to business, commercial (including consumer) and governmental matters. Consequently, transactions with no relation to business, commercial or governmental transactions would not be subject to this Act. Unilaterally generated electronic records and signatures which are not part of a transaction also are not covered by this Act. See Section 2, Comment 12.

2. This Act affects the medium in which information, records and signatures may be presented and retained under current legal requirements. While this Act covers all electronic records and signatures which are used in a business, commercial (including consumer) or governmental transaction, the operative provisions of the Act relate to requirements for writings and signatures under other laws. Accordingly, the exclusions in subsection (b) focus on those legal rules imposing certain writing and signature requirements which will *not* be affected by this Act.

3. The exclusions listed in subsection (b) provide clarity and certainty regarding the laws which are and are not affected by this Act. This section provides that transactions subject to specific laws are unaffected by this Act and leaves the balance subject to this Act.

4. Paragraph (1) excludes wills, codicils and testamentary trusts. This

exclusion is largely salutary given the unilateral context in which such records are generally created and the unlikely use of such records in a transaction as defined in this Act (i.e., actions taken by two or more persons in the context of business, commercial or governmental affairs). Paragraph (2) excludes all of the Uniform Commercial Code other than UCC Sections 1-107 and 1-206, and Articles 2 and 2A. This Act does not apply to the excluded UCC articles, whether in "current" or "revised" form. The Act does apply to UCC Articles 2 and 2A and to UCC Sections 1-107 and 1-206.

5. Articles 3, 4 and 4A of the UCC impact payment systems and have specifically been removed from the coverage of this Act. The check collection and electronic fund transfer systems governed by Articles 3, 4 and 4A involve systems and relationships involving numerous parties beyond the parties to the underlying contract. The impact of validating electronic media in such systems involves considerations beyond the scope of this Act. Articles 5, 8 and 9 have been excluded because the revision process relating to those Articles included significant consideration of electronic practices. Paragraph 4 provides for exclusion from this Act of the Uniform Computer Information Transactions Act (UCITA) because the drafting process of that Act also included significant consideration of electronic contracting provisions.

6. The very limited application of this Act to Transferable Records in Section 16 does not affect payment systems, and the section is designed to apply to a transaction only through express agreement of the parties. The exclusion of Articles 3 and 4 will not affect the Act's coverage of Transferable Records. Section 16 is designed to allow for the development of systems which will provide "control" as defined in Section 16. Such control is necessary as a substitute for the idea of possession which undergirds negotiable instrument law. The technology has yet to be developed which will allow for the possession of a unique electronic token embodying the rights associated with a negotiable promissory note. Section 16's concept of control is intended as a substitute for possession.

The provisions in Section 16 operate as free standing rules, establishing the rights of parties using Transferable Records *under this Act*. The references in Section 16 to UCC Sections 3-302, 7-501, and 9-308 (R9-330(d)) are designed to incorporate the substance of those provisions into this Act for the limited purposes noted in Section 16(c). Accordingly, an electronic record which is also a Transferable Record, would not be used for purposes of a transaction governed by Articles 3, 4, or 9, but would be an electronic record used for purposes of a transaction governed by Section 16. However, it is important to remember that those UCC Articles will still apply to the transferable record in their own right. Accordingly any other substantive requirements, e.g., method and manner of perfection under Article 9, must be complied with under those other laws. See Comments to Section 16.

7. This Act does apply, *in toto*, to transactions under unrevised Articles 2 and 2A. There is every reason to validate electronic contracting in these situations. Sale and lease transactions do not implicate broad systems beyond the parties to the underlying transaction, such as are present in check collection and electronic funds transfers. Further sales and leases generally do not have as far reaching effect on the rights of third parties beyond the contracting parties, such as exists in the secured transactions system. Finally, it is in the area of sales, licenses and leases that electronic commerce is occurring to its greatest extent today. To exclude these transactions would largely gut the purpose of this Act.

In the event that Articles 2 and 2A are revised and adopted in the future, UETA will only apply to the extent provided in those Acts.

8. An electronic record/signature may be used for purposes of more than one legal requirement, or may be covered by more than one law. Consequently, it is important to make clear, despite any apparent redundancy, in subsection (c) that an electronic record used for purposes of a law which is *not* affected by this Act under subsection (b) may nonetheless be used and validated for purposes of other laws not excluded by subsection (b). For example, this Act does not apply to an electronic record of a check when used for purposes of a transaction governed by Article 4 of the Uniform Commercial Code, i.e., the Act does not validate so-called electronic checks. However, for purposes of check retention statutes, the same electronic record of the check is covered by this Act, so that retention of an electronic image/record of a check will satisfy such retention statutes, so long as the requirements of Section 12 are fulfilled.

In another context, subsection (c) would operate to allow this Act to apply to what would appear to be an excluded transaction under subsection (b). For example, Article 9 of the Uniform Commercial Code applies generally to any transaction that creates a security interest in personal property. However, Article 9 excludes landlord's liens. Accordingly, although this Act excludes from its application transactions subject to Article 9, this Act would apply to the creation of a landlord lien if the law otherwise applicable to landlord's liens did not provide otherwise, because the landlord's lien transaction is excluded from Article 9.

9. Additional exclusions under subparagraph (b)(4) should be limited to laws which govern electronic records and signatures which may be used in transactions as defined in Section 2(16). Records used unilaterally, or which do not relate to business, commercial (including consumer), or governmental affairs are not governed by this Act in any event, and exclusion of laws relating to such records may create unintended inferences about whether other records and signatures are covered by this Act.

It is also important that additional exclusions, if any, be incorporated under subsection (b)(4). As noted in Comment 8 above, an electronic record used in a transaction excluded under subsection (b), e.g., a check used to pay one's taxes, will nonetheless be validated for purposes of other, non-excluded laws under subsection (c), e.g., the check when used as proof of payment. It is critical that additional exclusions, if any, be incorporated into subsection (b) so that the salutary effect of subsection (c) apply to validate those records in other, non-excluded transactions. While a legislature may determine that a particular notice, such as a utility shutoff notice, be provided to a person in writing on paper, it is difficult to see why the utility should not be entitled to use electronic media for storage and evidentiary purposes. *Legislative Note Regarding Possible Additional Exclusions under Section 3(b)(4).*

The following discussion is derived from the Report dated September 21, 1998 of The Task Force on State Law Exclusions (the "Task Force") presented to the Drafting Committee. After consideration of the Report, the Drafting Committee determined that exclusions other than those specified in the Act were not warranted. In addition, other inherent limitations on the applicability of the Act (the definition of transaction, the requirement that the parties acquiesce in the use of an electronic format) also militate against additional exclusions. Nonetheless, the Drafting Committee recognized that some legislatures may wish to exclude additional transactions from the Act, and determined that guidance in some major areas would be helpful to those legislatures considering additional areas for exclusion.

Because of the overwhelming number of references in state law to writings and signatures, the following list of possible transactions is not exhaustive. However, they do represent those areas most commonly raised during the course of the drafting process as areas that might be inappropriate for an electronic medium. It is important to keep in mind however, that the Drafting Committee determined that exclusion of these additional areas was not warranted.

1. **Trusts** (other than testamentary trusts). Trusts can be used for both business and personal purposes. By virtue of the definition of transaction, trusts used outside the area of business and commerce would not be governed by this Act. With respect to business or commercial trusts, the laws governing their formation contain few or no requirements for paper or signatures. Indeed, in most jurisdictions trusts of any kind may be created orally. Consequently, the Drafting Committee believed that the Act should apply to any transaction where the law leaves to the parties the decision of whether to use a writing. Thus, in the absence of legal requirements for writings, there is no sound reason to exclude laws governing trusts from the application of this Act.

2. **Powers of Attorney.** A power of attorney is simply a formalized type of agency agreement. In general, no formal requirements for paper or execution were found to be applicable to the validity of powers of attorney.

Special health powers of attorney have been established by statute in some States. These powers may have special requirements under state law regarding execution, acknowledgment and possibly notarization. In the normal case such powers will not arise in a transactional context and so would not be covered by this Act. However, even if such a record were to arise in a transactional context, this Act operates simply to remove the barrier to the use of an electronic medium, and preserves other requirements of applicable substantive law, avoiding any necessity to exclude such laws from the operation of this Act. Especially in light of the provisions of Sections 8 and 11, the substantive requirements under such laws will be preserved and may be satisfied in an electronic format.

3. **Real Estate Transactions.** It is important to distinguish between the efficacy of paper documents involving real estate between the parties, as opposed to their effect on third parties. As between the parties it is unnecessary to maintain existing barriers to electronic contracting. There are no unique characteristics to contracts relating to real property as opposed to other business and commercial (including consumer) contracts. Consequently, the decision whether to use an electronic medium for their agreements should be a matter for the parties to determine. Of course, to be effective against third parties state law generally requires filing with a governmental office. Pending adoption of electronic filing systems by States, the need for a piece of paper to file to perfect rights against third parties, will be a consideration for the parties. In the event notarization and acknowledgment are required under other laws, Section 11 provides a means for such actions to be accomplished electronically.

With respect to the requirements of government filing, those are left to the individual States in the decision of whether to adopt and implement electronic filing systems. (See optional Sections 17-19.) However, government recording systems currently require paper deeds including notarized, manual signatures. Although California and Illinois are experimenting with electronic filing systems, until such systems become widespread, the parties likely will choose to use, at the least, a paper deed for filing purposes. Nothing in this Act precludes the parties from selecting the medium best suited to the needs of the particular transaction.

Parties may wish to consummate the transaction using electronic media in order to avoid expensive travel. Yet the actual deed may be in paper form to assure compliance with existing recording systems and requirements. The critical point is that nothing in this Act prevents the parties from selecting paper or electronic media for all or part of their transaction.

4. **Consumer Protection Statutes.** Consumer protection provisions in state law often require that information be disclosed or provided to a consumer in writing. Because this Act does apply to such transactions, the question of whether such laws should be specifically excluded was considered. Exclusion of consumer transactions would eliminate a huge group of commercial transactions which benefit consumers by enabling the efficiency of the electronic medium. Commerce over the internet is driven by consumer demands and concerns and must be included.

At the same time, it is important to recognize the protective effects of many consumer statutes. Consumer statutes often require that information be provided in writing, or may require that the consumer separately sign or initial a particular provision to evidence that the consumer's attention was brought to the provision. Subsection (1) requires electronic records to be retainable by a person whenever the law requires information to be delivered in writing. The section imposes a significant burden on the sender of information. The sender must assure that the information system of the recipient is compatible with, and capable of retaining the information sent by, the sender's system. Furthermore, nothing in this Act permits the avoidance of legal requirements of separate signatures or initialing. The Act simply permits the signature or initialing to be done electronically.

Other consumer protection statutes require (expressly or implicitly) that certain information be presented in a certain manner or format. Laws requiring information to be presented in particular fonts, formats or in similar fashion, as well as laws requiring conspicuous displays of information are preserved. Section 8(b)(3) specifically preserves the applicability of such requirements in an electronic environment. In the case of legal requirements that information be presented or appear conspicuous, the determination of what is conspicuous will be left to other law. Section 8 was included to specifically preserve the protective functions of such disclosure statutes, while at the same time allowing the use of electronic media if the substantive requirements of the other laws could be satisfied in the electronic medium.

Formatting and separate signing requirements serve a critical purpose in much consumer protection legislation, to assure that information is not slipped past the unsuspecting consumer. Not only does this Act not disturb those requirements, it preserves those requirements. In addition, other bodies of substantive law continue to operate to allow the courts to police any such bad conduct or overreaching, e.g., unconscionability, fraud, duress, mistake and the like. These bodies of law remain applicable regardless of the medium in which a record appears.

The requirement that both parties agree to conduct a transaction electronically also prevents the imposition of an electronic medium on unwilling parties See Section 5(b). In addition, where the law requires inclusion of specific terms or language, those requirements are preserved broadly by Section 5(e).

Requirements that information be sent to, or received by, someone have been preserved in Section 15. As in the paper world, obligations to send do not impose any duties on the sender to assure receipt, other than reasonable methods of dispatch. In those cases where receipt is required legally,

Sections 5, 8, and 15 impose the burden on the sender to assure delivery to the recipient if satisfaction of the legal requirement is to be fulfilled.

The preservation of existing safeguards, together with the ability to opt out of the electronic medium entirely, demonstrate the lack of any need generally to exclude consumer protection laws from the operation of this Act. Legislatures may wish to focus any review on those statutes which provide for post-contract formation and post-breach notices to be in paper. However, any such consideration must also balance the needed protections against the potential burdens which may be imposed. Consumers and others will not be well served by restrictions which preclude the employment of electronic technologies sought and desired by consumers.

SECTION 4. PROSPECTIVE APPLICATION. This [Act] applies to any electronic record or electronic signature created, generated, sent, communicated, received, or stored on or after the effective date of this [Act].

Comment

This section makes clear that the Act only applies to validate electronic records and signatures which arise subsequent to the effective date of the Act. Whether electronic records and electronic signatures arising before the effective date of this Act are valid is left to other law.

SECTION 5. USE OF ELECTRONIC RECORDS AND ELECTRONIC SIGNATURES; VARIATION BY AGREEMENT.

(a) This [Act] does not require a record or signature to be created, generated, sent, communicated, received, stored, or otherwise processed or used by electronic means or in electronic form.

(b) This [Act] applies only to transactions between parties each of which has agreed to conduct transactions by electronic means. Whether the parties agree to conduct a transaction by electronic means is determined from the context and surrounding circumstances, including the parties' conduct.

(c) A party that agrees to conduct a transaction by electronic means may refuse to conduct other transactions by electronic means. The right granted by this subsection may not be waived by agreement.

(d) Except as otherwise provided in this [Act], the effect of any of its provisions may be varied by agreement. The presence in certain provisions of this [Act] of the words "unless otherwise agreed", or words of similar import, does not imply that the effect of other provisions may not be varied by agreement.

(e) Whether an electronic record or electronic signature has legal consequences is determined by this [Act] and other applicable law.

Comment

This section limits the applicability of this Act to transactions which parties have agreed to conduct electronically. Broad interpretation of the term agreement is necessary to assure that this Act has the widest possible application consistent with its purpose of removing barriers to electronic commerce.

1. This section makes clear that this Act is intended to facilitate the use of electronic means, but does not require the use of electronic records and signatures. This fundamental principle is set forth in subsection (a) and elaborated by subsections (b) and (c), which require an intention to conduct transactions electronically and preserve the right of a party to refuse to use electronics in any subsequent transaction.

2. The paradigm of this Act is two willing parties doing transactions electronically. It is therefore appropriate that the Act is voluntary and preserves the greatest possible party autonomy to refuse electronic transactions. The requirement that party agreement be found from all the surrounding circumstances is a limitation on the scope of this Act.

3. If this Act is to serve to facilitate electronic transactions, it must be applicable under circumstances not rising to a full fledged contract to use electronics. While absolute certainty can be accomplished by obtaining an explicit contract before relying on electronic transactions, such an explicit contract should not be necessary before one may feel safe in conducting transactions electronically. Indeed, such a requirement would itself be an unreasonable barrier to electronic commerce, at odds with the fundamental purpose of this Act. Accordingly, the requisite agreement, express or implied, must be determined from all available circumstances and evidence.

4. Subsection (b) provides that the Act applies to transactions in which the parties have agreed to conduct the transaction electronically. In this context it is essential that the parties' actions and words be broadly construed in determining whether the requisite agreement exists. Accordingly, the Act expressly provides that the party's agreement is to be found from all circumstances, including the parties' conduct. The critical element is the intent of a party to conduct a transaction electronically. Once that intent is established, this Act applies. See Restatement 2d Contracts, Sections 2, 3, and 19.

Examples of circumstances from which it may be found that parties have reached an agreement to conduct transactions electronically include the following:

A.   Automaker and supplier enter into a Trading Partner Agreement setting forth the terms, conditions and methods for the conduct of business between them electronically.

B.   Joe gives out his business card with his business e-mail address. It may be reasonable, under the circumstances, for a recipient of the card to infer that Joe has agreed to communicate electronically for business purposes. However, in the absence of additional facts, it would not necessarily be reasonable to infer Joe's agreement to communicate electronically for purposes outside the scope of the business indicated by use of the business card.

C.   Sally may have several e-mail addresses—home, main office, office of a non-profit organization on whose board Sally sits. In each case, it may be reasonable to infer that Sally is willing to communicate electronically with respect to business related to the business/purpose associated with the respective e-mail addresses. However, depending on the circumstances, it may not be reasonable to communicate with Sally for purposes other than those related to the purpose for which she maintained a particular e-mail account.

D. Among the circumstances to be considered in finding an agreement would be the time when the assent occurred relative to the timing of the use of electronic communications. If one orders books from an online vendor, such as Bookseller.com, the intention to conduct that transaction and to receive any correspondence related to the transaction electronically can be inferred from the conduct. Accordingly, as to information related to that transaction it is reasonable for Bookseller to deal with the individual electronically.

The examples noted above are intended to focus the inquiry on the party's agreement to conduct a transaction electronically. Similarly, if two people are at a meeting and one tells the other to send an e-mail to confirm a transaction—the requisite agreement under subsection (b) would exist. In each case, the use of a business card, statement at a meeting, or other evidence of willingness to conduct a transaction electronically must be viewed in light of all the surrounding circumstances with a view toward broad validation of electronic transactions.

5. Just as circumstances may indicate the existence of agreement, express or implied from surrounding circumstances, circumstances may also demonstrate the absence of true agreement. For example:

A. If Automaker, Inc. were to issue a recall of automobiles via its Internet website, it would not be able to rely on this Act to validate that notice in the case of a person who never logged on to the website, or indeed, had no ability to do so, notwithstanding a clause in a paper purchase contract by which the buyer agreed to receive such notices in such a manner.

B. Buyer executes a standard form contract in which an agreement to receive all notices electronically in set forth on page 3 in the midst of other fine print. Buyer has never communicated with Seller electronically, and has not provided any other information in the contract to suggest a willingness to deal electronically. Not only is it unlikely that any but the most formalistic of agreements may be found, but nothing in this Act prevents courts from policing such form contracts under common law doctrines relating to contract formation, unconscionability and the like.

6. Subsection (c) has been added to make clear the ability of a party to refuse to conduct a transaction electronically, even if the person has conducted transactions electronically in the past. The effectiveness of a party's refusal to conduct a transaction electronically will be determined under other applicable law in light of all surrounding circumstances. Such circumstances must include an assessment of the transaction involved.

A party's right to decline to act electronically under a specific contract, on the ground that each action under that contract amounts to a separate "transaction," must be considered in light of the purpose of the contract and the action to be taken electronically. For example, under a contract for the purchase of goods, the giving and receipt of notices electronically, as provided in the contract, should not be viewed as discreet transactions. Rather such notices amount to separate actions which are part of the "transaction" of purchase evidenced by the contract. Allowing one party to require a change of medium in the middle of the transaction evidenced by that contract is not the purpose of this subsection. Rather this subsection is intended to preserve the party's right to conduct the next purchase in a non- electronic medium.

7. Subsection (e) is an essential provision in the overall scheme of this Act. While this Act validates and effectuates electronic records and electronic signatures, the legal effect of such records and signatures is left to existing substantive law outside this Act except in very narrow circumstances. See, e.g., Section 16. Even when this Act operates to validate records and signatures in an electronic medium, it expressly preserves the substantive rules of other law applicable to such records. See, e.g., Section 11.

For example, beyond validation of records, signatures and contracts based on the medium used, Section 7 (a) and (b) should not be interpreted as establishing the legal effectiveness of any given record, signature or contract. Where a rule of law requires that the record contain minimum substantive content, the legal effect of such a record will depend on whether the record meets the substantive requirements of other applicable law.

Section 8 expressly preserves a number of legal requirements in currently existing law relating to the presentation of information in writing. Although this Act now would allow such information to be presented in an electronic record, Section 8 provides that the other substantive requirements of law must be satisfied in the electronic medium as well.

SECTION 6.   CONSTRUCTION AND APPLICATION.

This [Act] must be construed and applied:

(1) to facilitate electronic transactions consistent with other applicable law;

(2) to be consistent with reasonable practices concerning electronic transactions and with the continued expansion of those practices; and

(3) to effectuate its general purpose to make uniform the law with respect to the subject of this [Act] among States enacting it.

Comment

1. The purposes and policies of this Act are

(a) to facilitate and promote commerce and governmental transactions by validating and authorizing the use of electronic records and electronic signatures;

(b) to eliminate barriers to electronic commerce and governmental transactions resulting from uncertainties relating to writing and signature requirements;

(c) to simplify, clarify and modernize the law governing commerce and governmental transactions through the use of electronic means;

(d) to permit the continued expansion of commercial and governmental electronic practices through custom, usage and agreement of the parties;

(e) to promote uniformity of the law among the States (and worldwide) relating to the use of electronic and similar technological means of effecting and performing commercial and governmental transactions;

(f) to promote public confidence in the validity, integrity and reliability of electronic commerce and governmental transactions; and

(g) to promote the development of the legal and business infrastructure necessary to implement electronic commerce and governmental transactions.

2. This Act has been drafted to permit flexible application consistent with its purpose to validate electronic transactions. The provisions of this Act validating and effectuating the employ of electronic media allow the courts to apply them to new and unforeseen technologies and practices. As time progresses, it is anticipated that what is new and unforeseen today will be commonplace tomorrow. Accordingly, this legislation is intended to set a framework for the validation of media which may be developed in the future and which demonstrate the same qualities as the electronic media contemplated and validated under this Act.

SECTION 7.   LEGAL RECOGNITION OF ELECTRONIC RECORDS, ELECTRONIC SIGNATURES, AND ELECTRONIC CONTRACTS.

(a) A record or signature may not be denied legal effect or enforceability solely because it is in electronic form.

(b) A contract may not be denied legal effect or enforceability solely because an electronic record was used in its formation.

(c) If a law requires a record to be in writing, an electronic record satisfies the law.

(d) If a law requires a signature, an electronic signature satisfies the law.

Source: UNCITRAL Model Law on Electronic Commerce, Articles 5, 6, and 7.

Comment

1. This section sets forth the fundamental premise of this Act: namely, that the medium in which a record, signature, or contract is created, presented or retained does not affect it's legal significance. Subsections (a) and (b) are designed to eliminate the single element of medium as a reason to deny effect or enforceability to a record, signature, or contract. The fact that the information is set forth in an electronic, as opposed to paper, record is irrelevant.

2. Under Restatement 2d Contracts Section 8, a contract may have legal effect and yet be unenforceable. Indeed, one circumstance where a record or contract may have effect but be unenforceable is in the context of the Statute of Frauds. Though a contract may be unenforceable, the records may have collateral effects, as in the case of a buyer that insures goods purchased under a contract unenforceable under the Statute of Frauds. The insurance company may not deny a claim on the ground that the buyer is not the owner, though the buyer may have no direct remedy against seller for failure to deliver. See Restatement 2d Contracts, Section 8, Illustration 4.

While this section would validate an electronic record for purposes of a statute of frauds, if an agreement to conduct the transaction electronically cannot reasonably be found (See Section 5(b)) then a necessary predicate to the applicability of this Act would be absent and this Act would not validate the electronic record. Whether the electronic record might be valid under other law is not addressed by this Act.

3. Subsections (c) and (d) provide the positive assertion that electronic records and signatures satisfy legal requirements for writings and

signatures. The provisions are limited to requirements in laws that a record be in writing or be signed. This section does not address requirements imposed by other law in addition to requirements for writings and signatures See, e.g., Section 8.

Subsections (c) and (d) are particularized applications of subsection (a). The purpose is to validate and effectuate electronic records and signatures as the equivalent of writings, subject to all of the rules applicable to the efficacy of a writing, except as such other rules are modified by the more specific provisions of this Act.

Illustration 1: A sends the following e-mail to B: "I hereby offer to buy widgets from you, delivery next Tuesday. /s/ A." B responds with the following e-mail: "I accept your offer to buy widgets for delivery next Tuesday. /s/ B." The e-mails may not be denied effect solely because they are electronic. In addition, the e-mails do qualify as records under the Statute of Frauds. However, because there is no quantity stated in either record, the parties' agreement would be unenforceable under existing UCC Section 2-201(1).

Illustration 2: A sends the following e-mail to B: "I hereby offer to buy 100 widgets for $1000, delivery next Tuesday. /s/ A." B responds with the following e-mail: "I accept your offer to purchase 100 widgets for $1000, delivery next Tuesday. /s/ B." In this case the analysis is the same as in Illustration 1 except that here the records otherwise satisfy the requirements of UCC Section 2-201(1). The transaction may not be denied legal effect solely because there is not a pen and ink "writing" or "signature".

4. Section 8 addresses additional requirements imposed by other law which may affect the legal effect or enforceability of an electronic record in a particular case. For example, in Section 8(a) the legal requirement addressed is *the provision of information* in writing. The section then sets forth the standards to be applied in determining whether the provision of information by an electronic record is the equivalent of the provision of information in writing. The requirements in Section 8 are in addition to the bare validation that occurs under this section.

5. Under the substantive law applicable to a particular transaction within this Act, the legal effect of an electronic record may be separate from the issue of whether the record contains a signature. For example, where notice must be given as part of a contractual obligation, the effectiveness of the notice will turn on whether the party provided the notice regardless of whether the notice was signed (See Section 15). An electronic record attributed to a party under Section 9 and complying with the requirements of Section 15 would suffice in that case, notwithstanding that it may not contain an electronic signature.

SECTION 8. PROVISION OF INFORMATION IN WRITING; PRESENTATION OF RECORDS.

(a) If parties have agreed to conduct a transaction by electronic means and a law requires a person to provide, send, or deliver information in writing to another person, the requirement is satisfied if the information is provided, sent, or delivered, as the case may be, in an electronic record capable of retention by the recipient at the time of receipt. An electronic record is not capable of retention by the recipient if the sender or its information processing system inhibits the ability of the recipient to print or store the electronic record.

(b) If a law other than this [Act] requires a record (i) to be posted or displayed in a certain manner, (ii) to be sent, communicated, or transmitted by a specified method, or (iii) to contain information that is formatted in a certain manner, the following rules apply:

(1) The record must be posted or displayed in the manner specified in the other law.

(2) Except as otherwise provided in subsection (d)(2), the record must be sent, communicated, or transmitted by the method specified in the other law.

(3) The record must contain the information formatted in the manner specified in the other law.

(c) If a sender inhibits the ability of a recipient to store or print an electronic record, the electronic record is not enforceable against the recipient.

(d) The requirements of this section may not be varied by agreement, but:

(1) to the extent a law other than this [Act] requires information to be provided, sent, or delivered in writing but permits that requirement to be varied by agreement, the requirement under subsection (a) that the information be in the form of an electronic record capable of retention may also be varied by agreement; and

(2) a requirement under a law other than this [Act] to send, communicate, or transmit a record by [first-class mail, postage prepaid] [regular United States mail], may be varied by agreement to the extent permitted by the other law.

Source: Canadian—Uniform Electronic Commerce Act

Comment

1. This section is a savings provision, designed to assure, consistent with the fundamental purpose of this Act, that otherwise applicable substantive law will not be overridden by this Act. The section makes clear that while the pen and ink provisions of such other law may be satisfied electronically, nothing in this Act vitiates the other requirements of such laws. The section addresses a number of issues related to disclosures and notice provisions in other laws.

2. This section is independent of the prior section. Section 7 refers to legal requirements for a writing. This section refers to legal requirements for the provision of information in writing or relating to the method or manner of presentation or delivery of information. The section addresses more specific legal requirements of other laws, provides standards for satisfying the more particular legal requirements, and defers to other law for satisfaction of requirements under those laws.

3. Under subsection (a), to meet a requirement of other law that information be provided in writing, the recipient of an electronic record of the

information must be able to get to the electronic record and read it, and must have the ability to get back to the information in some way at a later date. Accordingly, the section requires that the electronic record be capable of retention for later review.

The section specifically provides that any inhibition on retention imposed by the sender or the sender's system will preclude satisfaction of this section. Use of technological means now existing or later developed which prevents the recipient from retaining a copy the information would result in a determination that information has not been provided under subsection (a). The policies underlying laws requiring the provision of information in writing warrant the imposition of an additional burden on the sender to make the information available in a manner which will permit subsequent reference. A difficulty does exist for senders of information because of the disparate systems of their recipients and the capabilities of those systems. However, in order to satisfy the *legal requirement* of other law to make information available, the sender must assure that the recipient receives and can retain the information. However, it is left for the courts to determine whether the sender has complied with this subsection if evidence demonstrates that it is something peculiar the recipient's system which precludes subsequent reference to the information.

4. Subsection (b) is a savings provision for laws which provide for the means of delivering or displaying information and which are not affected by the Act. For example, if a law requires delivery of notice by first class US mail, that means of delivery would not be affected by this Act. The information to be delivered may be provided on a disc, i.e., in electronic form, but the particular means of delivery must still be via the US postal service. Display, delivery and formatting requirements will continue to be applicable to electronic records and signatures. If those legal requirements can be satisfied in an electronic medium, e.g., the information can be presented in the equivalent of 20 point bold type as required by other law, this Act will validate the use of the medium, leaving to the other applicable law the question of whether the particular electronic record meets the other legal requirements. If a law requires that particular records be delivered together, or attached to other records, this Act does not preclude the delivery of the records together in an electronic communication, so long as the records are connected or associated with each other in a way determined to satisfy the other law.

5. Subsection (c) provides incentives for senders of information to use systems which will not inhibit the other party from retaining the information. However, there are circumstances where a party providing certain information may wish to inhibit retention in order to protect intellectual property rights or prevent the other party from retaining confidential information about the sender. In such cases inhibition is understandable, but if the sender wishes to enforce the record in which the information is contained, the sender may not inhibit its retention by the recipient. Unlike subsection (a), subsection (c) applies in all transactions and simply provides for unenforceability against the recipient. Subsection (a) applies only where another law imposes the writing requirement, and subsection (a) imposes a broader responsibility on the sender to assure retention capability by the recipient.

6. The protective purposes of this section justify the non-waivability provided by subsection (d). However, since the requirements for sending and formatting and the like are imposed by other law, to the extent other law permits waiver of such protections, there is no justification for imposing a more severe burden in an electronic environment.

SECTION 9. ATTRIBUTION AND EFFECT OF ELECTRONIC RECORD AND ELECTRONIC SIGNATURE.

(a) An electronic record or electronic signature is attributable to a person if it was the act of the person. The act of the person may be shown in any manner, including a showing of the efficacy of any security procedure applied to determine the person to which the electronic record or electronic signature was attributable.

(b) The effect of an electronic record or electronic signature attributed to a person under subsection (a) is determined from the context and surrounding circumstances at the time of its creation, execution, or adoption, including the parties' agreement, if any, and otherwise as provided by law.

Comment

1. Under subsection (a), so long as the electronic record or electronic signature resulted from a person's action it will be attributed to that person—the legal effect of that attribution is addressed in subsection (b). This section does not alter existing rules of law regarding attribution. The section assures that such rules will be applied in the electronic environment. A person's actions include actions taken by human agents of the person, as well as actions taken by an electronic agent, i.e., the tool, of the person. Although the rule may appear to state the obvious, it assures that the record or signature is not ascribed to a machine, as opposed to the person operating or programing the machine.

In each of the following cases, both the electronic record and electronic signature would be attributable to a person under subsection (a):

A. The person types his/her name as part of an e-mail purchase order;

B. The person's employee, pursuant to authority, types the person's name as part of an e-mail purchase order;

C. The person's computer, programmed to order goods upon receipt of inventory information within particular parameters, issues a purchase order which includes the person's name, or other identifying information, as part of the order.

In each of the above cases, law other than this Act would ascribe both the signature and the action to the person if done in a paper medium. Subsection (a) expressly provides that the same result will occur when an electronic medium is used.

2. Nothing in this section affects the use of a signature as a device for attributing a record to a person. Indeed, a signature is often the primary method for attributing a record to a person. In the foregoing examples, once the electronic signature is attributed to the person, the electronic record would also be attributed to the person, unless the person established fraud, forgery, or other invalidating cause. However, a signature is not the only method for attribution.

3. The use of facsimile transmissions provides a number of examples of attribution using information other than a signature. A facsimile may be attributed to a person because of the information printed across the top of

the page that indicates the machine from which it was sent. Similarly, the transmission may contain a letterhead which identifies the sender. Some cases have held that the letterhead actually constituted a signature because it was a symbol adopted by the sender with intent to authenticate the facsimile. However, the signature determination resulted from the necessary finding of intention in that case. Other cases have found facsimile letterheads NOT to be signatures because the requisite intention was not present. The critical point is that with or without a signature, information within the electronic record may well suffice to provide the facts resulting in attribution of an electronic record to a particular party.

In the context of attribution of records, normally the content of the record will provide the necessary information for a finding of attribution. It is also possible that an established course of dealing between parties may result in a finding of attribution Just as with a paper record, evidence of forgery or counterfeiting may be introduced to rebut the evidence of attribution.

4. Certain information may be present in an electronic environment that does not appear to attribute but which clearly links a person to a particular record. Numerical codes, personal identification numbers, public and private key combinations all serve to establish the party to whom an electronic record should be attributed. Of course security procedures will be another piece of evidence available to establish attribution.

The inclusion of a specific reference to security procedures as a means of proving attribution is salutary because of the unique importance of security procedures in the electronic environment. In certain processes, a technical and technological security procedure may be the best way to convince a trier of fact that a particular electronic record or signature was that of a particular person. In certain circumstances, the use of a security procedure to establish that the record and related signature came from the person's business might be necessary to overcome a claim that a hacker intervened. The reference to security procedures is not intended to suggest that other forms of proof of attribution should be accorded less persuasive effect. It is also important to recall that the particular strength of a given procedure does not affect the procedure's status as a security procedure, but only affects the weight to be accorded the evidence of the security procedure as tending to establish attribution.

5. This section does apply in determining the effect of a "click-through" transaction. A "click-through" transaction involves a process which, if executed with an intent to "sign," will be an electronic signature. See definition of Electronic Signature. In the context of an anonymous "click-through," issues of proof will be paramount. This section will be relevant to establish that the resulting electronic record is attributable to a particular person upon the requisite proof, including security procedures which may track the source of the click-through.

6. Once it is established that a record or signature is attributable to a particular party, the effect of a record or signature must be determined in light of the context and surrounding circumstances, including the parties' agreement, if any. Also informing the effect of any attribution will be other legal requirements considered in light of the context. Subsection (b) addresses the effect of the record or signature once attributed to a person.

SECTION 10.   EFFECT OF CHANGE OR ERROR. If a change or error in an electronic record occurs in a transmission between parties to a transaction, the following rules apply:

(1) If the parties have agreed to use a security procedure to detect changes or errors and one party has conformed to the procedure, but the other party has not, and the nonconforming party would have detected the change or error had that party also conformed, the conforming party may avoid the effect of the changed or erroneous electronic record.

(2) In an automated transaction involving an individual, the individual may avoid the effect of an electronic record that resulted from an error made by the individual in dealing with the electronic agent of another person if the electronic agent did not provide an opportunity for the prevention or correction of the error and, at the time the individual learns of the error, the individual:

(A) promptly notifies the other person of the error and that the individual did not intend to be bound by the electronic record received by the other person;

(B) takes reasonable steps, including steps that conform to the other person's reasonable instructions, to return to the other person or, if instructed by the other person, to destroy the consideration received, if any, as a result of the erroneous electronic record; and

(C) has not used or received any benefit or value from the consideration, if any, received from the other person.

(3) If neither paragraph (1) nor paragraph (2) applies, the change or error has the effect provided by other law, including the law of mistake, and the parties' contract, if any.

(4) Paragraphs (2) and (3) may not be varied by agreement.

Source: Restatement 2d Contracts, Sections 152-155.

Comment

1. This section is limited to changes and errors occurring in transmissions between parties—whether person-person (paragraph 1) or in an automated transaction involving an individual and a machine (paragraphs 1 and 2). The section focuses on the effect of changes and errors occurring when records are exchanged between parties. In cases where changes and errors occur in contexts other than transmission, the law of mistake is expressly made applicable to resolve the conflict.

The section covers both changes and errors. For example, if Buyer sends a message to Seller ordering 100 widgets, but Buyer's information processing system changes the order to 1000 widgets, a "change" has occurred between what Buyer transmitted and what Seller received. If on the other hand, Buyer typed in 1000 intending to order only 100, but sent the message before noting the mistake, an error would have occurred which would also be covered by this section.

2. Paragraph (1) deals with any transmission where the parties have agreed to use a security procedure to detect changes and errors. It operates against the non- conforming party, i.e., the party in the best position to have avoided the change or error, regardless of whether that person is the sender or recipient. The source of the error/change is not indicated, and so both human and machine errors/changes would be covered. With respect to errors or changes that would not be detected by the security procedure even if applied, the parties are left to the general law of mistake to resolve the dispute.

3. Paragraph (1) applies only in the situation where a security procedure would detect the error/change but one party fails to use the procedure and does not detect the error/change. In such a case, consistent with the law of mistake generally, the record is made avoidable at the instance of the party who took all available steps to avoid the mistake. See Restatement 2d Contracts Sections 152-154.

Making the erroneous record avoidable by the conforming party is consistent with Sections 153 and 154 of the Restatement 2d Contracts because the non-conforming party was in the best position to avoid the problem, and would bear the risk of mistake. Such a case would constitute mistake by one party. The mistaken party (the conforming party) would be entitled to avoid any resulting contract under Section 153 because s/he does not have the risk of mistake and the non-conforming party had reason to know of the mistake.

4. As with paragraph (1), paragraph (2), when applicable, allows the mistaken party to avoid the effect of the erroneous electronic record. However, the subsection is limited to human error on the part of an individual when dealing with the electronic agent of the other party. In a transaction between individuals there is a greater ability to correct the error before parties have acted on it. However, when an individual makes an error while dealing with the electronic agent of the other party, it may not be possible to correct the error before the other party has shipped or taken other action in reliance on the erroneous record.

Paragraph (2) applies only to errors made by individuals. If the error results from the electronic agent, it would constitute a system error. In such a case the effect of that error would be resolved under paragraph (1) if applicable, otherwise under paragraph (3) and the general law of mistake.

5. The party acting through the electronic agent/machine is given incentives by this section to build in safeguards which enable the individual to prevent the sending of an erroneous record, or correct the error once sent. For example, the electronic agent may be programed to provide a "confirmation screen" to the individual setting forth all the information the individual initially approved. This would provide the individual with the ability to prevent the erroneous record from ever being sent. Similarly, the electronic agent might receive the record sent by the individual and then send back a confirmation which the individual must again accept before the transaction is completed. This would allow for correction of an erroneous record. In either case, the electronic agent would "provide an opportunity for prevention or correction of the error," *and the subsection would not apply*. Rather, the affect of any error is governed by other law.

6. Paragraph (2) also places additional requirements on the mistaken individual before the paragraph may be invoked to avoid an erroneous electronic record. The individual must take prompt action to advise the other party of the error and the fact that the individual did not intend the electronic record. Whether the action is prompt must be determined from

all the circumstances including the individual's ability to contact the other party. The individual should advise the other party both of the error and of the lack of intention to be bound (i.e., avoidance) by the electronic record received. Since this provision allows avoidance by the mistaken party, that party should also be required to expressly note that it is seeking to avoid the electronic record, i.e., lacked the intention to be bound.

Second, restitution is normally required in order to undo a mistaken transaction. Accordingly, the individual must also return or destroy any consideration received, adhering to instructions from the other party in any case. This is to assure that the other party retains control over the consideration sent in error.

Finally, and most importantly in regard to transactions involving intermediaries which may be harmed because transactions cannot be unwound, the individual cannot have received any benefit from the transaction. This section prevents a party from unwinding a transaction after the delivery of value and consideration which cannot be returned or destroyed. For example, if the consideration received is information, it may not be possible to avoid the benefit conferred. While the information itself could be returned, mere access to the information, or the ability to redistribute the information would constitute a benefit precluding the mistaken party from unwinding the transaction. It may also occur that the mistaken party receives consideration which changes in value between the time of receipt and the first opportunity to return. In such a case restitution cannot be made adequately, and the transaction would not be avoidable. In each of the foregoing cases, under subparagraph (2)(c), the individual would have received the benefit of the consideration and would NOT be able to avoid the erroneous electronic record under this section.

7. In all cases not covered by paragraphs (1) or (2), where error or change to a record occur, the parties contract, or other law, specifically including the law of mistake, applies to resolve any dispute. In the event that the parties' contract and other law would achieve different results, the construction of the parties' contract is left to the other law. If the error occurs in the context of record retention, Section 12 will apply. In that case the standard is one of accuracy and retrievability of the information.

8. Paragraph (4) makes the error correction provision in paragraph (2) and the application of the law of mistake in paragraph (3) non-variable. Paragraph (2) provides incentives for parties using electronic agents to establish safeguards for individuals dealing with them. It also avoids unjustified windfalls to the individual by erecting stringent requirements before the individual may exercise the right of avoidance under the paragraph. Therefore, there is no reason to permit parties to avoid the paragraph by agreement. Rather, parties should satisfy the paragraph's requirements.

SECTION 11. NOTARIZATION AND ACKNOWLEDGMENT. If a law requires a signature or record to be notarized, acknowledged, verified, or made under oath, the requirement is satisfied if the electronic signature of the person authorized to perform those acts, together with all other information required to be included by other applicable law, is attached to or logically associated with the signature or record.

Comment

This section permits a notary public and other authorized officers to act electronically, effectively removing the stamp/seal requirements. However, the section does not eliminate any of the other requirements of notarial laws, and consistent with the entire thrust of this Act, simply allows the signing and information to be accomplished in an electronic medium.

For example, Buyer wishes to send a notarized Real Estate Purchase Agreement to Seller via e-mail. The notary must appear in the room with the Buyer, satisfy him/herself as to the identity of the Buyer, and swear to that identification. All that activity must be reflected as part of the electronic Purchase Agreement and the notary's electronic signature must appear as a part of the electronic real estate purchase contract.

As another example, Buyer seeks to send Seller an affidavit averring defects in the products received. A court clerk, authorized under state law to administer oaths, is present with Buyer in a room. The Clerk administers the oath and includes the statement of the oath, together with any other requisite information, in the electronic record to be sent to the Seller. Upon administering the oath and witnessing the application of Buyer's electronic signature to the electronic record, the Clerk also applies his electronic signature to the electronic record. So long as all substantive requirements of other applicable law have been fulfilled and are reflected in the electronic record, the sworn electronic record of Buyer is as effective as if it had been transcribed on paper.

SECTION 12. RETENTION OF ELECTRONIC RE-CORDS; ORIGINALS.

(a) If a law requires that a record be retained, the requirement is satisfied by retaining an electronic record of the information in the record which:

(1) accurately reflects the information set forth in the record after it was first generated in its final form as an electronic record or otherwise; and

(2) remains accessible for later reference.

(b) A requirement to retain a record in accordance with subsection (a) does not apply to any information the sole purpose of which is to enable the record to be sent, communicated, or received.

(c) A person may satisfy subsection (a) by using the services of another person if the requirements of that subsection are satisfied.

(d) If a law requires a record to be presented or retained in its original form, or provides consequences if the record is not presented or retained in its original form, that law is satisfied by an electronic record retained in accordance with subsection (a).

(e) If a law requires retention of a check, that requirement is satisfied by retention of an electronic record of the information on the front and back of the check in accordance with subsection (a).

(f) A record retained as an electronic record in accordance with subsection (a) satisfies a law requiring a person to retain a record for evidentiary, audit, or like purposes, unless a law enacted after the effective date of this [Act] specifically prohibits the use of an electronic record for the specified purpose.

(g) This section does not preclude a governmental agency of this State from specifying additional requirements for the retention of a record subject to the agency's jurisdiction.

Source: UNCITRAL Model Law On Electronic Commerce Articles 8 and 10.

Comment

1. This section deals with the serviceability of electronic records as retained records and originals. So long as there exists reliable assurance that the electronic record accurately reproduces the information, this section continues the theme of establishing the functional equivalence of electronic and paper-based records. This is consistent with Fed.R.Evid. 1001(3) and Unif.R.Evid. 1001(3) (1974). This section assures that information stored electronically will remain effective for all audit, evidentiary, archival and similar purposes.

2. In an electronic medium, the concept of an original document is problematic. For example, as one drafts a document on a computer the "original" is either on a disc or the hard drive to which the document has been initially saved. If one periodically saves the draft, the fact is that at times a document may be first saved to disc then to hard drive, and at others vice versa. In such a case the "original" may change from the information on the disc to the information on the hard drive. Indeed, it may be argued that the "original" exists solely in RAM and, in a sense, the original is destroyed when a "copy" is saved to a disc or to the hard drive. In any event, in the context of record retention, the concern focuses on the integrity of the information, and not with its "originality."

3. Subsection (a) requires accuracy and the ability to access at a later time. The requirement of accuracy is derived from the Uniform and Federal Rules of Evidence. The requirement of continuing accessibility addresses the issue of technology obsolescence and the need to update and migrate information to developing systems. It is not unlikely that within the span of 5-10 years (a period during which retention of much information is required) a corporation may evolve through one or more generations of technology. More to the point, this technology may be incompatible with each other necessitating the reconversion of information from one system to the other.

For example, certain operating systems from the early 1980's, e.g., memory typewriters, became obsolete with the development of personal computers. The information originally stored on the memory typewriter would need to be converted to the personal computer system in a way meeting the standards for accuracy contemplated by this section. It is also possible that the medium on which the information is stored is less stable. For example, information stored on floppy discs is generally less stable, and subject to a greater threat of disintegration, that information stored on a computer hard drive. In either case, the continuing accessibility issue must be satisfied to validate information stored by electronic means under this section.

This section permits parties to convert original written records to electronic records for retention so long as the requirements of subsection (a) are satisfied. Accordingly, in the absence of specific requirements to retain written records, written records may be destroyed once saved as electronic records satisfying the requirements of this section.

The subsection refers to the information contained in an electronic record, rather than relying on the term electronic record, as a matter of clarity that the critical aspect in retention is the information itself. What information must be retained is determined by the purpose for which the information is needed. If the addressing and pathway information regarding an e-mail is relevant, then that information should also be retained. However if it is the substance of the e-mail that is relevant, only that information need be retained. Of course, wise record retention would include all such information since what information will be relevant at a later time will not be known.

4. Subsections (b) and (c) simply make clear that certain ancillary information or the use of third parties, does not affect the serviceability of records and information retained electronically. Again, the relevance of particular information will not be known until that information is required at a subsequent time.

5. Subsection (d) continues the theme of the Act as validating electronic records as originals where the law requires retention of an original. The validation of electronic records and electronic information as originals is consistent with the Uniform Rules of Evidence. See Uniform Rules of Evidence 1001(3), 1002, 1003 and 1004.

6. Subsection (e) specifically addresses particular concerns regarding check retention statutes in many jurisdictions. A Report compiled by the Federal Reserve Bank of Boston identifies hundreds of state laws which require the retention or production of original canceled checks. Such requirements preclude banks and their customers from realizing the benefits and efficiencies related to truncation processes otherwise validated under current law. The benefits to banks and their customers from electronic check retention are effectuated by this provision.

7. Subsections (f) and (g) generally address other record retention statutes. As with check retention, all businesses and individuals may realize significant savings from electronic record retention. So long as the standards in Section 12 are satisfied, this section permits all parties to obtain those benefits. As always the government may require records in any medium, however, these subsections require a governmental agency to specifically identify the types of records and requirements that will be imposed.

SECTION 13. ADMISSIBILITY IN EVIDENCE. In a proceeding, evidence of a record or signature may not be excluded solely because it is in electronic form.

Source: UNCITRAL Model Law on Electronic Commerce Article 9.

Comment

Like Section 7, this section prevents the nonrecognition of electronic records and signatures solely on the ground of the media in which information is presented.

Nothing in this section relieves a party from establishing the necessary foundation for the admission of an electronic record. See Uniform Rules of Evidence 1001(3), 1002, 1003 and 1004.

SECTION 14. AUTOMATED TRANSACTION. In an automated transaction, the following rules apply:

(1) A contract may be formed by the interaction of electronic agents of the parties, even if no individual was aware of or reviewed the electronic agents' actions or the resulting terms and agreements.

(2) A contract may be formed by the interaction of an electronic agent and an individual, acting on the individual's own behalf or for another person, including by an interaction in which the individual performs actions that the individual is free to refuse to perform and which the individual knows or has reason to know will cause the electronic agent to complete the transaction or performance.

(3) The terms of the contract are determined by the substantive law applicable to it.

Source: UNICTRAL Model Law on Electronic Commerce Article 11.

Comment

1. This section confirms that contracts can be formed by machines functioning as electronic agents for parties to a transaction. It negates any claim that lack of human intent, at the time of contract formation, prevents contract formation. When machines are involved, the requisite intention flows from the programing and use of the machine. As in other cases, these are salutary provisions consistent with the fundamental purpose of the Act to remove barriers to electronic transactions while leaving the substantive law, e.g., law of mistake, law of contract formation, unaffected to the greatest extent possible.

2. The process in paragraph (2) validates an anonymous click-through transaction. It is possible that an anonymous click-through process may simply result in no recognizable legal relationship, e.g., A goes to a person's website and acquires access without in any way identifying herself, or otherwise indicating agreement or assent to any limitation or obligation, and the owner's site grants A access. In such a case no legal relationship has been created.

On the other hand it may be possible that A's actions indicate agreement to a particular term. For example, A goes to a website and is confronted by an initial screen which advises her that the information at this site is proprietary, that A may use the information for her own personal purposes, but that, by clicking below, A agrees that any other use without the site owner's permission is prohibited. If A clicks "agree" and downloads the information and then uses the information for other, prohibited purposes, should not A be bound by the click? It seems the answer properly should be, and would be, yes.

If the owner can show that the only way A could have obtained the information was from his website, and that the process to access the subject information required that A must have clicked the "I agree" button after having the ability to see the conditions on use, A has performed actions which A was free to refuse, which A knew would cause the site to grant her access, i.e., "complete the transaction." The terms of the resulting contract will be determined under general contract principles, but will include the limitation on A's use of the information, as a condition precedent to granting her access to the information.

3. In the transaction set forth in Comment 2, the record of the transac-

tion also will include an electronic signature. By clicking "I agree" A adopted a process with the intent to "sign," i.e., bind herself to a legal obligation, the resulting record of the transaction. If a "signed writing" were required under otherwise applicable law, this transaction would be enforceable. If a "signed writing" were not required, it may be sufficient to establish that the electronic record is attributable to A under Section 9. Attribution may be shown in any manner reasonable including showing that, of necessity, A could only have gotten the information through the process at the website.

SECTION 15.   TIME AND PLACE OF SENDING AND RECEIPT.

(a) Unless otherwise agreed between the sender and the recipient, an electronic record is sent when it:

(1) is addressed properly or otherwise directed properly to an information processing system that the recipient has designated or uses for the purpose of receiving electronic records or information of the type sent and from which the recipient is able to retrieve the electronic record;

(2) is in a form capable of being processed by that system; and

(3) enters an information processing system outside the control of the sender or of a person that sent the electronic record on behalf of the sender or enters a region of the information processing system designated or used by the recipient which is under the control of the recipient.

(b) Unless otherwise agreed between a sender and the recipient, an electronic record is received when:

(1) it enters an information processing system that the recipient has designated or uses for the purpose of receiving electronic records or information of the type sent and from which the recipient is able to retrieve the electronic record; and

(2) it is in a form capable of being processed by that system.

(c) Subsection (b) applies even if the place the information processing system is located is different from the place the electronic record is deemed to be received under subsection (d).

(d) Unless otherwise expressly provided in the electronic record or agreed between the sender and the recipient, an electronic record is deemed to be sent from the sender's place of business and to be received at the recipient's place of business. For purposes of this subsection, the following rules apply:

(1) If the sender or recipient has more than one place of business, the place of business of that person is the place having the closest relationship to the underlying transaction.

(2) If the sender or the recipient does not have a place of business, the place of business is the sender's or recipient's residence, as the case may be.

(e) An electronic record is received under subsection (b) even if no individual is aware of its receipt.

(f) Receipt of an electronic acknowledgment from an information processing system described in subsection (b) establishes that a record was received but, by itself, does not establish that the content sent corresponds to the content received.

(g) If a person is aware that an electronic record purportedly sent under subsection (a), or purportedly received under subsection (b), was not actually sent or received, the legal effect of the sending or receipt is determined by other applicable law. Except to the extent permitted by the other law, the requirements of this subsection may not be varied by agreement.

Source: UNCITRAL Model Law on Electronic Commerce Article 15.

Comment

1. This section provides default rules regarding when and from where an electronic record is sent and when and where an electronic record is received. This section does not address the efficacy of the record that is sent or received. That is, whether a record is unintelligible or unusable by a recipient is a separate issue from whether that record was sent or received. The effectiveness of an illegible record, whether it binds any party, are questions left to other law.

2. Subsection (a) furnishes rules for determining when an electronic record is sent. The effect of the sending and its import are determined by other law once it is determined that a sending has occurred.

In order to have a proper sending, the subsection requires that information be properly addressed or otherwise directed to the recipient. In order to send within the meaning of this section, there must be specific information which will direct the record to the intended recipient. Although mass electronic sending is not precluded, a general broadcast message, sent to systems rather than individuals, would not suffice as a sending.

The record will be considered sent once it leaves the control of the sender, or comes under the control of the recipient. Records sent through e-mail or the internet will pass through many different server systems. Accordingly, the critical element when more than one system is involved is the loss of control by the sender.

However, the structure of many message delivery systems is such that electronic records may actually never leave the control of the sender. For example, within a university or corporate setting, e-mail sent within the system to another faculty member is technically not out of the sender's control since it never leaves the organization's server. Accordingly, to qualify as a sending, the e-mail must arrive at a point where the recipient has control. This section does not address the effect of an electronic record that is thereafter "pulled back," e.g., removed from a mailbox. The analog in the paper world would be removing a letter from a person's mailbox. As in the case of providing information electronically under Section 8, the recipient's ability to receive a message should be judged from the perspective of whether the sender has done any action which would preclude retrieval. This is especially the case in regard to sending, since the sender must direct the record to a system designated or used by the recipient.

3. Subsection (b) provides simply that when a record enters the system which the recipient has designated or uses and to which it has access, in a form capable of being processed by that system, it is received. Keying receipt to a system accessible by the recipient removes the potential for a recipient leaving messages with a server or other service in order to avoid receipt. However, the section does not resolve the issue of how the sender proves the time of receipt.

To assure that the recipient retains control of the place of receipt, subsection (b) requires that the system be specified or used by the recipient, and that the system be used or designated for the type of record being sent. Many people have multiple e-mail addresses for different purposes. Subsection (b) assures that recipients can designate the e-mail address or system to be used in a particular transaction. For example, the recipient retains the ability to designate a home e-mail for personal matters, work e-mail for official business, or a separate organizational e-mail solely for the business purposes of that organization. If A sends B a notice at his home which relates to business, it may not be deemed received if B designated his business address as the sole address for business purposes. Whether actual knowledge upon seeing it at home would qualify as receipt is determined under the otherwise applicable substantive law.

4. Subsections (c) and (d) provide default rules for determining where a record will be considered to have been sent or received. The focus is on the place of business of the recipient and not the physical location of the information processing system, which may bear absolutely no relation to the transaction between the parties. It is not uncommon for users of electronic commerce to communicate from one State to another without knowing the location of information systems through which communication is operated. In addition, the location of certain communication systems may change without either of the parties being aware of the change. Accordingly, where the place of sending or receipt is an issue under other applicable law, e.g., conflict of laws issues, tax issues, the relevant location should be the location of the sender or recipient and not the location of the information processing system.

Subsection (d) assures individual flexibility in designating the place from which a record will be considered sent or at which a record will be considered received. Under subsection (d) a person may designate the place of sending or receipt unilaterally in an electronic record. This ability, as with the ability to designate by agreement, may be limited by otherwise applicable law to places having a reasonable relationship to the transaction.

5. Subsection (e) makes clear that receipt is not dependent on a person having notice that the record is in the person's system. Receipt occurs when the record reaches the designated system whether or not the recipient ever retrieves the record. The paper analog is the recipient who never reads a mail notice.

6. Subsection (f) provides legal certainty regarding the effect of an

electronic acknowledgment. It only addresses the fact of receipt, not the quality of the content, nor whether the electronic record was read or "opened."

7. Subsection (g) limits the parties' ability to vary the method for sending and receipt provided in subsections (a) and (b), when there is a legal requirement for the sending or receipt. As in other circumstances where legal requirements derive from other substantive law, to the extent that the other law permits variation by agreement, this Act does not impose any additional requirements, and provisions of this Act may be varied to the extent provided in the other law.

SECTION 16. TRANSFERABLE RECORDS.

(a) In this section, "transferable record" means an electronic record that:

(1) would be a note under [Article 3 of the Uniform Commercial Code] or a document under [Article 7 of the Uniform Commercial Code] if the electronic record were in writing; and

(2) the issuer of the electronic record expressly has agreed is a transferable record.

(b) A person has control of a transferable record if a system employed for evidencing the transfer of interests in the transferable record reliably establishes that person as the person to which the transferable record was issued or transferred.

(c) A system satisfies subsection (b), and a person is deemed to have control of a transferable record, if the transferable record is created, stored, and assigned in such a manner that:

(1) a single authoritative copy of the transferable record exists which is unique, identifiable, and, except as otherwise provided in paragraphs (4), (5), and (6), unalterable;

(2) the authoritative copy identifies the person asserting control as:

(A) the person to which the transferable record was issued; or

(B) if the authoritative copy indicates that the transferable record has been transferred, the person to which the transferable record was most recently transferred;

(3) the authoritative copy is communicated to and maintained by the person asserting control or its designated custodian;

(4) copies or revisions that add or change an identi-

179

fied assignee of the authoritative copy can be made only with the consent of the person asserting control;

(5) each copy of the authoritative copy and any copy of a copy is readily identifiable as a copy that is not the authoritative copy; and

(6) any revision of the authoritative copy is readily identifiable as authorized or unauthorized.

(d) Except as otherwise agreed, a person having control of a transferable record is the holder, as defined in [Section 1-201(20) of the Uniform Commercial Code], of the transferable record and has the same rights and defenses as a holder of an equivalent record or writing under [the Uniform Commercial Code], including, if the applicable statutory requirements under [Section 3-302(a), 7-501, or 9-308 of the Uniform Commercial Code] are satisfied, the rights and defenses of a holder in due course, a holder to which a negotiable document of title has been duly negotiated, or a purchaser, respectively. Delivery, possession, and indorsement are not required to obtain or exercise any of the rights under this subsection.

(e) Except as otherwise agreed, an obligor under a transferable record has the same rights and defenses as an equivalent obligor under equivalent records or writings under [the Uniform Commercial Code].

(f) If requested by a person against which enforcement is sought, the person seeking to enforce the transferable record shall provide reasonable proof that the person is in control of the transferable record. Proof may include access to the authoritative copy of the transferable record and related business records sufficient to review the terms of the transferable record and to establish the identity of the person having control of the transferable record.

Source: Revised Article 9, Section 9-105.

Comment

1. Paper negotiable instruments and documents are unique in the fact that a tangible token—a piece of paper—actually embodies intangible rights and obligations. The extreme difficulty of creating a unique electronic token which embodies the singular attributes of a paper negotiable document or instrument dictates that the rules relating to negotiable documents and instruments not be simply amended to allow the use of an electronic record for the requisite paper writing. However, the desirability of establishing rules by which business parties might be able to acquire some of the benefits of negotiability in an electronic environment is recognized by the inclusion of this section on Transferable Records.

This section provides legal support for the creation, transferability and enforceability of electronic note and document equivalents, as against the issuer/obligor. The certainty created by the section provides the requisite incentive for industry to develop the systems and processes, which involve significant expenditures of time and resources, to enable the use of such electronic documents.

The importance of facilitating the development of systems which will permit electronic equivalents is a function of cost, efficiency and safety for the records. The storage cost and space needed for the billions of paper notes and documents is phenomenal. Further, natural disasters can wreak havoc on the ability to meet legal requirements for retaining, retrieving and delivering paper instruments. The development of electronic systems meeting the rigorous standards of this section will permit retention of copies which reflect the same integrity as the original. As a result storage, transmission and other costs will be reduced, while security and the ability to satisfy legal requirements governing such paper records will be enhanced.

Section 16 provides for the creation of an electronic record which may be controlled by the holder, who in turn may obtain the benefits of holder in due course and good faith purchaser status. If the benefits and efficiencies of electronic media are to be realized in this industry it is essential to establish a means by which transactions involving paper promissory notes may be accomplished completely electronically. Particularly as other aspects of such transactions are accomplished electronically, the drag on the transaction of requiring a paper note becomes evident. In addition to alleviating the logistical problems of generating, storing and retrieving paper, the mailing and transmission costs associated with such transactions will also be reduced.

2. The definition of transferable record is limited in two significant ways. First, only the equivalent of paper promissory notes and paper documents of title can be created as transferable records. Notes and Documents of Title do not impact the broad systems that relate to the broader payments mechanisms related, for example, to checks. Impacting the check collection system by allowing for "electronic checks" has ramifications well beyond the ability of this Act to address. Accordingly, this Act excludes from its scope transactions governed by UCC Articles 3 and 4. The limitation to promissory note equivalents in Section 16 is quite important in that regard because of the ability to deal with many enforcement issues by contract without affecting such systemic concerns.

Second, not only is Section 16 limited to electronic records which would qualify as negotiable promissory notes or documents if they were in writing, but the issuer of the electronic record must expressly agree that the electronic record is to be considered a transferable record. The definition of transferable record as "an electronic record that . . . the issuer of the electronic record expressly has agreed is a transferable record" indicates that the electronic record itself will likely set forth the issuer's agreement, though it may be argued that a contemporaneous electronic or written record might set forth the issuer's agreement. However, conversion of a paper note issued as such would not be possible because the issuer would not be the issuer, in such a case, of an electronic record. The purpose of such a restriction is to assure that transferable records can only be created at the time of issuance by the obligor. The possibility that a paper note might be converted to an electronic record and then intentionally destroyed, and the effect of such action, was not intended to be covered by Section 16.

The requirement that the obligor expressly agree in the electronic record to its treatment as a transferable record does not otherwise affect the characterization of a transferable record (i.e., does not affect what would be a paper note) because it is a statutory condition. Further, it does not obligate the issuer to undertake to do any other act than the payment of the obligation evidenced by the transferable record. Therefore, it does not make the transferable record "conditional" within the meaning of Section 3-104(a)(3) of the Uniform Commercial Code.

3. Under Section 16 acquisition of "control" over an electronic record serves as a substitute for "possession" in the paper analog. More precisely, "control" under Section 16 serves as the substitute for delivery, indorsement and possession of a negotiable promissory note or negotiable document of title. Section 16(b) allows control to be found so long as "a system employed for evidencing the transfer of interests in the transferable record reliably establishes [the person claiming control] as the person to which the transferable record was issued or transferred." The key point is that a system, whether involving third party registry or technological safeguards, must be shown to reliably establish the identity of *the* person entitled to payment. Section 16(c) then sets forth a safe harbor list of very strict requirements for such a system. The specific provisions listed in Section 16(c) are derived from Section 105 of Revised Article 9 of the Uniform Commercial Code. Generally, the transferable record must be unique, identifiable, and except as specifically permitted, unalterable. That "authoritative copy" must (i) identify the person claiming control as the person to whom the record was issued or most recently transferred, (ii) be maintained by the person claiming control or its designee, and (iii) be unalterable except with the permission of the person claiming control. In addition any copy of the authoritative copy must be readily identifiable as a copy and all revisions must be readily identifiable as authorized or unauthorized.

The control requirements may be satisfied through the use of a trusted third party registry system. Such systems are currently in place with regard to the transfer of securities entitlements under Article 8 of the Uniform Commercial Code, and in the transfer of cotton warehouse receipts under the program sponsored by the United States Department of Agriculture. This Act would recognize the use of such a system so long as the standards of subsection (c) were satisfied. In addition, a technological system which met such exacting standards would also be permitted under Section 16.

For example, a borrower signs an electronic record which would be a promissory note or document if it were paper. The borrower specifically agrees in the electronic record that it will qualify as a transferable record under this section. The lender implements a newly developed technological system which dates, encrypts, and stores all the electronic information in the transferable record in a manner which lender can demonstrate reliably establishes lender as the person to which the transferable record was issued. In the alternative, the lender may contract with a third party to act as a registry for all such transferable records, retaining records establishing the party to whom the record was issued and all subsequent transfers of the record. An example of this latter method for assuring control is the system established for the issuance and transfer of electronic cotton warehouse receipts under 7 C.F.R. section 735 et seq.

Of greatest importance in the system used is the ability to securely and demonstrably be able to transfer the record to others in a manner which assures that only one "holder" exists. The need for such certainty and security resulted in the very stringent standards for a system outlined in subsection (c). A system relying on a third party registry is likely the most effective way to satisfy the requirements of subsection (c) that the transferable record remain unique, identifiable and unalterable, while also providing the means to assure that the transferee is clearly noted and identified.

It must be remembered that Section 16 was drafted in order to provide sufficient legal certainty regarding the rights of those in control of such electronic records, that legal incentives would exist to warrant the development of systems which would establish the requisite control. During the drafting of Section 16, representatives from the Federal Reserve carefully scrutinized the impact of any electronicization of any aspect of the national payment system. Section 16 represents a compromise position which, as noted, serves as a bridge pending more detailed study and consideration of what legal changes, if any, are necessary or appropriate in the context of the payment systems impacted. Accordingly, Section 16 provides limited scope for the attainment of important rights derived from the concept of negotiability, in order to permit the development of systems which will satisfy its strict requirements for control.

4. It is important to note what the section does not provide. Issues related to enforceability against intermediate transferees and transferors (i.e., indorser liability under a paper note), warranty liability that would attach in a paper note, and issues of the effect of taking a transferable record on the underlying obligation, are NOT addressed by this section. Such matters must be addressed, if at all, by contract between and among the parties in the chain of transmission and transfer of the transferable record. In the event that such matters are not addressed by the contract, the issues would need to be resolved under otherwise applicable law. Other law may include general contract principles of assignment and assumption, or may include rules from Article 3 of the Uniform Commercial Code applied by analogy.

For example, Issuer agrees to pay a debt by means of a transferable record issued to A. Unless there is agreement between issuer and A that the transferable record "suspends" the underlying obligation (see Section 3-310 of the Uniform Commercial Code), A would not be prevented from enforcing the underlying obligation without the transferable record. Similarly, if A transfers the transferable record to B by means granting B control, B may obtain holder in due course rights against the obligor/issuer, but B's recourse against A would not be clear unless A agreed to remain liable under the transferable record. Although the rules of Article 3 may be applied by analogy in an appropriate context, in the absence of an express agreement in the transferable record or included by applicable system rules, the liability of the transferor would not be clear.

5. Current business models exist which rely for their efficacy on the benefits of negotiability. A principal example, and one which informed much of the development of Section 16, involves the mortgage backed securities industry. Aggregators of commercial paper acquire mortgage secured promissory notes following a chain of transfers beginning with the origination of the mortgage loan by a mortgage broker. In the course of the transfers of this paper, buyers of the notes and lenders/secured parties for these buyers will intervene. For the ultimate purchaser of the paper, the ability to rely on holder in due course and good faith purchaser status creates the legal security necessary to issue its own investment securities which are backed by the obligations evidenced by the notes purchased. Only through their HIDC status can these purchasers be assured that third party claims will be barred. Only through their HIDC status can the end purchaser avoid the incredible burden of requiring and assuring that each person in the chain of transfer has waived any and all defenses to performance which may be created during the chain of transfer.

6. This section is a stand-alone provision. Although references are made to specific provisions in Article 3, Article 7, and Article 9 of the Uniform Commercial Code, these provisions are incorporated into this Act and made the applicable rules for purposes of this Act. The rights of parties to transferable records are established under subsections (d) and (e). Subsection (d) provides rules for determining the rights of a party in control of a transferable record. The subsection makes clear that the rights are determined under this section, and not under other law, by incorporating the rules on the manner of acquisition into this statute. The last sentence of subsection (d) is intended to assure that requirements related to notions of possession, which are inherently inconsistent with the idea of an electronic record, are not incorporated into this statute.

If a person establishes control, Section 16(d) provides that that person is the "holder" of the transferable record which is equivalent to a holder of an analogous paper negotiable instrument. More importantly, if the person acquired control in a manner which would make it a holder in due course of an equivalent paper record, the person acquires the rights of a HIDC. The person in control would therefore be able to enforce the transferable record against the obligor regardless of intervening claims and defenses. However, by pulling these rights into Section 16, this Act does NOT validate the wholesale electrification of promissory notes under Article 3 of the Uniform Commercial Code.

Further, it is important to understand that a transferable record under Section 16, while having no counterpart under Article 3 of the Uniform Commercial Code, would be an "account," "general intangible," or "payment intangible" under Article 9 of the Uniform Commercial Code. Accordingly, two separate bodies of law would apply to that asset of the obligee. A taker of the transferable record under Section 16 may acquire purchaser rights under Article 9 of the Uniform Commercial Code, however, those rights may be defeated by a trustee in bankruptcy of a prior person in control unless perfection under Article 9 of the Uniform Commercial Code by filing is achieved. If the person in control also takes control in a manner granting it holder in due course status, of course that person would take free of any claim by a bankruptcy trustee or lien creditor.

7. Subsection (e) accords to the obligor of the transferable record rights equal to those of an obligor under an equivalent paper record. Accordingly, unless a waiver of defense clause is obtained in the electronic record, or the transferee obtains HDC rights under subsection (d), the obligor has all the rights and defenses available to it under a contract assignment. Additionally, the obligor has the right to have the payment noted or otherwise included as part of the electronic record.

8. Subsection (f) grants the obligor the right to have the transferable record and other information made available for purposes of assuring the correct person to pay. This will allow the obligor to protect its interest and obtain the defense of discharge by payment or performance. This is particularly important because a person receiving subsequent control under the appropriate circumstances may well qualify as a holder in course who can enforce payment of the transferable record.

9. Section 16 is a singular exception to the thrust of this Act to simply validate electronic media used in commercial transactions. Section 16 actually provides a means for expanding electronic commerce. It provides certainty to lenders and investors regarding the enforceability of a new class of financial services. It is hoped that the legal protections afforded by

Section 16 will engender the development of technological and business models which will permit realization of the significant cost savings and efficiencies available through electronic transacting in the financial services industry. Although only a bridge to more detailed consideration of the broad issues related to negotiability in an electronic context, Section 16 provides the impetus for that broader consideration while allowing continuation of developing technological and business models.

[SECTION 17. CREATION AND RETENTION OF ELECTRONIC RECORDS AND CONVERSION OF WRITTEN RE-CORDS BY GOVERNMENTAL AGENCIES.

[Each governmental agency] [The [designated state officer]] of this State shall determine whether, and the extent to which, [it] [a governmental agency] will create and retain electronic records and convert written records to electronic records.]

Comment

See Comments following Section 19.

[SECTION 18. ACCEPTANCE AND DISTRIBUTION OF ELECTRONIC RECORDS BY GOVERNMENTAL AGENCIES.

(a) Except as otherwise provided in Section 12(f), [each governmental agency] [the [designated state officer]] of this State shall determine whether, and the extent to which, [it] [a governmental agency] will send and accept electronic records and electronic signatures to and from other persons and otherwise create, generate, communicate, store, process, use, and rely upon electronic records and electronic signatures.

(b) To the extent that a governmental agency uses electronic records and electronic signatures under subsection (a), the [governmental agency] [designated state officer], giving due consideration to security, may specify:

(1) the manner and format in which the electronic records must be created, generated, sent, communicated, received, and stored and the systems established for those purposes;

(2) if electronic records must be signed by electronic means, the type of electronic signature required, the manner and format in which the electronic signature must be affixed to the electronic record, and the identity of, or criteria that must be met by, any third party used by a person filing a document to facilitate the process;

(3) control processes and procedures as appropriate to ensure adequate preservation, disposition, integrity, se-

curity, confidentiality, and auditability of electronic records; and

(4) any other required attributes for electronic records which are specified for corresponding nonelectronic records or reasonably necessary under the circumstances.

(c) Except as otherwise provided in Section 12(f), this [Act] does not require a governmental agency of this State to use or permit the use of electronic records or electronic signatures.]

Source: Illinois Act Section 25-101; Florida Electronic Signature Act, Chapter 96-324, Section 7 (1996).

Comment

See Comments following Section 19.

[SECTION 19. INTEROPERABILITY. The [governmental agency] [designated officer] of this State which adopts standards pursuant to Section 18 may encourage and promote consistency and interoperability with similar requirements adopted by other governmental agencies of this and other States and the federal government and nongovernmental persons interacting with governmental agencies of this State. If appropriate, those standards may specify differing levels of standards from which governmental agencies of this State may choose in implementing the most appropriate standard for a particular application.]

Source: Illinois Act Section 25-115.

See Legislative Note below—Following Comments.

Comment

1. Sections 17-19 have been bracketed as optional provisions to be considered for adoption by each State. Among the barriers to electronic commerce are barriers which exist in the use of electronic media by state governmental agencies—whether among themselves or in external dealing with the private sector. In those circumstances where the government acts as a commercial party, e.g., in areas of procurement, the general validation provisions of this Act will apply. That is to say, the government must agree to conduct transactions electronically with vendors and customers of government services.

However, there are other circumstances when government ought to establish the ability to proceed in transactions electronically. Whether in regard to records and communications within and between governmental agencies, or with respect to information and filings which must be made with governmental agencies, these sections allow a State to establish the ground work for such electronicization.

2. The provisions in Sections 17-19 are broad and very general. In many States they will be unnecessary because enacted legislation designed to facilitate governmental use of electronic records and communications is in place. However, in many States broad validating rules are needed and desired. Accordingly, this Act provides these sections as a baseline.

Of paramount importance in all States however, is the need for States to assure that whatever systems and rules are adopted, the systems established are compatible with the systems of other governmental agencies and with common systems in the private sector. A very real risk exists that implementation of systems by myriad governmental agencies and offices may create barriers because of a failure to consider compatibility, than would be the case otherwise.

3. The provisions in Section 17-19 are broad and general to provide the greatest flexibility and adaptation to the specific needs of the individual States. The differences and variations in the organization and structure of governmental agencies mandates this approach. However, it is imperative that each State always keep in mind the need to prevent the erection of barriers through appropriate coordination of systems and rules within the parameters set by the State.

4. Section 17 authorizes state agencies to use electronic records and electronic signatures generally for intra-governmental purposes, and to convert written records and manual signatures to electronic records and electronic signatures. By its terms the section gives enacting legislatures the option to leave the decision to use electronic records or convert written records and signatures to the governmental agency or assign that duty to a designated state officer. It also authorizes the destruction of written records after conversion to electronic form.

5. Section 18 broadly authorizes state agencies to send and receive electronic records and signatures in dealing with non-governmental persons. Again, the provision is permissive and not obligatory (see subsection (c)). However, it does provide specifically that with respect to electronic records used for evidentiary purposes, Section 12 will apply unless a particular agency expressly opts out.

6. Section 19 is the most important section of the three. It requires governmental agencies or state officers to take account of consistency in applications and interoperability to the extent practicable when promulgating standards. This section is critical in addressing the concern that inconsistent applications may promote barriers greater than currently exist. Without such direction the myriad systems that could develop independently would be new barriers to electronic commerce, not a removal of barriers. The key to interoperability is flexibility and adaptability. The requirement of a single system may be as big a barrier as the proliferation of many disparate systems.

Legislative Note Regarding Adoption of Sections 17-19

1. Sections 17-19 are optional sections for consideration by individual legislatures for adoption, and have been bracketed to make this clear. The inclusion or exclusion of Sections 17-19 will not have a detrimental impact on the uniformity of adoption of this Act, so long as Sections 1-16 are adopted uniformly as presented. In some States Sections 17-19 will be unnecessary because legislation is already in place to authorize and implement government use of electronic media. However, the general authorization provided by Sections 17-19 may be critical in some States which desire to move forward in this area.

2. In the event that a state legislature chooses to adopt Sections 17-19, a number of issues must be addressed:

A. Is the general authorization to adopt electronic media, provided by Sections 17-19 sufficient for the needs of the particular jurisdiction, or is more detailed and specific authorization necessary? This determination may be affected by the decision regarding the appropriate entity or person to oversee implementation of the use of electronic media (See next paragraph). Sections 17-19 are broad and general in the authorization granted. Certainly greater specificity can be added subsequent to adoption of these sections. The question for the legislature is whether greater direction and specificity is needed at this time. If so, the legislature should not enact Sections 17-19 at this time.

B.   Assuming a legislature decides to enact Sections 17-19, what entity or person should oversee implementation of the government's use of electronic media? As noted in each of Sections 17-19, again by brackets, a choice must be made regarding the entity to make critical decisions regarding the systems and rules which will govern the use of electronic media by the State. Each State will need to consider its particular structure and administration in making this determination. However, legislatures are strongly encouraged to make compatibility and interoperability considerations paramount in making this determination.

C.   Finally, a decision will have to be made regarding the process by which coordination of electronic systems will occur between the various branches of state government and among the various levels of government within the State. Again this will require consideration of the unique situation in each State.

3. If a State chooses not to enact Sections 17-19, UETA Sections 1-16 will still apply to governmental entities when acting as a "person" engaging in "transactions" within its scope. The definition of transaction includes "governmental affairs." Of course, like any other party, the circumstances surrounding a transaction must indicate that the governmental actor has agreed to act electronically (See Section 5(b)), but otherwise all the provisions of Sections 1-16 will apply to validate the use of electronic records and signatures in transactions involving governmental entities.

If a State does choose to enact Sections 17-19, Sections 1-16 will continue to apply as above. In addition, Sections 17-19 will provide authorization for intra- governmental uses of electronic media. Finally, Sections 17-19 provide a broader authorization for the State to develop systems and procedures for the use of electronic media in its relations with non-governmental entities and persons.

SECTION 20.   SEVERABILITY CLAUSE. If any provision of this [Act] or its application to any person or circumstance is held invalid, the invalidity does not affect other provisions or applications of this [Act] which can be given effect without the invalid provision or application, and to this end the provisions of this [Act] are severable.

SECTION 21.   EFFECTIVE DATE. This [Act] takes effect . . . .

APPENDIX B

Electronic Signatures in Global and National Commerce Act

PL 106-229, June 30, 2000, 114 Stat 464

UNITED STATES PUBLIC LAWS

106th Congress—Second Session

Convening January 24, 2000

Additions and Deletions are not identified in this database.

Vetoed provisions within tabular material are not displayed

PL 106-229 (S 761)

June 30, 2000

ELECTRONIC SIGNATURES IN GLOBAL AND
NATIONAL COMMERCE ACT

An Act To facilitate the use of electronic records and signatures in interstate or foreign commerce.

Be it enacted by the Senate and House of Representatives of the United States of America in Congress assembled,

«15 USCA § 7001 NOTE»

SECTION 1. SHORT TITLE.

This Act may be cited as the "Electronic Signatures in Global and National Commerce Act".

«15 USCA § 7001 prec. NOTE»

TITLE I—ELECTRONIC RECORDS AND SIGNATURES IN COMMERCE

«15 USCA § 7001»

SEC. 101.   GENERAL RULE OF VALIDITY.

(a) IN GENERAL.— Notwithstanding any statute, regulation, or other rule of law (other than this title and title II), with respect to any transaction in or affecting interstate or foreign commerce—

(1) a signature, contract, or other record relating to such transaction may not be denied legal effect, validity, or enforceability solely because it is in electronic form; and

(2) a contract relating to such transaction may not be denied legal effect, validity, or enforceability solely because an electronic signature or electronic record was used in its formation.

(b) PRESERVATION   OF   RIGHTS   AND OBLIGATIONS.— This title does not—

(1) limit, alter, or otherwise affect any requirement imposed by a statute, regulation, or rule of law relating to the rights and obligations of persons under such statute, regulation, or rule of law other than a requirement that contracts or other records be written, signed, or in nonelectronic form; or

(2) require any person to agree to use or accept electronic records or electronic signatures, other than a governmental agency with respect to a record other than a contract to which it is a party.

(c) CONSUMER DISCLOSURES.—

(1) CONSENT TO ELECTRONIC RECORDS.— Notwithstanding subsection (a), if a statute, regulation, or other rule of law requires that information relating to a transaction or transactions in or affecting interstate or foreign commerce be provided or made available to a consumer in writing, the use of an electronic record to provide or make available (whichever is required) such information satisfies the requirement that such information be in writing if—

(A) the consumer has affirmatively consented to such use and has not withdrawn such consent;

(B)   the consumer, prior to consenting, is provided with a clear and conspicuous statement—

(i)   informing the consumer of (I) any right or option of the consumer to have the record provided or made available on paper or in nonelectronic form, and (II) the right of the consumer to withdraw the consent to have the record provided or made available in an electronic form and of any conditions, consequences (which may include termination of the parties' relationship), or fees in the event of such withdrawal;

(ii)   informing the consumer of whether the consent applies (I) only to the particular transaction which gave rise to the obligation to provide the record, or (II) to identified categories of records that may be provided or made available during the course of the parties' relationship;

(iii)   describing the procedures the consumer must use to withdraw consent as provided in clause (i) and to update information needed to contact the consumer electronically; and

(iv)   informing the consumer (I) how, after the consent, the consumer may, upon request, obtain a paper copy of an electronic record, and (II) whether any fee will be charged for such copy;

(C)   the consumer—

(i)   prior to consenting, is provided with a statement of the hardware and software requirements for access to and retention of the electronic records; and

(ii)   consents electronically, or confirms his or her consent electronically, in a manner that reasonably demonstrates that the consumer can access information in the electronic form that will be used to provide the information that is the subject of the consent; and

(D)   after the consent of a consumer in accordance with subparagraph (A), if a change in the hardware or software requirements needed to access or retain electronic records creates a material risk that the consumer will not be able to access or retain a subsequent electronic record that was the subject of the consent, the person providing the electronic record—

(i)   provides the consumer with a statement of (I)

191

the revised hardware and software requirements for access to and retention of the electronic records, and (II) the right to withdraw consent without the imposition of any fees for such withdrawal and without the imposition of any condition or consequence that was not disclosed under subparagraph (B)(i); and

(ii)   again complies with subparagraph (C).

(2) OTHER RIGHTS.—

(A) PRESERVATION   OF   CONSUMER PROTECTIONS.— Nothing in this title affects the content or timing of any disclosure or other record required to be provided or made available to any consumer under any statute, regulation, or other rule of law.

(B) VERIFICATION OR ACKNOWLEDGMENT.— If a law that was enacted prior to this Act expressly requires a record to be provided or made available by a specified method that requires verification or acknowledgment of receipt, the record may be provided or made available electronically only if the method used provides verification or acknowledgment of receipt (whichever is required).

(3) EFFECT OF FAILURE TO OBTAIN ELEC-TRONIC CONSENT OR CONFIRMATION OF CONSENT.— The legal effectiveness, validity, or enforceability of any contract executed by a consumer shall not be denied solely because of the failure to obtain electronic consent or confirmation of consent by that consumer in accordance with paragraph (1)(C)(ii).

(4) PROSPECTIVE EFFECT.— Withdrawal of consent by a consumer shall not affect the legal effectiveness, validity, or enforceability of electronic records provided or made available to that consumer in accordance with paragraph (1) prior to implementation of the consumer's withdrawal of consent. A consumer's withdrawal of consent shall be effective within a reasonable period of time after receipt of the withdrawal by the provider of the record. Failure to comply with paragraph (1)(D) may, at the election of the consumer, be treated as a withdrawal of consent for purposes of this paragraph.

(5) PRIOR CONSENT.— This subsection does not apply to any records that are provided or made available to a consumer who has consented prior to the effective

date of this title to receive such records in electronic form as permitted by any statute, regulation, or other rule of law.

(6) ORAL COMMUNICATIONS.— An oral communication or a recording of an oral communication shall not qualify as an electronic record for purposes of this subsection except as otherwise provided under applicable law.

(d) RETENTION OF CONTRACTS AND RECORDS.—

(1) ACCURACY AND ACCESSIBILITY.— If a statute, regulation, or other rule of law requires that a contract or other record relating to a transaction in or affecting interstate or foreign commerce be retained, that requirement is met by retaining an electronic record of the information in the contract or other record that—

(A) accurately reflects the information set forth in the contract or other record; and

(B) remains accessible to all persons who are entitled to access by statute, regulation, or rule of law, for the period required by such statute, regulation, or rule of law, in a form that is capable of being accurately reproduced for later reference, whether by transmission, printing, or otherwise.

(2) EXCEPTION.— A requirement to retain a contract or other record in accordance with paragraph (1) does not apply to any information whose sole purpose is to enable the contract or other record to be sent, communicated, or received.

(3) ORIGINALS.— If a statute, regulation, or other rule of law requires a contract or other record relating to a transaction in or affecting interstate or foreign commerce to be provided, available, or retained in its original form, or provides consequences if the contract or other record is not provided, available, or retained in its original form, that statute, regulation, or rule of law is satisfied by an electronic record that complies with paragraph (1).

(4) CHECKS.— If a statute, regulation, or other rule of law requires the retention of a check, that requirement is satisfied by retention of an electronic record of the information on the front and back of the check in accordance with paragraph (1).

(e) ACCURACY AND ABILITY TO RETAIN CONTRACTS AND OTHER RECORDS.— Notwithstanding subsection (a), if a statute, regulation, or other rule of law requires that a contract or other record relating to a transaction in or affecting interstate or foreign commerce be in writing, the legal effect, validity, or enforceability of an electronic record of such contract or other record may be denied if such electronic record is not in a form that is capable of being retained and accurately reproduced for later reference by all parties or persons who are entitled to retain the contract or other record.

(f) PROXIMITY.— Nothing in this title affects the proximity required by any statute, regulation, or other rule of law with respect to any warning, notice, disclosure, or other record required to be posted, displayed, or publicly affixed.

(g) NOTARIZATION AND ACKNOWLEDGMENT.— If a statute, regulation, or other rule of law requires a signature or record relating to a transaction in or affecting interstate or foreign commerce to be notarized, acknowledged, verified, or made under oath, that requirement is satisfied if the electronic signature of the person authorized to perform those acts, together with all other information required to be included by other applicable statute, regulation, or rule of law, is attached to or logically associated with the signature or record.

(h) ELECTRONIC AGENTS.— A contract or other record relating to a transaction in or affecting interstate or foreign commerce may not be denied legal effect, validity, or enforceability solely because its formation, creation, or delivery involved the action of one or more electronic agents so long as the action of any such electronic agent is legally attributable to the person to be bound.

(i) INSURANCE.— It is the specific intent of the Congress that this title and title II apply to the business of insurance.

(j) INSURANCE AGENTS AND BROKERS.— An insurance agent or broker acting under the direction of a party that enters into a contract by means of an electronic record or electronic signature may not be held liable for any deficiency in the electronic procedures agreed to by the parties under that contract if—

(1) the agent or broker has not engaged in negligent, reckless, or intentional tortious conduct;

(2) the agent or broker was not involved in the

development or establishment of such electronic procedures; and

(3) the agent or broker did not deviate from such procedures.

«15 USCA § 7002»

SEC. 102. EXEMPTION TO PREEMPTION.

(a) IN GENERAL.— A State statute, regulation, or other rule of law may modify, limit, or supersede the provisions of section 101 with respect to State law only if such statute, regulation, or rule of law—

(1) constitutes an enactment or adoption of the Uniform Electronic Transactions Act as approved and recommended for enactment in all the States by the National Conference of Commissioners on Uniform State Laws in 1999, except that any exception to the scope of such Act enacted by a State under section 3(b)(4) of such Act shall be preempted to the extent such exception is inconsistent with this title or title II, or would not be permitted under paragraph (2)(A)(ii) of this subsection; or

(2) (A) specifies the alternative procedures or requirements for the use or acceptance (or both) of electronic records or electronic signatures to establish the legal effect, validity, or enforceability of contracts or other records, if—

(i) such alternative procedures or requirements are consistent with this title and title II; and

(ii) such alternative procedures or requirements do not require, or accord greater legal status or effect to, the implementation or application of a specific technology or technical specification for performing the functions of creating, storing, generating, receiving, communicating, or authenticating electronic records or electronic signatures; and

(B) if enacted or adopted after the date of the enactment of this Act, makes specific reference to this Act.

(b) EXCEPTIONS FOR ACTIONS BY STATES AS MARKET PARTICIPANTS.— Subsection (a)(2)(A)(ii) shall not apply to the statutes, regulations, or other rules of law governing procurement by any State, or any agency or instrumentality thereof.

(c) PREVENTION OF CIRCUMVENTION.— Subsection (a) does not permit a State to circumvent this title or title II through the imposition of nonelectronic delivery methods under section 8(b)(2) of the Uniform Electronic Transactions Act.

«15 USCA § 7003»

SEC. 103.   SPECIFIC EXCEPTIONS.

(a) EXCEPTED REQUIREMENTS.— The provisions of section 101 shall not apply to a contract or other record to the extent it is governed by—

(1) a statute, regulation, or other rule of law governing the creation and execution of wills, codicils, or testamentary trusts;

(2) a State statute, regulation, or other rule of law governing adoption, divorce, or other matters of family law; or

(3) the Uniform Commercial Code, as in effect in any State, other than sections 1–107 and 1–206 and Articles 2 and 2A.

(b) ADDITIONAL EXCEPTIONS.— The provisions of section 101 shall not apply to—

(1) court orders or notices, or official court documents (including briefs, pleadings, and other writings) required to be executed in connection with court proceedings;

(2) any notice of—

(A)   the cancellation or termination of utility services (including water, heat, and power);

(B)   default, acceleration, repossession, foreclosure, or eviction, or the right to cure, under a credit agreement secured by, or a rental agreement for, a primary residence of an individual;

(C)   the cancellation or termination of health insurance or benefits or life insurance benefits (excluding annuities); or

(D)   recall of a product, or material failure of a product, that risks endangering health or safety; or

(3) any document required to accompany any transportation or handling of hazardous materials, pesticides, or other toxic or dangerous materials.

(c) REVIEW OF EXCEPTIONS.—

(1) EVALUATION REQUIRED.— The Secretary of Commerce, acting through the Assistant Secretary for

Communications and Information, shall review the operation of the exceptions in subsections (a) and (b) to evaluate, over a period of 3 years, whether such exceptions continue to be necessary for the protection of consumers. Within 3 years after the date of enactment of this Act, the Assistant Secretary shall submit a report to the Congress on the results of such e valuation.

(2) DETERMINATIONS.— If a Federal regulatory agency, with respect to matter within its jurisdiction, determines after notice and an opportunity for public comment, and publishes a finding, that one or more such exceptions are no longer necessary for the protection of consumers and eliminating such exceptions will not increase the material risk of harm to consumers, such agency may extend the application of section 101 to the exceptions identified in such finding.

«15 USCA § 7004»

SEC. 104. APPLICABILITY TO FEDERAL AND STATE GOVERNMENTS.

(a) FILING AND ACCESS REQUIREMENTS.— Subject to subsection (c)(2), nothing in this title limits or supersedes any requirement by a Federal regulatory agency, self-regulatory organization, or State regulatory agency that records be filed with such agency or organization in accordance with specified standards or formats.

(b) PRESERVATION OF EXISTING RULEMAKING AUTHORITY.—

(1) USE OF AUTHORITY TO INTERPRET.— Subject to paragraph (2) and subsection (c), a Federal regulatory agency or State regulatory agency that is responsible for rulemaking under any other statute may interpret section 101 with respect to such statute through—

(A) the issuance of regulations pursuant to a statute; or

(B) to the extent such agency is authorized by statute to issue orders or guidance, the issuance of orders or guidance of general applicability that are publicly available and published (in the Federal Register in the case of an order or guidance issued by a Federal regulatory agency).

This paragraph does not grant any Federal regulatory agency or State regulatory agency authority to issue regulations, orders, or guidance pursuant to any statute that does not authorize such issuance.

(2) LIMITATIONS ON INTERPRETATION AUTHORITY.— Notwithstanding paragraph (1), a Federal regulatory agency shall not adopt any regulation, order, or guidance described in paragraph (1), and a State regulatory agency is preempted by section 101 from adopting any regulation, order, or guidance described in paragraph (1), unless—

(A)   such regulation, order, or guidance is consistent with section 101;

(B)   such regulation, order, or guidance does not add to the requirements of such section; and

(C)   such agency finds, in connection with the issuance of such regulation, order, or guidance, that—

(i)   there is a substantial justification for the regulation, order, or guidance;

(ii)   the methods selected to carry out that purpose—

(I)   are substantially equivalent to the requirements imposed on records that are not electronic records; and

(II)   will not impose unreasonable costs on the acceptance and use of electronic records; and

(iii)   the methods selected to carry out that purpose do not require, or accord greater legal status or effect to, the implementation or application of a specific technology or technical specification for performing the functions of creating, storing, generating, receiving, communicating, or authenticating electronic records or electronic signatures.

(3) PERFORMANCE STANDARDS.—

(A) ACCURACY, RECORD INTEGRITY, ACCESSIBILITY.— Notwithstanding paragraph (2)(C)(iii), a Federal regulatory agency or State regulatory agency may interpret section 101(d) to specify performance standards to assure accuracy, record integrity, and accessibility of records that are required to be retained. Such performance standards may be specified in a manner that imposes a requirement in violation of paragraph (2)(C)(iii) if the requirement (i) serves an important governmental objective; and (ii) is substantially related to the achievement of that objective. Nothing in this paragraph shall be construed to grant any Federal regulatory agency or State regulatory agency authority to require use of a particular type of software or hardware in order to comply with section 101(d).

(B) PAPER OR PRINTED FORM.— Notwithstanding subsection (c)(1), a Federal regulatory agency or State regulatory agency may interpret section 101(d) to require retention of a record in a tangible printed or paper form if—

(i) there is a compelling governmental interest relating to law enforcement or national security for imposing such requirement; and

(ii) imposing such requirement is essential to attaining such interest.

(4) EXCEPTIONS FOR ACTIONS BY GOVERNMENT AS MARKET PARTICIPANT.— Paragraph (2)(C)(iii) shall not apply to the statutes, regulations, or other rules of law governing procurement by the Federal or any State government, or any agency or instrumentality thereof.

(c) ADDITIONAL LIMITATIONS.—

(1) REIMPOSING PAPER PROHIBITED.— Nothing in subsection (b) (other than paragraph (3)(B) thereof) shall be construed to grant any Federal regulatory agency or State regulatory agency authority to impose or reimpose any requirement that a record be in a tangible printed or paper form.

(2) CONTINUING OBLIGATION UNDER GOVERNMENT PAPERWORK ELIMINATION ACT.— Nothing in subsection (a) or (b) relieves any Federal regulatory agency of its obligations under the Government Paperwork Elimination Act (title XVII of Public Law 105-277).

(d) AUTHORITY TO EXEMPT FROM CONSENT PROVISION.—

(1) IN GENERAL.— A Federal regulatory agency may, with respect to matter within its jurisdiction, by regulation or order issued after notice and an opportunity for public comment, exempt without condition a specified category or type of record from the requirements relating to consent in section 101(c) if such exemption is necessary to eliminate a substantial burden on electronic commerce and will not increase the material risk of harm to consumers.

(2) PROSPECTUSES.— Within 30 days after the date

of enactment of this Act, the Securities and Exchange Commission shall issue a regulation or order pursuant to paragraph (1) exempting from section 101(c) any records that are required to be provided in order to allow advertising, sales literature, or other information concerning a security issued by an investment company that is registered under the Investment Company Act of 1940, or concerning the issuer thereof, to be excluded from the definition of a prospectus under section 2(a)(10)(A) of the Securities Act of 1933.

(e) ELECTRONIC LETTERS OF AGENCY.— The Federal Communications Commission shall not hold any contract for telecommunications service or letter of agency for a preferred carrier change, that otherwise complies with the Commission's rules, to be legally ineffective, invalid, or unenforceable solely because an electronic record or electronic signature was used in its formation or authorization.

«15 USCA § 7005»

SEC. 105. STUDIES.

(a) DELIVERY.— Within 12 months after the date of the enactment of this Act, the Secretary of Commerce shall conduct an inquiry regarding the effectiveness of the delivery of electronic records to consumers using electronic mail as compared with delivery of written records via the United States Postal Service and private express mail services. The Secretary shall submit a report to the Congress regarding the results of such inquiry by the conclusion of such 12–month period.

(b) STUDY OF ELECTRONIC CONSENT.— Within 12 months after the date of the enactment of this Act, the Secretary of Commerce and the Federal Trade Commission shall submit a report to the Congress evaluating any benefits provided to consumers by the procedure required by section 101(c)(1)(C)(ii); any burdens imposed on electronic commerce by that provision; whether the benefits outweigh the burdens; whether the absence of the procedure required by section 101(c)(1)(C)(ii) would increase the incidence of fraud directed against consumers; and suggesting any revisions to the provision deemed appropriate by the Secretary and the Commission. In conducting this evaluation, the Secretary and the Commission shall solicit comment from the general public, consumer representatives, and electronic commerce businesses.

«15 USCA § 7006»

SEC. 106. DEFINITIONS.

For purposes of this title:

(1) CONSUMER.— The term "consumer" means an individual who obtains, through a transaction, products or services which are used primarily for personal, family, or household purposes, and also means the legal representative of such an individual.

(2) ELECTRONIC.— The term "electronic" means relating to technology having electrical, digital, magnetic, wireless, optical, electromagnetic, or similar capabilities.

(3) ELECTRONIC AGENT.— The term "electronic agent" means a computer program or an electronic or other automated means used independently to initiate an action or respond to electronic records or performances in whole or in part without review or action by an individual at the time of the action or response.

(4) ELECTRONIC RECORD.— The term "electronic record" means a contract or other record created, generated, sent, communicated, received, or stored by electronic means.

(5) ELECTRONIC SIGNATURE.— The term "electronic signature" means an electronic sound, symbol, or process, attached to or logically associated with a contract or other record and executed or adopted by a person with the intent to sign the record.

(6) FEDERAL REGULATORY AGENCY.— The term "Federal regulatory agency" means an agency, as that term is defined in section 552(f) of title 5, United States Code.

(7) INFORMATION.— The term "information" means data, text, images, sounds, codes, computer programs, software, databases, or the like.

(8) PERSON.— The term "person" means an individual, corporation, business trust, estate, trust, partnership, limited liability company, association, joint venture, governmental agency, public corporation, or any other legal or commercial entity.

(9) RECORD.— The term "record" means information that is inscribed on a tangible medium or that is stored in an electronic or other medium and is retrievable in perceivable form.

(10) REQUIREMENT.— The term "requirement" includes a prohibition.

(11) SELF–REGULATORY ORGANIZATION.— The term "self-regulatory organization" means an organization or entity that is not a Federal regulatory agency or a State, but that is under the supervision of a Federal regulatory agency and is authorized under Federal law to adopt and administer rules applicable to its members that are enforced by such organization or entity, by a Federal regulatory agency, or by another self-regulatory organization.

(12) STATE.— The term "State" includes the District of Columbia and the territories and possessions of the United States.

(13) TRANSACTION.— The term "transaction" means an action or set of actions relating to the conduct of business, consumer, or commercial affairs between two or more persons, including any of the following types of conduct—

(A) the sale, lease, exchange, licensing, or other disposition of (i) personal property, including goods and intangibles, (ii) services, and (iii) any combination thereof; and

(B) the sale, lease, exchange, or other disposition of any interest in real property, or any combination thereof.

«15 USCA § 7001 NOTE»

SEC. 107.   EFFECTIVE DATE.

(a) IN GENERAL.— Except as provided in subsection (b), this title shall be effective on October 1, 2000.

(b) EXCEPTIONS.—

(1) RECORD RETENTION.—

(A) IN GENERAL.— Subject to subparagraph (B), this title shall be effective on March 1, 2001, with respect to a requirement that a record be retained imposed by—

(i) a Federal statute, regulation, or other rule of law, or

(ii) a State statute, regulation, or other rule of law administered or promulgated by a State regulatory agency.

(B) DELAYED   EFFECT   FOR   PENDING

RULEMAKINGS.— If on March 1, 2001, a Federal regulatory agency or State regulatory agency has announced, proposed, or initiated, but not completed, a rulemaking proceeding to prescribe a regulation under section 104(b)(3) with respect to a requirement described in subparagraph (A), this title shall be effective on June 1, 2001, with respect to such requirement.

(2) CERTAIN GUARANTEED AND INSURED LOANS.— With regard to any transaction involving a loan guarantee or loan guarantee commitment (as those terms are defined in section 502 of the Federal Credit Reform Act of 1990), or involving a program listed in the Federal Credit Supplement, Budget of the United States, FY 2001, this title applies only to such transactions entered into, and to any loan or mortgage made, insured, or guaranteed by the United States Government thereunder, on and after one year after the date of enactment of this Act.

(3) STUDENT LOANS.— With respect to any records that are provided or made available to a consumer pursuant to an application for a loan, or a loan made, pursuant to title IV of the Higher Education Act of 1965, section 101(c) of this Act shall not apply until the earlier of—

(A) such time as the Secretary of Education publishes revised promissory notes under section 432(m) of the Higher Education Act of 1965; or

(B) one year after the date of enactment of this Act.

«15 USCA § 7021 prec. NOTE»

TITLE II—TRANSFERABLE RECORDS

«15 USCA § 7021»

SEC. 201. TRANSFERABLE RECORDS.

(a) DEFINITIONS.— For purposes of this section:

(1) TRANSFERABLE RECORD.— The term "transferable record" means an electronic record that—

(A) would be a note under Article 3 of the Uniform Commercial Code if the electronic record were in writing;

(B) the issuer of the electronic record expressly has agreed is a transferable record; and

(C) relates to a loan secured by real property.

A transferable record may be executed using an electronic signature.

(2) OTHER DEFINITIONS.— The terms "electronic record", "electronic signature", and "person" have the same meanings provided in section 106 of this Act.

(b) CONTROL.— A person has control of a transferable record if a system employed for evidencing the transfer of interests in the transferable record reliably establishes that person as the person to which the transferable record was issued or transferred.

(c) CONDITIONS.— A system satisfies subsection (b), and a person is deemed to have control of a transferable record, if the transferable record is created, stored, and assigned in such a manner that—

(1) a single authoritative copy of the transferable record exists which is unique, identifiable, and, except as otherwise provided in paragraphs (4), (5), and (6), unalterable;

(2) the authoritative copy identifies the person asserting control as—

(A) the person to which the transferable record was issued; or

(B) if the authoritative copy indicates that the transferable record has been transferred, the person to which the transferable record was most recently transferred;

(3) the authoritative copy is communicated to and maintained by the person asserting control or its designated custodian;

(4) copies or revisions that add or change an identified assignee of the authoritative copy can be made only with the consent of the person asserting control;

(5) each copy of the authoritative copy and any copy of a copy is readily identifiable as a copy that is not the authoritative copy; and

(6) any revision of the authoritative copy is readily identifiable as authorized or unauthorized.

(d) STATUS AS HOLDER.— Except as otherwise agreed, a person having control of a transferable record is the holder, as defined in section 1-201(20) of the Uniform Commercial Code, of the transferable record and has the same rights and defenses as a holder of an equivalent record or writing under the Uniform Commercial Code, including, if the applicable statutory requirements under section 3–302(a), 9–308, or revised section 9-330 of the Uniform Commercial Code are satisfied, the rights and defenses of a holder in due course or a purchaser, respectively. Delivery, possession, and endorsement are not required to obtain or exercise any of the rights under this subsection.

(e) OBLIGOR RIGHTS.— Except as otherwise agreed, an obligor under a transferable record has the same rights and defenses as an equivalent obligor under equivalent records or writings under the Uniform Commercial Code.

(f) PROOF OF CONTROL.— If requested by a person against which enforcement is sought, the person seeking to enforce the transferable record shall provide reasonable proof that the person is in control of the transferable record. Proof may include access to the authoritative copy of the transferable record and related business records sufficient to review the terms of the transferable record and to establish the identity of the person having control of the transferable record.

(g) UCC REFERENCES.— For purposes of this subsection, all references to the Uniform Commercial Code are to the Uniform Commercial Code as in effect in the jurisdiction the law of which governs the transferable record.

«15 USCA § 7021 NOTE»

SEC. 202. EFFECTIVE DATE.

This title shall be effective 90 days after the date of enactment of this Act.

«15 USCA § 7031 prec. NOTE»

TITLE III—PROMOTION OF INTERNATIONAL ELECTRONIC COMMERCE

«15 USCA § 7031»

SEC. 301. PRINCIPLES GOVERNING THE USE OF ELECTRONIC SIGNATURES IN INTERNATIONAL TRANSACTIONS.

(a) PROMOTION OF ELECTRONIC SIGNATURES.—

(1) REQUIRED ACTIONS.— The Secretary of Commerce shall promote the acceptance and use, on an international basis, of electronic signatures in accordance with the principles specified in paragraph (2) and

in a manner consistent with section 101 of this Act. The Secretary of Commerce shall take all actions necessary in a manner consistent with such principles to eliminate or reduce, to the maximum extent possible, the impediments to commerce in electronic signatures, for the purpose of facilitating the development of interstate and foreign commerce.

(2) PRINCIPLES.— The principles specified in this paragraph are the following:

(A) Remove paper-based obstacles to electronic transactions by adopting relevant principles from the Model Law on Electronic Commerce adopted in 1996 by the United Nations Commission on International Trade Law.

(B) Permit parties to a transaction to determine the appropriate authentication technologies and implementation models for their transactions, with assurance that those technologies and implementation models will be recognized and enforced.

(C) Permit parties to a transaction to have the opportunity to prove in court or other proceedings that their authentication approaches and their transactions are valid.

(D) Take a nondiscriminatory approach to electronic signatures and authentication methods from other jurisdictions.

(b) CONSULTATION.— In conducting the activities required by this section, the Secretary shall consult with users and providers of electronic signature products and services and other interested persons.

(c) DEFINITIONS.— As used in this section, the terms "electronic record" and "electronic signature" have the same meanings provided in section 106 of this Act.

TITLE IV—COMMISSION ON ONLINE CHILD PROTECTION

«47 USCA § 231 NOTE»

SEC. 401. AUTHORITY TO ACCEPT GIFTS.

Section 1405 of the Child Online Protection Act (47 U.S.C. 231 note) is amended by inserting after subsection (g) the following new subsection:

"(h) GIFTS, BEQUESTS, AND DEVISES.—The Commission may accept, use, and dispose of gifts, bequests, or devises of services or property, both real (including the use of office space) and personal, for the purpose of aiding or facilitating the work of the Commission. Gifts or grants not used at the termination of the Commission shall be returned to the donor or grantee.".

Approved June 30, 2000.

APPENDIX C

N.Y. BitLicense

NEW YORK STATE DEPARTMENT OF FINANCIAL SERVICES

NEW YORK CODES, RULES AND REGULATIONS

TITLE 23. DEPARTMENT OF FINANCIAL SERVICES

CHAPTER I. REGULATIONS OF THE SUPERINTENDENT OF FINANCIAL SERVICES

PART 200. VIRTUAL CURRENCIES
(ALL MATERIAL IS NEW)

Statutory Authority: Financial Services Law Sections 102, 104, 201, 206, 301, 302, 309, and 408

Section 200.1. Introduction

This Part contains regulations relating to the conduct of business involving Virtual Currency, as defined herein, in accordance with the superintendent's powers pursuant to the above-stated authority.

Section 200.2. Definitions

For purposes of this Part only, the following definitions shall apply:

(a) *Affiliate* means any Person that directly or indirectly controls, is controlled by, or is under common control with, another Person;

(b) *Cyber Security Event* means any act or attempt, successful or unsuccessful, to gain unauthorized access to, disrupt, or misuse a Licensee's electronic systems or information stored on such systems;

(c) *Department* means the New York State Department of Financial Services;

(d) *Exchange Service* means the conversion or exchange of Fiat Currency or other value into Virtual Currency, the conversion or exchange of Virtual Currency into Fiat Currency or other value, or the conversion or exchange of one form of Virtual Currency into another form of Virtual Currency;

(e) *Fiat Currency* means government-issued currency that is designated as legal tender in its country of issuance through government decree, regulation, or law;

(f) *Licensee* means any Person duly licensed by the superintendent pursuant to this Part;

(g) *New York* means the State of New York;

(h) *New York Resident* means any Person that resides, is located, has a place of business, or is conducting business in New York;

(i) *Person* means an individual, partnership, corporation, association, joint stock association, trust, or other entity, however organized;

(j) *Prepaid Card* means an electronic payment device that: (i) is usable at a single merchant or an affiliated group of merchants that share the same name, mark, or logo, or is usable at multiple, unaffiliated merchants or service providers; (ii) is issued in and for a specified amount of Fiat Currency; (iii) can be reloaded in and for only Fiat Currency, if at all; (iv) is issued and/or reloaded on a prepaid basis for the future purchase or delivery of goods or services; (v) is honored upon presentation; and (vi) can be redeemed in and for only Fiat Currency, if at all;

(k) *Principal Officer* means an executive officer of an entity, including, but not limited to, the chief executive, financial, operating, and compliance officers, president, general counsel, managing partner, general partner, controlling partner, and trustee, as applicable;

(l) *Principal Stockholder* means any Person that directly or indirectly owns, controls, or holds with power to vote ten percent or more of any class of outstanding capital stock or other equity interest of an entity or possesses the power to direct or cause the direction of the management or policies of the entity;

(m) *Principal Beneficiary* means any Person entitled to ten percent or more of the benefits of a trust;

(n) *Qualified Custodian* means a bank, trust company, national bank, savings bank, savings and loan association, federal savings association, credit union, or federal credit union in the State of New York, subject to the prior approval of the superintendent. To the extent applicable, terms used in this definition shall have the meaning ascribed by the Banking Law;

(o) *Transmission* means the transfer, by or through a third party, of Virtual Currency from a Person to a Person, including the transfer from the account or storage repository of a Person to the account or storage repository of a Person;

(p) *Virtual Currency* means any type of digital unit that is used as a medium of exchange or a form of digitally stored value. Virtual Currency shall be broadly construed to include digital units of exchange that (i) have a centralized repository or administrator; (ii) are decentralized and have no centralized repository or administrator; or (iii) may be created or obtained by computing or manufacturing effort. Virtual Currency shall not be construed to include any of the following:

(1)   digital units that (i) are used solely within online gaming platforms, (ii) have no market or application outside of those gaming platforms, (iii) cannot be converted into, or redeemed for, Fiat Currency or Virtual Currency, and (iv) may or may not be redeemable for real-world goods, services, discounts, or purchases.

(2)   digital units that can be redeemed for goods, services, discounts, or purchases as part of a customer affinity or rewards program with the issuer and/or other designated merchants or can be redeemed for digital units in another customer affinity or rewards program, but cannot be converted into, or redeemed for, Fiat Currency or Virtual Currency; or

(3)   digital units used as part of Prepaid Cards;

(q) *Virtual Currency Business Activity* means the conduct of any one of the following types of activities involving New York or a New York Resident:

(1)   receiving Virtual Currency for Transmission or Transmitting Virtual Currency, except where the transaction is undertaken for non-financial purposes and does not involve the transfer of more than a nominal amount of Virtual Currency;

(2)   storing, holding, or maintaining custody or control of Virtual Currency on behalf of others;

(3)   buying and selling Virtual Currency as a customer business;

(4)   performing Exchange Services as a customer business; or

(5)   controlling, administering, or issuing a Virtual Currency.

The development and dissemination of software in and of itself does not constitute Virtual Currency Business Activity.

Section 200.3.   License

(a) License required. No Person shall, without a license obtained from the superintendent as provided in this Part, engage in any Virtual Currency Business Activity. Licensees are not authorized to exercise fiduciary powers, as defined under Section 100 of the Banking Law.

(b) Unlicensed agents prohibited. Each Licensee is prohibited from conducting any Virtual Currency Business Activity through an agent or agency arrangement when the agent is not a Licensee.

(c) Exemption from licensing requirements. The following Persons are exempt from the licensing requirements otherwise applicable under this Part:

(1) Persons that are chartered under the New York Banking Law and are approved by the superintendent to engage in Virtual Currency Business Activity; and

(2) merchants and consumers that utilize Virtual Currency solely for the purchase or sale of goods or services or for investment purposes.

Section 200.4. Application

(a) Application for a license required under this Part shall be in writing, under oath, and in a form prescribed by the superintendent, and shall contain the following:

(1) the exact name of the applicant, including any doing business as name, the form of organization, the date of organization, and the jurisdiction where organized or incorporated;

(2) a list of all of the applicant's Affiliates and an organization chart illustrating the relationship among the applicant and such Affiliates;

(3) a list of, and detailed biographical information for, each individual applicant and each director, Principal Officer, Principal Stockholder, and Principal Beneficiary of the applicant, as applicable, including such individual's name, physical and mailing addresses, and information and documentation regarding such individual's personal history, experience, and qualification, which shall be accompanied by a form of authority, executed by such individual, to release information to the Department;

(4) a background report prepared by an independent investigatory agency acceptable to the superintendent for each individual applicant, and each Principal Officer, Principal Stockholder, and Principal Beneficiary of the applicant, as applicable;

(5) for each individual applicant; for each Principal Officer, Principal Stockholder, and Principal Beneficiary of the applicant, as applicable; and for all individuals to be employed by the applicant who have access to any

customer funds, whether denominated in Fiat Currency or Virtual Currency: (i) a set of completed fingerprints, or a receipt indicating the vendor (which vendor must be acceptable to the superintendent) at which, and the date when, the fingerprints were taken, for submission to the State Division of Criminal Justice Services and the Federal Bureau of Investigation; (ii) if applicable, such processing fees as prescribed by the superintendent; and (iii) two portrait-style photographs of the individuals measuring not more than two inches by two inches;

(6) an organization chart of the applicant and its management structure, including its Principal Officers or senior management, indicating lines of authority and the allocation of duties among its Principal Officers or senior management;

(7) a current financial statement for the applicant and each Principal Officer, Principal Stockholder, and Principal Beneficiary of the applicant, as applicable, and a projected balance sheet and income statement for the following year of the applicant's operation;

(8) a description of the proposed, current, and historical business of the applicant, including detail on the products and services provided and to be provided, all associated website addresses, the jurisdictions in which the applicant is engaged in business, the principal place of business, the primary market of operation, the projected customer base, any specific marketing targets, and the physical address of any operation in New York;

(9) details of all banking arrangements;

(10) all written policies and procedures required by, or related to, the requirements of this Part;

(11) an affidavit describing any pending or threatened administrative, civil, or criminal action, litigation, or proceeding before any governmental agency, court, or arbitration tribunal against the applicant or any of its directors, Principal Officers, Principal Stockholders, and Principal Beneficiaries, as applicable, including the names of the parties, the nature of the proceeding, and the current status of the proceeding;

(12) verification from the New York State Department of Taxation and Finance that the applicant is compliant with all New York State tax obligations in a form acceptable to the superintendent;

(13) if applicable, a copy of any insurance policies maintained for the benefit of the applicant, its directors or officers, or its customers;

(14) an explanation of the methodology used to calculate the value of Virtual Currency in Fiat Currency; and

(15) such other additional information as the superintendent may require.

(b) As part of such application, the applicant shall demonstrate that it will be compliant with all of the requirements of this Part upon licensing.

(c) Notwithstanding Subsection (b) of this Section, the superintendent may in his or her sole discretion and consistent with the purposes and intent of the Financial Services Law and this Part approve an application by granting a conditional license.

(1) A conditional license may be issued to an applicant that does not satisfy all of the regulatory requirements upon licensing.

(2) A Licensee that holds a conditional license may be subject to heightened review, whether in regard to the scope and frequency of examination or otherwise.

(3) Unless the superintendent removes the conditional status of or renews a conditional license, said license shall expire two years after its date of issuance.

i) The superintendent may in his or her sole discretion and consistent with the purposes and intent of the Financial Services Law and this Part:

(A) renew a conditional license for an additional length of time; or

(B) remove the conditional status from a conditional license.

(4) A conditional license may be suspended or revoked pursuant to Section 200.6 of this Part.

(5) A conditional license may impose any reasonable condition or conditions, as determined by the superintendent in his or her sole discretion.

(6) The superintendent may remove any condition or conditions from a conditional license that has been issued.

(7) In determining whether to issue a conditional license, renew or remove the conditional status of a

conditional license, or impose or remove any specific conditions on a conditional license, the superintendent may consider any relevant factor or factors. Relevant factors may include but are not limited to:

i) the nature and scope of the applicant's or Licensee's business;

ii) the anticipated volume of business to be transacted by the applicant or Licensee;

iii) the nature and scope of the risks that the applicant's or Licensee's business presents to consumers, Virtual Currency markets, financial markets, and the general public;

iv) the measures which the applicant or Licensee has taken to limit or mitigate the risks its business presents;

v) whether the applicant or Licensee is registered with FinCEN;

vi) whether the applicant or Licensee is licensed, registered, or otherwise authorized by any governmental or self-regulatory authority to engage in financial services or other business activities;

vii) the applicant's or Licensee's financial services or other business experience; and

viii) the Licensee's history as a holder of a conditional license issued by the superintendent.

(d) The superintendent may permit that any application for a license under this Part, or any other submission required by this Part, be made or executed by electronic means.

Section 200.5. Application fees

As part of an application for licensing under this Part, each applicant must submit an initial application fee, in the amount of five thousand dollars, to cover the cost of processing the application, reviewing application materials, and investigating the financial condition and responsibility, financial and business experience, and character and general fitness of the applicant. If the application is denied or withdrawn, such fee shall not be refunded. Each Licensee may be required to pay fees to the Department to process additional applications related to the license.

Section 200.6. Action by superintendent

(a) Generally. Upon the filing of an application for licensing under this Part, payment of the required fee, and demonstration by the applicant of its ability to comply with the provisions of this Part upon licensing, the superintendent shall investigate the financial condition and responsibility, financial and business experience, and character and general fitness of the applicant. If the superintendent finds these qualities are such as to warrant the belief that the applicant's business will be conducted honestly, fairly, equitably, carefully, and efficiently within the purposes and intent of this Part, and in a manner commanding the confidence and trust of the community, the superintendent shall advise the applicant in writing of his or her approval of the application, and shall issue to the applicant a license to conduct Virtual Currency Business Activity, subject to the provisions of this Part and such other conditions as the superintendent shall deem appropriate; or the superintendent may deny the application.

(b) Approval or denial of application. The superintendent shall approve or deny every application for a license hereunder within 90 days from the filing of an application deemed by the superintendent to be complete. Such period of 90 days may be extended at the discretion of the superintendent for such additional reasonable period of time as may be required to enable compliance with this Part. A license issued pursuant to this Part shall remain in full force and effect until it is surrendered by the Licensee, is revoked or suspended, or expires as provided in this Part.

(c) Suspension or revocation of license. The superintendent may suspend or revoke a license issued under this Part on any ground on which the superintendent might refuse to issue an original license, for a violation of any provision of this Part, for good cause shown, or for failure of the Licensee to pay a judgment, recovered in any court, within or without this State, by a claimant or creditor in an action arising out of, or relating to, the Licensee's Virtual Currency Business Activity, within thirty days after the judgment becomes final or within thirty days after expiration or termination of a stay of execution thereon; provided, however, that if execution on the judgment is stayed, by court order or operation of law or otherwise, then proceedings to suspend or revoke the license (for failure of the Licensee to pay such judgment) may not be commenced by the superintendent during the time of such stay, and for thirty days thereafter. "Good cause" shall exist when a Licensee has defaulted or is likely to default in performing its obligations or financial engagements or engages in unlawful, dishonest, wrongful, or inequitable conduct or practices that may cause harm to the public.

(d) Hearing. No license issued under this Part shall be revoked or suspended except after a hearing thereon. The superintendent shall give a Licensee no less than ten days' written notice of the time and place of such hearing by registered or certified mail addressed to the principal place of business of such Licensee. Any order of the superintendent suspending or revoking such license shall state the grounds upon which it is based and be sent by registered or certified mail to the Licensee at its principal place of business as shown in the records of the Department.

(e) Preliminary injunction. The superintendent may, when deemed by the superintendent to be in the public interest, seek a preliminary injunction to restrain a Licensee from continuing to perform acts that violate any provision of this Part, the Financial Services Law, Banking Law, or Insurance Law.

(f) Preservation of powers. Nothing in this Part shall be construed as limiting any power granted to the superintendent under any other provision of the Financial Services Law, Banking Law, or Insurance Law, including any power to investigate possible violations of law, rule, or regulation or to impose penalties or take any other action against any Person for violation of such laws, rules, or regulations.

Section 200.7. Compliance

(a) Generally. Each Licensee is required to comply with all applicable federal and state laws, rules, and regulations.

(b) Compliance officer. Each Licensee shall designate a qualified individual or individuals responsible for coordinating and monitoring compliance with this Part and all other applicable federal and state laws, rules, and regulations.

(c) Compliance policy. Each Licensee shall maintain and enforce written compliance policies, including policies with respect to anti-fraud, anti-money laundering, cyber security, privacy and information security, and any other policy required under this Part, which must be reviewed and approved by the Licensee's board of directors or an equivalent governing body.

Section 200.8. Capital requirements

(a) Each Licensee shall maintain at all times such capital in an amount and form as the superintendent determines is sufficient to ensure the financial integrity of the Licensee and its ongoing operations based on an assessment of the specific risks applicable to each Licensee. In determining the minimum amount of capital that must be maintained by a Licensee, the superintendent may consider a variety of factors, including but not limited to:

(1) the composition of the Licensee's total assets, including the position, size, liquidity, risk exposure, and price volatility of each type of asset;

(2) the composition of the Licensee's total liabilities, including the size and repayment timing of each type of liability;

(3) the actual and expected volume of the Licensee's Virtual Currency Business Activity;

(4) whether the Licensee is already licensed or regulated by the superintendent under the Financial Services Law, Banking Law, or Insurance Law, or otherwise subject to such laws as a provider of a financial product or service, and whether the Licensee is in good standing in such capacity;

(5) the amount of leverage employed by the Licensee;

(6) the liquidity position of the Licensee;

(7) the financial protection that the Licensee provides for its customers through its trust account or bond;

(8) the types of entities to be serviced by the Licensee; and

(9) the types of products or services to be offered by the Licensee.

(b) Each Licensee shall hold capital required to be maintained in accordance with this Section in the form of cash, virtual currency, or high-quality, highly liquid, investment-grade assets, in such proportions as are acceptable to the superintendent.

Section 200.9. Custody and protection of customer assets

(a) Each Licensee shall maintain a surety bond or trust account in United States dollars for the benefit of its customers in such form and amount as is acceptable to the superintendent for the protection of the Licensee's customers. To the extent a Licensee maintains a trust account in accordance with this section, such trust account must be maintained with a Qualified Custodian.

(b) To the extent a Licensee stores, holds, or maintains custody or control of Virtual Currency on behalf of another

Person, such Licensee shall hold Virtual Currency of the same type and amount as that which is owed or obligated to such other Person.

(c) Each Licensee is prohibited from selling, transferring, assigning, lending, hypothecating, pledging, or otherwise using or encumbering assets, including Virtual Currency, stored, held, or maintained by, or under the custody or control of, such Licensee on behalf of another Person except for the sale, transfer, or assignment of such assets at the direction of such other Person.

Section 200.10. Material change to business

(a) Each Licensee must obtain the superintendent's prior written approval for any plan or proposal to introduce or offer a materially new product, service, or activity, or to make a material change to an existing product, service, or activity, involving New York or New York Residents.

(b) A "materially new product, service, or activity" or a "material change" may occur where:

(1) the proposed new product, service, or activity, or the proposed change may raise a legal or regulatory issue about the permissibility of the product, service, or activity;

(2) the proposed new product, service, or activity, or the proposed change may raise safety and soundness or operational concerns; or

(3) a change is proposed to an existing product, service, or activity that may cause such product, service, or activity to be materially different from that previously listed on the application for licensing by the superintendent.

(c) The Licensee shall submit a written plan describing the proposed materially new product, service, or activity, or the proposed material change, including a detailed description of the business operations, compliance policies, and the impact on the overall business of the Licensee, as well as such other information as requested by the superintendent.

(d) If a Licensee has any questions about the materiality of any proposed new product, service, or activity, or of any proposed change, the Licensee may seek clarification from the Department prior to introducing or offering that new product, service, or activity or making that change.

Section 200.11. Change of control; mergers and acquisitions

(a) Change of Control. No action shall be taken, except with the prior written approval of the superintendent, that may result in a change of control of a Licensee.

(1) Prior to any change of control, the Person seeking to acquire control of a Licensee shall submit a written application to the superintendent in a form and substance acceptable to the superintendent, including but not limited to detailed information about the applicant and all directors, Principal Officers, Principal Stockholders, and Principal Beneficiaries of the applicant, as applicable.

(2) For purposes of this Section, the term "control" means the possession, directly or indirectly, of the power to direct or cause the direction of the management and policies of a Licensee whether through the ownership of stock of such Licensee, the stock of any Person that possesses such power, or otherwise. Control shall be presumed to exist if a Person, directly or indirectly, owns, controls, or holds with power to vote ten percent or more of the voting stock of a Licensee or of any Person that owns, controls, or holds with power to vote ten percent or more of the voting stock of such Licensee. No Person shall be deemed to control another Person solely by reason of his being an officer or director of such other Person.

(3) The superintendent may determine upon application that any Person does not or will not upon the taking of some proposed action control another Person. Such determination shall be made within 30 days or such further period as the superintendent may prescribe. The filing of an application pursuant to this Subsection in good faith by any Person shall relieve the applicant from any obligation or liability imposed by this Section with respect to the subject of the application until the superintendent has acted upon the application. The superintendent may revoke or modify his or her determination, after notice and opportunity to be heard, whenever in his or her judgment revocation or modification is consistent with this Part. The superintendent may consider the following factors in making such a determination:

i) whether such Person's purchase of common stock is made solely for investment purposes and not to acquire control over the Licensee;

ii) whether such Person could direct, or cause the direction of, the management or policies of the Licensee;

iii) whether such Person could propose directors in opposition to nominees proposed by the management or board of directors of the Licensee;

iv) whether such Person could seek or accept representation on the board of directors of the Licensee;

v) whether such Person could solicit or participate in soliciting proxy votes with respect to any matter presented to the shareholders of the Licensee; or

vi) any other factor that indicates such Person would or would not exercise control of the Licensee.

(4) The superintendent shall approve or deny every application for a change of control of a Licensee hereunder within 120 days from the filing of an application deemed by the superintendent to be complete. Such period of 120 days may be extended by the superintendent, for good cause shown, for such additional reasonable period of time as may be required to enable compliance with the requirements and conditions of this Part.

(5) In determining whether to approve a proposed change of control, the superintendent shall, among other factors, take into consideration the public interest and the needs and convenience of the public.

(b) Mergers and Acquisitions. No action shall be taken, except with the prior written approval of the superintendent, that may result in a merger or acquisition of all or a substantial part of the assets of a Licensee.

(1) Prior to any such merger or acquisition, an application containing a written plan of merger or acquisition shall be submitted to the superintendent by the entities that are to merge or by the acquiring entity, as applicable. Such plan shall be in form and substance satisfactory to the superintendent, and shall specify each entity to be merged, the surviving entity, or the entity acquiring all or substantially all of the assets of the Licensee, as applicable, and shall describe the terms and conditions of the merger or acquisition and the mode of carrying it into effect.

(2) The superintendent shall approve or deny a proposed merger or a proposed acquisition of all or a substantial part of the assets of a Licensee within 120

days after the filing of an application that contains a written plan of merger or acquisition and is deemed by the superintendent to be complete. Such period of 120 days may be extended by the superintendent, for good cause shown, for such additional reasonable period of time as may be required to enable compliance with the requirements and conditions of this Part.

(3) In determining whether to so approve a proposed merger or acquisition, the superintendent shall, among other factors, take into consideration the public interest and the needs and convenience of the public.

Section 200.12. Books and records

(a) Each Licensee shall, in connection with its Virtual Currency Business Activity, make, keep, and preserve all of its books and records in their original form or native file format for a period of at least seven years from the date of their creation and in a condition that will allow the superintendent to determine whether the Licensee is complying with all applicable laws, rules, and regulations. The books and records maintained by each Licensee shall, without limitation, include:

(1) for each transaction, the amount, date, and precise time of the transaction, any payment instructions, the total amount of fees and charges received and paid to, by, or on behalf of the Licensee, and the names, account numbers, and physical addresses of (i) the party or parties to the transaction that are customers or accountholders of the Licensee; and (ii) to the extent practicable, any other parties to the transaction;

(2) a general ledger containing all asset, liability, ownership equity, income, and expense accounts;

(3) bank statements and bank reconciliation records;

(4) any statements or valuations sent or provided to customers and counterparties;

(5) records or minutes of meetings of the board of directors or an equivalent governing body;

(6) records demonstrating compliance with applicable state and federal anti-money laundering laws, rules, and regulations, including customer identification and verification documents, records linking customers to their respective accounts and balances, and a record of all compliance breaches;

(7) communications and documentation related to

223

investigations of customer complaints and transaction error resolution or concerning facts giving rise to possible violations of laws, rules, or regulations;

(8) all other records required to be maintained in accordance with this Part; and

(9) all other records as the superintendent may require.

(b) Each Licensee shall provide the Department, upon request, immediate access to all facilities, books, records, documents, or other information maintained by the Licensee or its Affiliates, wherever located.

(c) Records of non-completed, outstanding, or inactive Virtual Currency accounts or transactions shall be maintained for at least five years after the time when any such Virtual Currency has been deemed, under the Abandoned Property Law, to be abandoned property.

Section 200.13.   Examinations

(a) Each Licensee shall permit and assist the superintendent to examine the Licensee whenever in the superintendent's judgment such examination is necessary or advisable, but not less than once every two calendar years, including, without limitation, to determine:

(1) the financial condition of the Licensee;

(2) the safety and soundness of the conduct of its business;

(3) the policies of its management;

(4) whether the Licensee has complied with the requirements of laws, rules, and regulations; and

(5) such other matters as the superintendent may determine, including, but not limited to, any activities of the Licensee outside the State of New York if in the opinion of the superintendent such activities may affect the Licensee's Virtual Currency Business Activity.

(b) Each Licensee shall permit and assist the superintendent at any time to examine all of the Licensee's books, records, accounts, documents, and other information.

(c) Each Licensee shall permit and assist the superintendent to make such special investigations as the superintendent shall deem necessary to determine whether a Licensee has violated any provision of the applicable laws, rules, or regulations and to the extent necessary shall permit and assist the superintendent to examine all relevant facilities, books, records, accounts, documents, and other information.

(d) For the purpose of determining the financial condition of the Licensee, its safety and soundness practices, or whether it has complied with the requirements of laws, rules, and regulations, the Licensee shall permit and assist the superintendent, when in the superintendent's judgment it is necessary or advisable, to examine an Affiliate of the Licensee.

Section 200.14. Reports and financial disclosures

(a) Each Licensee shall submit to the superintendent quarterly financial statements within 45 days following the close of the Licensee's fiscal quarter in the form, and containing such information, as the superintendent shall prescribe, including without limitation, the following information:

(1) a statement of the financial condition of the Licensee, including a balance sheet, income statement, statement of comprehensive income, statement of change in ownership equity, cash flow statement, and statement of net liquid assets;

(2) a statement demonstrating compliance with any financial requirements established under this Part;

(3) financial projections and strategic business plans;

(4) a list of all off-balance sheet items;

(5) a chart of accounts, including a description of each account; and

(6) a report of permissible investments by the Licensee as permitted under this Part.

(b) Each Licensee shall submit audited annual financial statements, together with an opinion and an attestation by an independent certified public accountant regarding the effectiveness of the Licensee's internal control structure. All such annual financial statements shall include:

(1) a statement of management's responsibilities for preparing the Licensee's annual financial statements, establishing and maintaining adequate internal controls and procedures for financial reporting, and complying with all applicable laws, rules, and regulations;

(2) an assessment by management of the Licensee's compliance with such applicable laws, rules, and regulations during the fiscal year covered by the financial statements; and

(3) certification of the financial statements by an of-

ficer or director of the Licensee attesting to the truth and correctness of those statements.

(c) Each Licensee shall notify the superintendent in writing of any criminal action or insolvency proceeding against the Licensee or any of its directors, Principal Stockholders, Principal Officers, and Principal Beneficiaries, as applicable, immediately after the commencement of any such action or proceeding.

(d) Each Licensee shall notify the superintendent in writing of any proposed change to the methodology used to calculate the value of Virtual Currency in Fiat Currency that was submitted to the Department in accordance with Section 200.4 or this Subsection.

(e) Each Licensee shall submit a report to the superintendent immediately upon the discovery of any violation or breach of law, rule, or regulation related to the conduct of activity licensed under this Part.

(f) Each Licensee shall make additional special reports to the superintendent, at such times and in such form, as the superintendent may request.

Section 200.15.   Anti-money laundering program

(a) All values in United States dollars referenced in this Section must be calculated using the methodology to determine the value of Virtual Currency in Fiat Currency that was provided to the Department under this Part.

(b) Each Licensee shall conduct an initial risk assessment that will consider legal, compliance, financial, and reputational risks associated with the Licensee's activities, services, customers, counterparties, and geographic location and shall establish, maintain, and enforce an anti-money laundering program based thereon. The Licensee shall conduct additional assessments on an annual basis, or more frequently as risks change, and shall modify its anti-money laundering program as appropriate to reflect any such changes.

(c) The anti-money laundering program shall, at a minimum:

(1) provide for a system of internal controls, policies, and procedures designed to ensure ongoing compliance with all applicable anti-money laundering laws, rules, and regulations;

(2) provide for independent testing for compliance with, and the effectiveness of, the anti-money laundering program to be conducted by qualified internal

personnel of the Licensee, who are not responsible for the design, installation, maintenance, or operation of the anti-money laundering program, or the policies and procedures that guide its operation, or a qualified external party, at least annually, the findings of which shall be summarized in a written report submitted to the superintendent;

(3) designate a qualified individual or individuals in compliance responsible for coordinating and monitoring day-to-day compliance with the anti-money laundering program; and

(4) provide ongoing training for appropriate personnel to ensure they have a fulsome understanding of anti-money laundering requirements and to enable them to identify transactions required to be reported and maintain records required to be kept in accordance with this Part.

(d) The anti-money laundering program shall include a written anti-money laundering policy reviewed and approved by the Licensee's board of directors or equivalent governing body.

(e) Each Licensee, as part of its anti-money laundering program, shall maintain records and make reports in the manner set forth below.

(1) Records of Virtual Currency transactions. Each Licensee shall maintain the following information for all Virtual Currency transactions involving the payment, receipt, exchange, conversion, purchase, sale, transfer, or transmission of Virtual Currency:

i) the identity and physical addresses of the party or parties to the transaction that are customers or accountholders of the Licensee and, to the extent practicable, any other parties to the transaction;

ii) the amount or value of the transaction, including in what denomination purchased, sold, or transferred;

iii) the method of payment;

iv) the date or dates on which the transaction was initiated and completed; and

v) a description of the transaction.

(2) Reports on transactions. When a Licensee is involved in a Virtual Currency to Virtual Currency transaction or series of Virtual Currency to Virtual Cur-

rency transactions that are not subject to currency transaction reporting requirements under federal law, including transactions for the payment, receipt, exchange, conversion, purchase, sale, transfer, or transmission of Virtual Currency, in an aggregate amount exceeding the United States dollar value of $10,000 in one day, by one Person, the Licensee shall notify the Department, in a manner prescribed by the superintendent, within 24 hours.

(3) Monitoring for suspicious activity. Each Licensee shall monitor for transactions that might signify money laundering, tax evasion, or other illegal or criminal activity.

(i) Each Licensee shall file Suspicious Activity Reports ("SARs") in accordance with applicable federal laws, rules, and regulations.

(ii) Each Licensee that is not subject to suspicious activity reporting requirements under federal law shall file with the superintendent, in a form prescribed by the superintendent, reports of transactions that indicate a possible violation of law or regulation within 30 days from the detection of the facts that constitute a need for filing. Continuing suspicious activity shall be reviewed on an ongoing basis and a suspicious activity report shall be filed within 120 days of the last filing describing continuing activity.

(f) No Licensee shall structure transactions, or assist in the structuring of transactions, to evade reporting requirements under this Part.

(g) No Licensee shall engage in, facilitate, or knowingly allow the transfer or transmission of Virtual Currency when such action will obfuscate or conceal the identity of an individual customer or counterparty. Nothing in this Section, however, shall be construed to require a Licensee to make available to the general public the fact or nature of the movement of Virtual Currency by individual customers or counterparties.

(h) Each Licensee shall also maintain, as part of its anti-money laundering program, a customer identification program.

(1) Identification and verification of account holders. When opening an account for, or establishing a service relationship with, a customer, each Licensee must, at a minimum, verify the customer's identity, to the extent reasonable and practicable, maintain records of the in-

formation used to verify such identity, including name, physical address, and other identifying information, and check customers against the Specially Designated Nationals ("SDNs") list maintained by the Office of Foreign Asset Control ("OFAC"), a part of the U.S. Treasury Department. Enhanced due diligence may be required based on additional factors, such as for high risk customers, high-volume accounts, or accounts on which a suspicious activity report has been filed.

(2) Enhanced due diligence for accounts involving foreign entities. Licensees that maintain accounts for non-U.S. Persons and non-U.S. Licensees must establish enhanced due diligence policies, procedures, and controls to detect money laundering, including assessing the risk presented by such accounts based on the nature of the foreign business, the type and purpose of the activity, and the anti-money laundering and supervisory regime of the foreign jurisdiction.

(3) Prohibition on accounts with foreign shell entities. Licensees are prohibited from maintaining relationships of any type in connection with their Virtual Currency Business Activity with entities that do not have a physical presence in any country.

(4) Identification required for large transactions. Each Licensee must require verification of the identity of any accountholder initiating a transaction with a value greater than $3,000.

(i) Each Licensee shall demonstrate that it has risk-based policies, procedures, and practices to ensure, to the maximum extent practicable, compliance with applicable regulations issued by OFAC.

(j) Each Licensee shall have in place appropriate policies and procedures to block or reject specific or impermissible transactions that violate federal or state laws, rules, or regulations.

(k) The individual or individuals designated by the Licensee, pursuant to Paragraph 200.15(c)(3), shall be responsible for day-to-day operations of the anti-money laundering program and shall, at a minimum:

(1) Monitor changes in anti-money laundering laws, including updated OFAC and SDN lists, and update the program accordingly;

(2) Maintain all records required to be maintained under this Section;

(3) Review all filings required under this Section before submission;

(4) Escalate matters to the board of directors, senior management, or appropriate governing body and seek outside counsel, as appropriate;

(5) Provide periodic reporting, at least annually, to the board of directors, senior management, or appropriate governing body; and

(6) Ensure compliance with relevant training requirements.

Section 200.16.   Cyber security program

(a) Generally. Each Licensee shall establish and maintain an effective cyber security program to ensure the availability and functionality of the Licensee's electronic systems and to protect those systems and any sensitive data stored on those systems from unauthorized access, use, or tampering. The cyber security program shall be designed to perform the following five core cyber security functions:

(1) identify internal and external cyber risks by, at a minimum, identifying the information stored on the Licensee's systems, the sensitivity of such information, and how and by whom such information may be accessed;

(2) protect the Licensee's electronic systems, and the information stored on those systems, from unauthorized access, use, or other malicious acts through the use of defensive infrastructure and the implementation of policies and procedures;

(3) detect systems intrusions, data breaches, unauthorized access to systems or information, malware, and other Cyber Security Events;

(4) respond to detected Cyber Security Events to mitigate any negative effects; and

(5) recover from Cyber Security Events and restore normal operations and services.

(b) Policy. Each Licensee shall implement a written cyber security policy setting forth the Licensee's policies and procedures for the protection of its electronic systems and customer and counterparty data stored on those systems, which shall be reviewed and approved by the Licensee's board of directors or equivalent governing body at least annually. The cyber security policy must address the following areas:

(1) information security;

(2) data governance and classification;

(3) access controls;

(4) business continuity and disaster recovery planning and resources;

(5) capacity and performance planning;

(6) systems operations and availability concerns;

(7) systems and network security;

(8) systems and application development and quality assurance;

(9) physical security and environmental controls;

(10) customer data privacy;

(11) vendor and third-party service provider management;

(12) monitoring and implementing changes to core protocols not directly controlled by the Licensee, as applicable; and

(13) incident response.

(c) Chief Information Security Officer. Each Licensee shall designate a qualified employee to serve as the Licensee's Chief Information Security Officer ("CISO") responsible for overseeing and implementing the Licensee's cyber security program and enforcing its cyber security policy.

(d) Reporting. Each Licensee shall submit to the Department a report, prepared by the CISO and presented to the Licensee's board of directors or equivalent governing body, at least annually, assessing the availability, functionality, and integrity of the Licensee's electronic systems, identifying relevant cyber risks to the Licensee, assessing the Licensee's cyber security program, and proposing steps for the redress of any inadequacies identified therein.

(e) Audit. Each Licensee's cyber security program shall, at a minimum, include audit functions as set forth below.

(1) Penetration testing. Each Licensee shall conduct penetration testing of its electronic systems, at least annually, and vulnerability assessment of those systems, at least quarterly.

(2) Audit trail. Each Licensee shall maintain audit trail systems that:

(i) track and maintain data that allows for the complete and accurate reconstruction of all financial transactions and accounting;

(ii)   protect the integrity of data stored and maintained as part of the audit trail from alteration or tampering;

(iii)   protect the integrity of hardware from alteration or tampering, including by limiting electronic and physical access permissions to hardware and maintaining logs of physical access to hardware that allows for event reconstruction;

(iv)   log system events including, at minimum, access and alterations made to the audit trail systems by the systems or by an authorized user, and all system administrator functions performed on the systems; and

(v)   maintain records produced as part of the audit trail in accordance with the recordkeeping requirements set forth in this Part.

(f) Application Security. Each Licensee's cyber security program shall, at minimum, include written procedures, guidelines, and standards reasonably designed to ensure the security of all applications utilized by the Licensee. All such procedures, guidelines, and standards shall be reviewed, assessed, and updated by the Licensee's CISO at least annually.

(g) Personnel and Intelligence. Each Licensee shall:

(1) employ cyber security personnel adequate to manage the Licensee's cyber security risks and to perform the core cyber security functions specified in Paragraph 200.16(a)(1)-(5);

(2) provide and require cyber security personnel to attend regular cyber security update and training sessions; and

(3) require key cyber security personnel to take steps to stay abreast of changing cyber security threats and countermeasures.

Section 200.17.   Business continuity and disaster recovery

(a) Each Licensee shall establish and maintain a written business continuity and disaster recovery ("BCDR") plan reasonably designed to ensure the availability and functionality of the Licensee's services in the event of an emergency or other disruption to the Licensee's normal business activities. The BCDR plan, at minimum, shall:

(1) identify documents, data, facilities, infrastructure, personnel, and competencies essential to the continued operations of the Licensee's business;

(2) identify the supervisory personnel responsible for implementing each aspect of the BCDR plan;

(3) include a plan to communicate with essential Persons in the event of an emergency or other disruption to the operations of the Licensee, including employees, counterparties, regulatory authorities, data and communication providers, disaster recovery specialists, and any other Persons essential to the recovery of documentation and data and the resumption of operations;

(4) include procedures for the maintenance of back-up facilities, systems, and infrastructure as well as alternative staffing and other resources to enable the timely recovery of data and documentation and to resume operations as soon as reasonably possible following a disruption to normal business activities;

(5) include procedures for the back-up or copying, with sufficient frequency, of documents and data essential to the operations of the Licensee and storing of the information off site; and

(6) identify third parties that are necessary to the continued operations of the Licensee's business.

(b) Each Licensee shall distribute a copy of the BCDR plan, and any revisions thereto, to all relevant employees and shall maintain copies of the BCDR plan at one or more accessible off-site locations.

(c) Each Licensee shall provide relevant training to all employees responsible for implementing the BCDR plan regarding their roles and responsibilities.

(d) Each Licensee shall promptly notify the superintendent of any emergency or other disruption to its operations that may affect its ability to fulfill regulatory obligations or that may have a significant adverse effect on the Licensee, its counterparties, or the market.

(e) The BCDR plan shall be tested at least annually by qualified, independent internal personnel or a qualified third party, and revised accordingly.

Section 200.18. Advertising and marketing

(a) Each Licensee engaged in Virtual Currency Business Activity shall not advertise its products, services, or activities in New York or to New York Residents without including the name of the Licensee and the legend that such Licensee is "Licensed to engage in Virtual Currency Business Activity by the New York State Department of Financial Services."

(b) Each Licensee shall maintain, for examination by the superintendent, all advertising and marketing materials for a period of at least seven years from the date of their creation, including but not limited to print media, internet media (including websites), radio and television advertising, road show materials, presentations, and brochures. Each Licensee shall maintain hard copy, website captures of material changes to internet advertising and marketing, and audio and video scripts of its advertising and marketing materials, as applicable.

(c) In all advertising and marketing materials, each Licensee shall comply with all disclosure requirements under federal and state laws, rules, and regulations.

(d) In all advertising and marketing materials, each Licensee and any person or entity acting on its behalf, shall not, directly or by implication, make any false, misleading, or deceptive representations or omissions.

Section 200.19. Consumer protection

(a) Disclosure of material risks. As part of establishing a relationship with a customer, and prior to entering into an initial transaction for, on behalf of, or with such customer, each Licensee shall disclose in clear, conspicuous, and legible writing in the English language and in any other predominant language spoken by the customers of the Licensee, all material risks associated with its products, services, and activities and Virtual Currency generally, including at a minimum, the following:

(1) Virtual Currency is not legal tender, is not backed by the government, and accounts and value balances are not subject to Federal Deposit Insurance Corporation or Securities Investor Protection Corporation protections;

(2) legislative and regulatory changes or actions at the state, federal, or international level may adversely affect the use, transfer, exchange, and value of Virtual Currency;

(3) transactions in Virtual Currency may be irreversible, and, accordingly, losses due to fraudulent or accidental transactions may not be recoverable;

(4) some Virtual Currency transactions shall be deemed to be made when recorded on a public ledger, which is not necessarily the date or time that the customer initiates the transaction;

(5) the value of Virtual Currency may be derived from the continued willingness of market participants to

exchange Fiat Currency for Virtual Currency, which may result in the potential for permanent and total loss of value of a particular Virtual Currency should the market for that Virtual Currency disappear;

(6) there is no assurance that a Person who accepts a Virtual Currency as payment today will continue to do so in the future;

(7) the volatility and unpredictability of the price of Virtual Currency relative to Fiat Currency may result in significant loss over a short period of time;

(8) the nature of Virtual Currency may lead to an increased risk of fraud or cyber attack;

(9) the nature of Virtual Currency means that any technological difficulties experienced by the Licensee may prevent the access or use of a customer's Virtual Currency; and

(10) any bond or trust account maintained by the Licensee for the benefit of its customers may not be sufficient to cover all losses incurred by customers.

(b) Disclosure of general terms and conditions. When opening an account for a new customer, and prior to entering into an initial transaction for, on behalf of, or with such customer, each Licensee shall disclose in clear, conspicuous, and legible writing in the English language and in any other predominant language spoken by the customers of the Licensee, all relevant terms and conditions associated with its products, services, and activities and Virtual Currency generally, including at a minimum, the following, as applicable:

(1) the customer's liability for unauthorized Virtual Currency transactions;

(2) the customer's right to stop payment of a preauthorized Virtual Currency transfer and the procedure to initiate such a stop-payment order;

(3) under what circumstances the Licensee will, absent a court or government order, disclose information concerning the customer's account to third parties;

(4) the customer's right to receive periodic account statements and valuations from the Licensee;

(5) the customer's right to receive a receipt, trade ticket, or other evidence of a transaction;

(6) the customer's right to prior notice of a change in the Licensee's rules or policies; and

(7) such other disclosures as are customarily given in connection with the opening of customer accounts.

(c) Disclosures of the terms of transactions. Prior to each transaction in Virtual Currency, for, on behalf of, or with a customer, each Licensee shall furnish to each such customer a written disclosure in clear, conspicuous, and legible writing in the English language and in any other predominant language spoken by the customers of the Licensee, containing the terms and conditions of the transaction, which shall include, at a minimum, to the extent applicable:

(1) the amount of the transaction;

(2) any fees, expenses, and charges borne by the customer, including applicable exchange rates;

(3) the type and nature of the Virtual Currency transaction;

(4) a warning that once executed the transaction may not be undone, if applicable; and

(5) such other disclosures as are customarily given in connection with a transaction of this nature.

(d) Acknowledgement of disclosures. Each Licensee shall ensure that all disclosures required in this Section are acknowledged as received by customers.

(e) Receipts. Upon completion of any transaction, each Licensee shall provide to a customer a receipt containing the following information:

(1) the name and contact information of the Licensee, including a telephone number established by the Licensee to answer questions and register complaints;

(2) the type, value, date, and precise time of the transaction;

(3) the fee charged;

(4) the exchange rate, if applicable;

(5) a statement of the liability of the Licensee for non-delivery or delayed delivery;

(6) a statement of the refund policy of the Licensee; and

(7) any additional information the superintendent may require.

(f) Each Licensee shall make available to the Department, upon request, the form of the receipts it is required to provide to customers in accordance with Subsection 200.19(e).

(g) Prevention of fraud. Licensees are prohibited from engaging in fraudulent activity. Additionally, each Licensee shall take reasonable steps to detect and prevent fraud, including by establishing and maintaining a written anti-fraud policy. The anti-fraud policy shall, at a minimum, include:

(1) the identification and assessment of fraud-related risk areas;

(2) procedures and controls to protect against identified risks;

(3) allocation of responsibility for monitoring risks; and

(4) procedures for the periodic evaluation and revision of the anti-fraud procedures, controls, and monitoring mechanisms.

Section 200.20. Complaints

(a) Each Licensee shall establish and maintain written policies and procedures to fairly and timely resolve complaints.

(b) Each Licensee must provide, in a clear and conspicuous manner, on its website or websites, in all physical locations, and in any other location as the superintendent may prescribe, the following disclosures:

(1) the Licensee's mailing address, email address, and telephone number for the receipt of complaints;

(2) a statement that the complainant may also bring his or her complaint to the attention of the Department;

(3) the Department's mailing address, website, and telephone number; and

(4) such other information as the superintendent may require.

(c) Each Licensee shall report to the superintendent any change in the Licensee's complaint policies or procedures within seven days.

Section 200.21. Transitional Period

A Person already engaged in Virtual Currency Business Activity must apply for a license in accordance with this Part within 45 days of the effective date of this regulation. In doing so, such applicant shall be deemed in compliance with the licensure requirements of this Part until it has been notified by the superintendent that its application has been denied, in which case it shall immediately cease operating in this state and doing business with New York State Residents. Any Person engaged in Virtual Currency Business Activity that fails to submit an application for a license within 45 days of the effective date of this regulation shall be deemed to be conducting unlicensed Virtual Currency Business Activity.

Section 200.22.   Severability

If any provision of this Part or the application thereof to any Person or circumstance is adjudged invalid by a court of competent jurisdiction, such judgment shall not affect or impair the validity of the other provisions of this Part or the application thereof to other Persons or circumstances.

Index